Crimes of the Powerful: A Reader

Readings in Criminology and Criminal Justice series
Series editor Sandra Walklate

Ethnicity and Crime: A Reader
Basia Spalek

Gender and Crime: A Reader
Karen Evans and Janet Jamieson

Crimes of the Powerful: A Reader
David Whyte

Crimes of the Powerful: A Reader

Edited by David Whyte

McGraw Hill

Open University Press

Open University Press
McGraw-Hill Education
McGraw-Hill House
Shoppenhangers Road
Maidenhead
Berkshire
England
SL6 2QL

email: enquiries@openup.co.uk
world wide web: www.openup.co.uk

and Two Penn Plaza, New York, NY 10121—2289, USA

First published 2009

A catalogue record of this book is available from the British Library

ISBN-13: 9780335223909 (pb) 9780335223893 (hb)
ISBN-10: 0335223907 (pb) 0335223893 (hb)

Typeset by Kerrypress, Luton, Bedfordshire
Printed by in the UK by Bell and Bain Ltd, Glasgow

The **McGraw·Hill** Companies

Contents

SECTION 3:
Capitalism and crimes of the powerful　　　　　　　61

The slow sacrifice of humanity　　　　　　　　　　61

SECTION 4
Law and the corporation　　　　　　　　　　　　99

Structures of irresponsibility　　　　　　　　　　99

Series editor's foreword

This is third collection of readings to be published as part of a new McGraw-Hill/Open University Press series, 'Reading in Criminology and Criminal Justice'. The purpose of this series is to offer student-friendly approach to the issues and debates that are central to the contemporary discipline of criminology. Despite the proliferation of textbooks claiming to offer wide coverage of criminology and the criminal justice system, such books inevitably do not do justice to the needs of the undergraduate curriculum beyond year one. The intention of this series is to fill this gap. Indeed, the changing nature of the criminology undergraduate market makes its own claims for a wide variety of readily available material beyond the standard textbook. In particular, the modular system of curriculum delivery means that in order to deliver courses of an appropriate standard, tutors require available, easily accessible, and student-friendly material to support their courses. In the modular system collections of readings that address the core features of the criminology curriculum provide an essential starting point for students and tutors alike, especially in the light of the increasing number of journals and other outlets which may not be easily accessible or subscribed to by all libraries, electronic developments notwithstanding. Lack of availability of a wider range of both historical and contemporary material has a detrimental effect on the discipline and the student experience. The intention of this series is not only to fill this gap, and as a result do better justice to the debates in the discipline, but also to provide the opportunity for the nominated editors to make a mark on the discipline, by both stretching and contributing to its boundaries. This collection, offered by David Whyte, achieves both of these aims.

Questions relating to corporate crime, white-collar crime, crimes of the powerful, state crime, however they are signified, have always played their part in the history and development of criminology as a discipline. Such questions, whilst still marginal in much of the policy arena and public discourse on crime, are now not as marginal as they once were to the discipline itself and the delivery of a criminology-based curriculum. Indeed, benchmarking requirements are suggestive of the necessity for such concerns to be reflected in the undergraduate experience. This collection of readings ensures that the coverage that might be given to such questions is both substantial and thought-provoking. Divided into seven sections, the readings offered here take us on an important journey in thinking about the relationship between the state, power and crime.

In Section 1 we are encouraged to think critically about what does and does not count as crime as well as who is and is not considered criminal when engaged in such activities captured by the phrase 'states of exception'. Consideration of these issues is developed further in Section 2 in which the more complex and fuzzy links between the role of the state, business and trade are mapped out for us. The famous comment made by Tilly (1985) of understanding the state's own 'protection racket' offers a flavour of the critical edge we are encouraged to embrace in the excerpts chosen here. These readings lead into and link well with those chosen for Section 3 in which the more conventional issues around white-collar crime and crimes of the powerful are covered. Some of these readings constitute 'classics' in the criminological agenda. In Sections 4 and 5 we are introduced to the more substantive questions of how the structures of the capitalist process permit irresponsibility, on the one hand, and result in (unrecognised) criminal behaviour and victimisation on the other. The readings in Sections 6 and 7 encourage us to consider the problem of how useful the concept of crime is and whether or not the notion of harm has greater value in capturing some of the concerns that pertain to or result from 'crimes of the powerful'. Furthermore, in Section 7, the value of appealing to the law when thinking about crime and power is subjected to thoughtful critical examination.

It is self-evident that this collection of readings has taken a different approach to the notion of a reader than others that have been published so far in the series. Those differences are reflected in both the content and the shape of this reader. In terms of content, there are more and shorter extracts, some of which are now very difficult to obtain. This will be particularly useful for tutors wishing to develop courses and course materials where resource issues dictate their scarcity. In terms of shape, it is clear that David Whyte wants to ensure that we join with him on a particular kind of journey through this material. This journey is a theoretical one as well as a substantive one. Whilst those who use this reader may not wish to embrace this particular theoretical journey, they will certainly be encouraged to think critically about it. In this latter respect, this collection pushes the boundaries of criminological thought in this area and as a consequence it will make a contribution to the furthering of criminological debates on these issues. The agenda that David Whyte has set for criminology here is a significant and important one. It is an agenda that the discipline constantly needs to be alerted to, and this collection will ensure that this will be the case. This collection offers a powerful statement on both the state and the state of play when we think about crime and power.

Sandra Walklate
Eleanor Rathbone Chair of Sociology
University of Liverpool
00

Reference

Tilly, C. (1985) 'War making and state making as organized crime' in P. Evans, D. Rueschemeyer and T. Skopol (eds) *Bringing the State Back In*. Cambridge: Cambridge University Press.

Publisher's Acknowledgements

Open University Press would like to thank the publishers of the following for permission to use copyright material.

Weber, Max (1919/1948) Politics as a Vocation, in Gerth, H and Wright Mills, C (eds.) *From Max Weber: essays in sociology*, London: Routledge and Kegan Paul.

Benjamin, Walter (1927/1978) Critique of Violence, in Demetz, P (ed.) *Reflections: Essays, Aphorisms, Autobiographical Writings*, New York: Schoken Books.

Proal, Louis (1898) *Political Crime*, London: T. Fisher Unwin

Arendt, Hanah (1965/1977) *Eichman in Jerusalem: a report on the banality of evil*, London: Penguin.

Agamben, Georgio (1991/2000) Sovereign Police, in Binetti, V and Casarino, C (trans.) *Means Without End: notes on politics*, Minneapolis: University of Minnesota Press.

Rolston, Bill (2000) *Unfinished Business: state killings and the quest for truth*, Belfast: Beyond the Pale.

Tilly, Charles (1985) 'War Making and State Making as Organized Crime', in Evans, P et. al. (eds.) *Bringing the State Back In*, Cambridge, Cambridge University Press.

Gallant, Thomas (1999) Brigandage, Piracy, Capitalism and State-formation: Transnational Crime in an Historical World-systems Perspective, in Heyman, J and Smart, A (eds) *States and Illegal Practices*, Oxford: Berg.

Butler, Smedley, D. (1935) In Time of Peace, *Common Sense,* vol. 4, no. 11.

Woodiwiss, Michael (2005) *Gangster Capitalism: the United States and the global rise of organised crime*, London: Constable.

Chablis, William (1989) State-Organised Crime, *Criminology,* vol. 27, no. 2.

Wonders, Nancy and Danner, Mona (2006) in Michalowski, R and Kramer, R (eds.) *State-Corporate Crime: wrongdoing at the intersection of business and government*, New Brunswick: Rutgers University Press.

Marx, Karl (1858) Free Trade and Monopoly, *New York Daily Tribune*, September 25th.

Marx, K (1887/1954) *Capital: a critical analysis of capitalist production, volume 1*, London: Lawrence and Wishart.

Casement, R (1910/1997) Mitchell, A ed. The Amazon Journal of Roger Casement, Dublin: Lillyput

Ross, E.A. (1907/1973) *Sin and Society: an analysis of latter-day iniquity*, New York: Harper and Row.

Josephson, Matthew (1934/1962) *The Robber Barrons*, New York: Harcourt, Brace and World.

Robb, G (1992) *White Collar Crime in Modern England: financial fraud and business morality 1845–1929*, Cambridge: Cambridge University Press,

Braithwaite, J (1984) *Corporate Crime in the Pharmaceutical Industry*, London: Routledge and Kegan Paul.

Pearce, F and Tombs, S (1998) *Toxic Capitalism: Corporate Crime and the Chemical Industry*, Aldershot: Ashgate.

Barkan, J (2004) *The Corporation: the pathological pursuit of profit and power*, London: Constable.

Pearce, Frank (2001) Crime and Capitalist Business Organisations, in Shover, N. and Wright, J.P. (eds.) *Crimes of Privilege: readings in White Collar Crime*, Oxford: Oxford University Press

Veblen, Thorstein (1978) *Theory of Business Enterprise*, Piscataway New Jersey: Transaction.

Wells, Celia (2001) *Corporations and Criminal Responsibility, 2nd edition*. Oxford: Oxford University Press

Glasbeek, Harry (2002)*Wealth by Stealth*, Toronto: Between the Lines.

Bauman, Zigmund (1989) *Modernity and the Holocaust*, Oxford, Polity Press.

Cohen, Stanley (1993) Human rights and crimes of the state: the culture of denial, *Australian and New Zealand Journal of Criminology*, vol. 26, no. 2.

Sutherland, Edwin (1949/1983) White-Collar Crime: the uncut version, New Haven.: Yale University Press,

Passas, Nicos (1990) Anomie and Corporate Crime, *Contemporary Crises*, vol. 14.

Pearce, F and Tombs, S (1998) Bounded Rationality and Corporate Crime, from Ideology, Hegemony and Empiricism, *British Journal of Criminology*,

Carson, W.G. (1980) The Other Price of Britain's Oil: regulating safety on offshore oil installations in the British sector of the North Sea, *Contemporary Crises*, vol. 4, 239–26

Simpson, Sally and Ellis, Lori (1996) Theoretical Perspectives on the Corporate Victimisation of Women, in Szockyj, E and Fox, J (eds.) *Corporate Victimisation of Women*, Boston: North Eastern University Press

Herman, Ed (1982) *The Real Terror Network*, Boston: South End Press.

Sutherland, Edwin (1940) White Collar Criminality, *American Sociological Review*, vol. 5, no. 1.

Tappan, Paul (1947) Who is the White Collar Criminal? *American Sociological Review*, vol. 12, no. 1.

Snider, Laureen (2001) The Sociology of Corporate Crime: an obituary (or: whose knowledge claims have legs?) *Theoretical Criminology*, vol. 4, no. 2.

Schwendinger, Herman and Schwendinger, Julia (1970) Defenders of Order or Guardians of Human Rights? *Issues in Criminology*, vol. 5., no. 2.

Green, Penny and Ward, Tony (2004) *State Crime, Human Rights and the Limits of Criminology*

Friedrichs, David O. and Friedrichs, Jessica (2002) The World Bank and Crimes of Globalization: A Case Study, *Social Justice*

Marx, K (1887/1954) *Capital: a critical analysis of capitalist production, volume 1*, London: Lawrence and Wishart.

Alvesalo, A (2002) Downsized by Law, Ideology and Pragmatics – policing white collar crime, in Potter, G (2002) *Controversies in White Collar Crime*, Cincinnati: Anderson.

Michalowski, R and Kramer, R (1987) The Space between Laws: The Problem of Corporate Crime in a Transnational *Context, Social* Problems, vol. 34, no.

MacKinnon, Catherine (2006) *Are Women Human? and other international dialogues*, Cambridge, Massachusetts: Harvard

Bowring, B (2005) The Degradation of International Law? In Strawson, J (ed.) *Law After Ground Zero*, London: Glasshouse.

Chomsky, Noam (2003) Preventive War 'the Supreme Crime', *Zmag*, August 11th, published online at: http://www.zmag.org/content/showarticle.cfm?ItemID=4030

The Publisher directs the reader to the original publications for a full list of references.

Every effort has been made to trace the copyright holders, but if any have been inadvertently overlooked the publisher will be pleased to make the necessary arrangement at the first opportunity.

Studying the Crimes of the Powerful

In criminology, state crime and corporate crime now tend to be routinely incorporated into course and textbooks, normally as a bolt-on chapter or lecture, included on the basis that they constitute one of a range of different crime problems or types. It has been pretty routine, almost to the point of tedium, to find in criminology textbooks an acknowledgement that goes something like 'state and corporate crime cause more deaths than all other forms of crime put together' or 'crime committed from behind a desk is a much more pressing problem than crime committed on the street'. More than 30 years after Frank Pearce coined the term, crimes of the powerful are now incorporated into criminology, recognised and defined as a legitimate subject of academic inquiry.

But despite incorporation in criminology courses and textbooks, the study of crimes of the powerful is still treated at best as a mildly interesting diversion from the real business of crime and criminal justice, or at worst as the renegade cousin of the family. Only very rarely have there been texts that fully integrate crimes of the powerful into their analysis of crime (for exceptions, see Cook, 1997; Reiman, 1979). So we are left with a criminology that is concerned broadly with two carefully segregated types of crime: the 'real' crimes committed by low-status offenders, and those other, more difficult to pin down or 'ambiguous', (Nelken, 2007) crimes committed by people of relatively high social status.

And criminology plays a key role in the construction of crimes of the powerful as a kind of curio, a subject matter that is vaguely interesting but odd – a subject matter that could never emerge to dominate the discipline. This is by and large because criminology has one overriding concern: to study, explain, analyse and propose theories to eradicate, the crimes of the poor – Criminology's gaze is overwhelmingly directed downwards at the relatively powerless, an enterprise that it shares with most criminal justice agencies. It is the downward gaze of criminology, then, that reinforces the idea that the real problems of society can be located in the lower stratum, the poor working class and 'underclass' or an undefined group that are (in private, of course) referred to as 'jailbait' or 'scum'.

Approaching the crimes of the powerful therefore means rejecting some common assumptions about what a typical 'crime' is. We cannot take the concept of crime for granted. Crime, if we apply the term used by the European abolitionist movement, has no 'ontological reality'. That is to say, it has no reality outside of itself. Rather, the understanding, definition and popular perception of what crime is depends on how the institutional framework of the criminal justice system defines crime. Put simply, if the government decides to criminalise something and the police and the courts fall into line, then it will have a good chance of gaining popular recognition as a crime. The harms and illegalities that are not prioritised by the state criminal justice processes and agencies are not likely to be criminalised. Of course, this is a generalisation and the state definition of crime is always contested. The point, however, is that we have to understand 'crime' as not merely something that the state controls or organises a war against, but something that the state creates by deciding what to prioritise and what not to prioritise. All of this means that crime is not, and could never be, understood without a detailed appreciation of who has the power to define it. What it also means is that our idea of 'crime' is not, and never could be, fixed. Crime is not something that corresponds to a predetermined definition.

Questioning a fixed notion of 'crime' also means questioning predominant assumptions about what typically causes 'crime'. As Edwin Sutherland (1949) noted more than half a century ago, the study of white-collar crime turns conventional criminology on its head. For if we accept the empirical evidence from studies of white-collar crime – that the social impact of this form of crime really does dwarf mainstream or 'street' crime – then we have to rethink conventional assumptions about the relationship between poverty and crime. If we take the research evidence at face value, then there appears to be a much more significant relationship between wealth and crime than between poverty and crime. And yet the key measures of crime (police-recorded crime figures and crime surveys) and the bulk of the work by most criminologists remains fixated on the crimes of the poor as if 'crime' *was* some kind of predetermined or 'wired-in' concept (Tombs and Whyte, 2003; Walters, 2004).

Perhaps those of us who study and write about the crimes of the powerful should stop moaning and just count our blessings. After all, we would not have to go back very far in time for it to be virtually impossible to find even a mention of state crime, corporate crime or white-collar crime in a textbook. The point of making this observation, however, is not to feel either aggrieved about, or grateful for, the recognition of the crimes of the powerful in the mainstream of criminology. Neither is it to argue for a theory that can explain all crime – both the crimes of the powerful and the crimes of the powerless. The point, following Geis and Meier (1977), is that by failing to fully comprehend the significance of crimes of the powerful, mainstream criminology texts will remain all the poorer. Moreover, Geis and Meier's call to criminologists to study 'white-collar' crime is important to bear in mind not only because white-collar crime challenges the banal, state-defined study of crime, but also because, as they argue, studies of white-collar crime can give us important insights into processes of social change and into the social distribution of power. Thus, the crime of the powerful 'portrays the manner in which power is exercised in our society. A review of upperworld violations and the manner in which they are prosecuted tells us who is able to control what in American society and indicates the extent to which such control is effective' (Geis and Meier, 1977: 19).

So this book is not merely about crime; it is really about power. And just as we need to take care with a concept of crime, we cannot take what is meant by 'power' for granted. Perhaps the best starting point in this respect is to recognise that *power is relational*. In other words power is a consequence of relationships between different social actors. We cannot say that one individual, or group, or institution is powerful unless its power is defined in relation to other, less powerful, individuals, groups or institutions. For example, a prison is a powerful institution in relation to the people that it imprisons, to many of its visitors and even to researchers who want to get inside the prison. But in relation to the government department that runs the prison or the government minister responsible for the prison who has the power to close it down or to take action to curtail its activities, it does not appear very powerful at all. It is therefore important to bear the relational aspect of power in mind when reading this book: who is it that is being described as powerful and how is this power defined in relation to other, relatively powerless groups?

This text is concerned with the *institutionally* powerful, that is, its focus is on the form of power that is transmitted through state institutions and private business organisations or corporations. As such, it could be said that the substantive *foci* of this text actually constitute a fairly narrow group of powerful actors. A broad definition of crimes of powerful could include a substantive focus upon gendered power and racialised power, or could explore age as a key mediator of power. Furthermore, an expansive view of the powerful might be concerned with the micro-dynamics of power that we find in other social institutions such as the family or the school. This book restricts the boundaries of its analysis to states and corporations, though some of those (gendered and racialised) aspects of institutional power are covered in this book.

State institutions and corporations are chosen as the focus here because they are key and central agents of power in contemporary societies. They are also an important focus for 'crimes of the powerful' partly because of the truisms noted above. Crimes committed by states and corporations undoubtedly *do* kill more people, maim more people, rip off and steal from more people than crimes committed by individuals (Box, 1983; Friedrichs, 1996; Tombs and Whyte, forthcoming). Moreover, processes of criminalisation are profoundly influenced by state institutions and corporations – and, importantly, by the relationship between the two sets of institutions. They are powerful agents that play a central role in defining the boundaries of their own crime. For this reason, those forms of institutionalised power reveal a great deal about how law and 'crime' provide a framework for configuring and reproducing social relations of power.

The format of this book is rather unconventional. In comparison to most 'readers', the extracts here are relatively short and there are more of them. This is done in order to provide you with a broad sweep of readings. But there are drawbacks with presenting texts in such an abbreviated format. Because they have been distilled down to the core of the argument, or, in some cases, present only fragments of the general argument, there are few extracts here that capture the significance or the scope of the original work. For this reason, you are encouraged to use this book as an introduction to the texts that are selected here. In order to help you use the book in this way, each section is preceded by an essay that explains the wider significance of the articles and points to other literature that you will find useful if you decide to commit more of your time to studying the crimes of the powerful.

If you do, or even if you are more generally interested in studying the relationship between power and crime then it will be necessary to redirect your attention *upwards* to the higher reaches of the social strata. For, as the readings together in this book show, when we study the crimes of the powerful, the *crème de la crème* of society begin to look rather more like the scum.

References

Box, S. (1983) *Power, Crime and Mystification*. London: Routledge.

Cook, D. (1997) *Poverty, Crime and Punishment*. London: Child Poverty Action Group.

Friedrichs, D (1996) *Trusted Criminals: White collar crime in contemporary society*. Belmont, CA: Wadsworth.

Geis, G. and Meier, R. (1977) Introduction, in G. Geis and R. Meier, (eds) *White-Collar Crime: Offences in business, politics and the professions*. New York: Free Press.

Nelken, D. (2007) 'White collar and corporate crime' in M. Maguire, R. Morgan and R. Reiner (eds) *Oxford Handbook of Criminology*, 4th edn. Oxford: Oxford University Press.

Reiman, J. (1979) *The Rich Get Richer and the Poor Get Prison*. Boston: Allyn & Bacon.

Sutherland, E. (1949) *White-Collar Crime*. New York: Holt, Reinhart and Winston.

Tombs, S. and Whyte, D. (2003) 'Scrutinising the powerful? Crime, contemporary political economy and critical social research' in S. Tombs and D. Whyte (eds) *Unmasking the Crimes of the Powerful: Scrutinising states and corporations*. New York: Peter Lang.

Tombs, S. and Whyte, D. (forthcoming) 'Corporate crime? Theft, violence and harm' in J. Muncie, D. Talbot and R. Walters (eds) *Crime: Local and global*. Maidenhead: Open University Press.

Walters, R. (2004) *Deviant Knowledge: Criminology, politics and policy*. Cullompton: Willan.

SECTION 1:

State, violence, crime

States of exception

This section is concerned with the complex relationship between states, violence and the rule of law. It provides a theoretical introduction that locates the origins of crimes of the powerful in the very foundations of state power and authority. Before we explore various dimensions of crimes of the powerful, the readings in this section raise more fundamental questions about the relationship between states and the rule of law.

The section begins with what is regarded in political science and in sociology as a classic statement on state violence. Max Weber's comments on the state monopoly of the legitimate use of force are reproduced to provide a summary outline of his famous formulation. For Weber, the question is first of all one of definition: the resort to the legitimate use of force or violence is what *defines* the modern state. But if this formulation is the most famous contribution made by *Politics as a Vocation*, its full significance is barely represented in the brief extract reproduced here. The essay in its entirety analyses the conditions required for states to secure the obedience of their functionaries and officials; the bureaucratic means by which the state organises its capacity for violence; and the ethical basis of a politics that is ultimately organised around the actual or potential use of violence. In this sense, the essay provides important insights into how what Stan Cohen calls 'crimes of obedience' (see Section 5). For this reason students interested in the crimes of the powerful are encouraged to use it as a key reference point.

Weber has been criticised for overstating the degree to which political authorities possess a genuine monopoly on the legitimate use of force. There are forms of violence that are not produced by political mechanisms, but still exist legitimately in the sense that they remain relatively untouched by social opprobrium or censure. It might be said, for example, that violence perpetrated against women by their husbands and partners in the home has, in the context of patriarchal societies, been a relatively unscandalised form of violence. Similarly, the violence suffered by workers as a result of the industrial deaths and injuries perpetrated against them by their employers generally fails to attract any generalised level of censure. Therefore, both can be understood as relatively legitimatised forms of violence, even though neither can be sourced directly to the political mechanisms of the state. But those who defend Weber's position point out that, in *Politics as a Vocation*, Weber makes it clear that the 'right to use physical force is ascribed to other institutions or to individuals only to the extent to which the state permits it'. In this context, the failure of the criminal justice system to intervene in domestic violence can be understood as state complicity. Indeed, in so far as domestic violence was in many jurisdictions legally permitted until relatively recently, this is a form of violence that received the (tacit) approval of the state (see also the MacKinnon reading in Section 7 of this volume). Similarly, deaths and injuries caused by employers are generally legitimised by the lack of legal intervention by the state and its refusal to acknowledge those incidents as cases of 'violence' (Tombs, 2007). Arguably, then, both domestic violence and violence at work fall squarely into the scope of Weber's definition of state political violence.

Walter Benjamin's contribution is not restricted to the question of the political authority of the state, but opens up a broader discussion about the centrality of violence to the rule of law. And it is from this position that we can better understand the dilemmas of state monopoly posed by Weber. When reading this extract, it is important to know precisely what Benjamin means by 'violence' (Derrida, 1990). The word *Gewalt* used by Benjamin in the original German version was translated as simply as 'violence'. However, this does not fully capture his meaning of the term. In the German language, it has a broader meaning that encompasses the exercise of legitimate power and authority. This is significant since Benjamin is interested in precisely what it is that distinguishes *legitimate* and *illegitimate* violence. It is therefore important to have both meanings in mind when reading this extract from *Critique of Violence* – to know that the meaning of violence for Benjamin also implies *legitimate* power and authority. This essay is consistent with Weber's perspective in so far as Benjamin asserts that the law-making powers that parliaments derive their authority from is always founded upon, and attended to by, (legitimate) violence (whether politicians realise this or not). So, the enforcement of the law is itself always founded upon the state's (legitimate) recourse to violence. Another important theme that runs through this extract is the idea that the purpose of the rule of law is not – as is commonly understood – to draw a distinction between 'justice' and 'injustice'. For Benjamin, the rule of law must be regarded as conceptually separate from 'justice'. Rather, law establishes a distinction between the legitimate and illegitimate means of reaching particular ends. In order to uphold this legal distinction, the state must seek to eradicate individual violence unless it corresponds closely to the ends sought by legitimate (state) violence.

In the essay Benjamin makes an important distinction between law-making violence and law-preserving violence. Law-making violence seeks an end (power) by using a particular means (violence or the threat of violence). Thus, Benjamin notes: '[l]awmaking is power making, and, to that extent, an immediate manifestation of violence' (extract: 295). Individual violence for Benjamin is potentially 'lawmaking' simply because – unless it is challenged by the state – it may allow private individuals to exercise authority that is not permitted by the state.

Law-preserving violence is the violence used by the state when its monopoly over law-making violence is challenged. So the institutions of the criminal justice system (police, courts, prisons, etc.) are all concrete manifestations of law-preserving violence. Where individual violence occurs, it must be punished by law-preserving violence. This explains why the line between the illegitimate (vigilante) violence and the legitimate violence (in self-defence, for example) used by individuals is always a blurred one.

In this sense the extract by Benjamin can be read as an important philosophical foundation for later work in criminology by Christie (1977) and McBarnet (1983). From slightly different perspectives, those authors argued that the primary function of the criminal justice system was to dispossess individuals of their conflicts, and assume complete control of and responsibility for the resolution of disputes. The court sanction constitutes, for Benjamin (as it does for Christie and McBarnet), the immediate manifestation of the state's capacity for law-preserving violence; a violent response to a threat to the state's monopoly on law-making violence. To view the rule of law in this way is to raise important questions about the legitimacy – even the necessity – of using violence in resisting state power. And in this respect Benjamin's influence upon revolutionary thinkers cannot be underestimated. Thirty-four years after *Critique of Violence* was published, the anti-Imperialist theorist and leader Frantz Fanon (2001: 32) demonstrated how colonialism relied upon a rule of law that always reached its logical conclusion in the violent suppression, torture and dehumanisation of native populations and used this to argue for the necessity of a violence of the oppressed.

Although it refrained from reaching a revolutionary conclusion, the brutality of the British state in the eighteenth and nineteenth centuries was recognised in similar terms in what was perhaps the first book to recognise 'political' or 'state' crime as a focus of study in criminology. Published in 1898, Louis Proal's groundbreaking work, *Political Crime*, was the fourth in a series that included Lombroso's *The Female Offender* and Ferri's *Criminal Sociology*. As the extract of *Political Crime* reproduced here shows, the law was used as a naked instrument of colonial power by the English. In its suppression of the Irish people, 'persecution and spoliation' were given 'a legal shape'. Proal's concern is with how law is corrupted by politics; how politics corrupts and manipulates an otherwise just and impartial system. Unjust laws – what he calls the 'laws of exception' – are those laws created to work in favour of political elites. In this sense, Proal displays a liberal commitment to making the political and legal system work. And in pointing to 'laws of exception', Proal's work recognises an intimate relationship between the state and the corruption of power that is an enduring theme in classical liberal thought.

Hannah Arendt, in her analysis of the crimes of the Third Reich and the legal reasoning used in the subsequent prosecutions of its leaders, ploughs deep into the relationship between the 'laws of exception' and state violence. The concept of 'laws of exception' is of importance to Arendt not merely because they reveal the dark side of state power, but also because of what they reveal about the vulnerability of the state. 'Laws of exception' support and are in turn supported by the claim that 'the existence of the state itself is at stake'. Arendt argues that states retain the right to impose 'laws of exception' both as an expression of, and as a source of, their power. The resort to laws of exception, she notes, is generally justified using a principle of *raison d'état* (literally 'reason of state'), – an overriding concern normally equated to the 'national interest') that requires the state to use extreme measures to defend its integrity. It is the urgency of defending the integrity of the state that necessitates laws of exception. So, as we saw in the 2003 invasion and occupation of Iraq, weapons of mass destruction acted as the *raison d'état*; and self-defence – sometimes refined as a ticking bomb scenario – acts as the *raison d'état* for the extension of counter-terrorism police powers and the legitimisation of torture under the guise of a 'war on terror'. It is not difficult to deconstruct those narratives of necessity and see how they are almost entirely fictional, but this is not the point. The point is that the state always needs to provide a legitimating narrative for its resort to exception, which is, by definition, a resort to extreme measures.

Arendt is concerned with the limits that extreme measures place upon state sovereignty. If the principle of *raison d'état* shows how states use the laws of exception as emergency measures, what happens to the sovereignty of the state when the emergency becomes the norm? In other words, what happens to its claim to sovereignty when, as in the case of the Third Reich, a state is founded on criminal principles?

The position taken by the Allies following the Second World War was that by virtue of its crimes the German Nazi state had forfeited its right to sovereignty. The juridical disposal of Hitler's regime has been characterised as the first time in history that a universal legal rationale emerged to challenge the sovereignty of the nation state.[1] Elsewhere in her book, Arendt shows how the Allies and the state of Israel in, respectively, the Nuremberg trials and the trial of Eichmann dealt with this dilemma by assuming the role of judge and jury on behalf of humanity. The concept of 'crimes against humanity', no matter how loosely defined at the time, provided a legal rationale to dispense with any residual Third Reich claims to sovereignty and to subjugate its leaders to the court at Nuremberg. The German Third Reich state was a state founded upon 'criminal principles' (Arendt, 1977: 291), and therefore had violated its right to sovereign parity with other nations and invalidated its claim to invoke a 'state of exception'.

This legal rationale was also influenced by the so-called 'Radbruch formula'. Gustav Radbruch, the Social Democratic jurist, provided a basis for judgments on the Nazi leadership to be applied retroactively (after the fact). Radbruch asserted that if state laws reach an intolerable level of injustice, or if in their enactment they deliberately disavow equality, then they cease to be law (Haldeman, 2005). Radbruch's formula therefore provided a basis for the application of *universal* legal principles that should always take precedent over state law. The Radbruch principles later enabled East German political and military leaders to be prosecuted after the fall of the Berlin Wall for their role in the deaths of people who were killed crossing the border between East and West (Miller, 2001). Honecker's East Germany had also been defined as a state founded upon criminal principles with no right to invoke a state of exception.

Georgio Agamben reinforces Arendt's understanding of the right to invoke a state of exception as a common feature of all sovereign states. The idea that in order to maintain sovereign rule, the state must stand simultaneously outside *and* inside its own rule of law is a key insight into state power that Agamben began to develop in the short piece reproduced here. But for Agamben, the state of exception represents something much more fundamental than it does for Arendt. Here he argues that 'the concept of sovereignty has been finally introduced into the figure of the police' (extract: 103). The piece was written very shortly after the 1991 invasion of Iraq, in which the US invoked a principle of *necessity*, claiming that it was the guardian of the global order and therefore had to act to defend this order (see also the Bowring and Chomsky readings in Section 7). Agamben is very clearly influenced by those events and the term 'police' here has a more general meaning ascribed to it that indicates the nakedness of state power. Agamben's meaning of 'police' closely approximates to what Poulantzas (1978) referred to as the 'repressive state apparatuses' and Gramsci (1996) referred to as the 'state as policeman' (see also Coleman et al., 2009). In other words, he is referring to the apparatuses of the state that use force openly (various forms of police, military, courts, prisons, immigration and border officials, and so on). Essentially, Agamben is arguing, *contra* Proal, that state violence is not merely a result of bad government, or the 'administrative function of law enforcement' (extract: 104) but, following Benjamin, that state violence *is* state power. The state of exception for Agamben is therefore the core of power in all states. Moreover, it has become a permanent condition in the most powerful and advanced states. This claim is developed in his later work, *Homo Sacer* (Agamben, 1998) and *State of Exception* (Agamben, 2005), where he argues that the US detention centres of Abu Ghraib and Guantánamo are the highest stage of development of the state of exception. In other words, he argues, under conditions of a so-called war on terrorism, the exception has become the rule. There is resonance here with an enduring characteristic of the state that has been brought to light by some key British criminology texts. In the classic *Policing the Crisis*, Hall et al. (1978: 288) document a shift towards the exceptional state in late 1970s Britain and Northern Ireland that culminated in the routine resort by the police to 'informal' (illegal) strategies of quasi-judicial swoops on suspects, detention and torture. And a decade and a half later, Paddy Hillyard's *Suspect Community* (1993) documented how the 'exceptional powers' invoked by the British state to fight terrorism were gradually normalised by practice and legislation.

The perspectives set out so far in this section provide us with important insights into the complexity of the concept of state crime. For they all point to a paradox that students of state crime are always impelled to come back to: if sovereign power is ultimately guaranteed by a state of exception (the right to suspend the rule of law), and this suspension is a normal and permanent condition, then can we really define this as state 'crime' or state 'deviance'? This raises a broader issue of the difficulty of labelling state crimes as 'crimes', a problem to which we will return in Sections 6 and 7 of the book.

The readings in this section have so far been primarily concerned with the *structure* of state/law/violence and less concerned with the conditions that allow this structure to reproduce itself. In other words, little attention so far has been paid to the process by which states maintain their own legitimacy and stability. Agamben (2005: 87) has argued more recently that the state of exception has reached a point of 'maximum worldwide deployment' to the point that

> '[t]he normative aspect of law can thus be obliterated and contradicted with impunity by a government violence that – while ignoring international law externally and producing a permanent state of exception internally – nevertheless still claims to be applying the law'.

Thus, if there is a theme that runs through the extracts so far, it is the implication that states derive their power from the technologies of violence at their disposal. What is missing from this analysis and from the extracts reproduced here, however, is a recognition of the fragility of state power. States cannot rule by violence alone. All states need to maintain some kind of semblance of legitimate authority that is based on something other than a crude 'might is right' principle.

The final reading in this section begins to raise fundamental questions about the problems of legitimacy and consent that are produced when states commit crimes of violence, or authorise acts of extreme violence on their behalf. Bill Rolston poses an enduring question: what does it mean when the state uses extreme violence against a section of the population it is supposed to represent and protect? This question allows us to see clearly how the authorised use of violence can profoundly undermine the legitimacy of the state, and raises perhaps a more fundamental contradiction in state power. Proal had noted in the context of the British colonisation of Ireland that '[l]egal proscription is more hateful than brutal violence, because upon iniquity it superimposes hypocrisy'. This captures well the form of legal subjugation Rolston describes in *Unfinished Business*. In some cases the state invokes a 'state of exception'; in other cases it simply does not admit to its complicity or role in killing its victims. The continuum of state violence, therefore, moves from visible, acknowledged events to hidden and denied events. Moreover, the control exerted by the state following the event ensures that the families of victims continue to be victimised by the state (in the form of refusal to investigate, refusal to release information, and very often in the form of deliberate misinformation about the victims and the circumstances in which they were killed). When violence is committed against the state 'everything that can be known is known' (extract: xiv); in the case of violence committed by, or on behalf of, the state, the victims are 'undeserving'; and vilification and harassment by the state often continues long after the event, amplifying the trauma experienced by victims and their families.

As well as recognising state violence as a seemingly insurmountable, or unstoppable expression of power, it is important to recognise that the structure of state/law/violence that we find at the core of all modern states cannot reproduce itself indefinitely. The struggles by families of those victims against ongoing state brutality documented in *Unfinished Business* opened up an important space for a more general challenge to the legitimacy of British rule in Northern Ireland. It is only by acknowledging those types of resistance to state power that we begin to understand that everywhere state violence is imposed, it is opposed. This is not to project a reductionist view of power that underestimates the ability of the state to manipulate and absorb resistance. But it is to recognise that the imposition of state power is a process that is never complete. The dominance of state or law is never final. And if this statement seems like too neat an academic or abstract way of dismissing state power, then we need to bear witness to countless ongoing struggles against the arbitrary violence of the state (see, for example, Goldson and Coles, 2005; Stanley, 2007; Ryan, 1997; Scraton and Chadwick, 1987; Fisher, 1990; Harbury, 2005; Pickering, 2002).

In highlighting the contradictions in the structure of state/law/power, this section has provided us with a starting point for understanding where the space to oppose state power can be found. In this sense, the extracts in this section provide important theoretical foundations for thinking about state crime as a structure of power, and are therefore key reference points that we shall return in the final section of this text and at various points in between.

Note

1   If this argument holds for the modern state system, it is important to note that the decimation of indigenous soveriegnty and its total subjugation to the sovereign authority of the invader was the legal principle that always stood behind colonialism (Meiksins Wood, 2003).

References

Agamben, G. (1998) *Homo Sacer*. Palo Alto, CA: Standford University Press.

Agamben, G. (2005) *State of Exception*. Chicago: Chicago University Press.

Christie, N. (1977) 'Conflicts as property', *British Journal of Criminology*, 17(1): 1–15.

Coleman, R., Sim, J., Tombs, S. and Whyte, D. (2009) 'Introduction' in R. Coleman, J. Sim, S. Tombs and D. Whyte (eds) *State, Power, Crime*. London: Sage.

Derrida, J. (1990) 'Force of law: "The mystical foundation of authority" ' in A. Sarat and T. Kearns (eds) *Justice and Injustice in Law and Legal Theory*. Ann Arbor: University of Michigan Press.

Fanon, F. (2001) *The Wretched of the Earth*. London: Penguin.

Fisher, J. (1990) *Mothers of the Disappeared*. Cambridge, MA: South End Press.

Goldson, B. and Coles, D. (2005) *In the Care of the State: Child deaths in penal custody in England and Wales*. London: Inquest.

Gramsci, A. (1996) *Selections from the Prison Notebooks, Vol. 1*. London: Lawrence and Wishart.

Haldeman, F. (2005) 'Gustav Radbruch vs. Hans Kelsen: A debate on Nazi law', *Ratio Juris*, 18(2).

Hall, S., Critchner, C., Jefferson, T., Clarke, J. and Roberts, B. (1978) *Policing the Crisis*. Basingstoke: Macmillan.

Harbury, J. (2005) Truth, *Torture and the American Way: The history and consequences of US involvement in torture*. Boston: Beacon.

Hillyard, P. (1993) *Suspect Community*. London: Pluto.

McBarnet, D. (1983) 'Victim in the Witness Box' – confronting victimology's stereotype. *Contemporary Crises*, 7: 279–303.

Meiksins Wood, E. (2003) *Empires of Capital*. London: Verso.

Miller, R. (2001) 'Rejecting Radbruch: The European Court of Human Rights and the crimes of East German leadership', *Leiden Journal of International Law*, 14: 653–663.

Pickering, S. (2002) *Women, Policing and Resistance in Northern Ireland*. Belfast: Beyond the Pale.

Poulantzas, N. (1978) *State, Power, Socialism*. London: New Left Books.

Ryan, M. (1997) *Lobbying from Below: INQUEST in defence of civil liberties*. London: Routledge.

Scraton, P. and Chadwick, C. (1987) *In the Arms of the Law: Coroner's inquests and deaths in custody*. London: Pluto.

Stanley, L (2007) *Torture Survivors: Their experiences of violation, truth and justice*. Dili, East Timor: Judicial System Monitoring Programme.

Tombs, S. (2007) 'Violence, Safety crimes and Criminology', *British Journal of Criminology*, 47(4).

1

Politics as a vocation
Max Weber

[...] What is a 'state'? Sociologically, the state cannot be defined in terms of its ends. There is scarcely any task that some political association has not taken in hand, and there is no task that one could say has always been exclusive and peculiar to those associations which are designated as political ones: today the state, or historically, those associations which have been the predecessors of the modern state. Ultimately, one can define the modern state sociologically only in terms of the specific *means* peculiar to it, as to every political association, namely, the use of physical force.

'Every state is founded on force,' said Trotsky at Brest-Litovsk. That is indeed right. If no social institutions existed which knew the use of violence, then the concept of 'state' would be eliminated, and a condition would emerge that could be designated as 'anarchy,' in the specific sense of this word. Of course, force is certainly not the normal or the only means of the state—nobody says that—but force is a means specific to the state. Today the relation between the state and violence is an especially intimate one. In the past, the most varied institutions—beginning with the sib—have known the use of physical force as quite normal. Today, however, we have to say that a state is a human community that (successfully) claims the *monopoly of the legitimate use of physical force* within a given territory. Note that 'territory' is one of the characteristics of the state. Specifically, at the present time, the right to use physical force is ascribed to other institutions or to individuals only to the extent to which the state permits it. The state is considered the sole source of the 'right' to use violence. Hence, 'politics' for us means striving to share power or striving to influence the distribution of power, either among states or among groups within a state.

This corresponds essentially to ordinary usage. When a question is said to be a 'political' question, when a cabinet minister or an official is said to be a 'political' official, or when a decision is said to be 'politically' determined, what is always meant is that interests in the distribution, maintenance, or transfer of power are decisive for answering the questions and determining the decision or the official's sphere of activity. He who is active in politics strives for power either as a means in serving other aims, ideal or egoistic, or as 'power for power's sake,' that is, in order to enjoy the prestige-feeling that power gives.

Like the political institutions historically preceding it, the state is a relation of men dominating men, a relation supported by means of legitimate (i.e. considered to be legitimate) violence. [...]

[...] Whosoever contracts with violent means for whatever ends—and every politician does—is exposed to its specific consequences. This holds especially for the crusader, religious and revolutionary alike. Let us confidently take the present as an example. He who wants to establish absolute justice on earth by force requires a following, a human 'machine.' He must hold out the necessary internal and external premiums, heavenly or worldly reward, to this 'machine' or else the machine will not function. Under the conditions of the modern class struggle, the internal premiums consist of the satisfying of hatred and the craving for revenge; above all, resentment and the need for pseudo-ethical self-righteousness: the opponents must be slandered and accused of heresy. The external rewards are adventure, victory, booty, power, and spoils. The leader and his success are completely dependent upon the functioning of his machine and hence not on his own motives. [...]

Note

'Politik als Beruf,' *Gesammelte Politische Schriffen* (Muenchen, 1921), pp. 396–450. Originally a speech at Munich University, 1918, published in 1919 by Duncker & Humblodt, Munich.

2

Critique of violence
Walter Benjamin

[...] This thesis of natural law that regards violence as a natural datum is diametrically opposed to that of positive law, which sees violence as a product of history. If natural law can judge all existing law only in criticizing its ends, so positive law can judge all evolving law only in criticizing its means. If justice is the criterion of ends, legality is that of means. Notwithstanding this antithesis, however, both schools meet in their common basic dogma: just ends can be attained by justified means, justified means used for just ends. Natural law attempts, by the justness of the ends, to "justify" the means, positive law to "guarantee" the justness of the ends through the justification of the means. This antinomy would prove insoluble if the common dogmatic assumption were false, if justified means on the one hand and just ends on the other were in irreconcilable conflict. No insight into this problem could be gained, however, until the circular argument had been broken, and mutually independent criteria both of just ends and of justified means were established.

The realm of ends, and therefore also the question of a criterion of justness, is excluded for the time being from this study. Instead, the central place is given to the question of the justification of certain means that constitute violence. Principles of natural law cannot decide this question, but can only lead to bottomless casuistry. For if positive law is blind to the absoluteness of ends, natural law is equally so to the contingency of means. On the other hand, the positive theory of law is acceptable as a hypothetical basis at the outset of this study, because it undertakes a fundamental distinction between kinds of violence independently of cases of their application. This distinction is between historically acknowledged, so-called sanctioned violence, and unsanctioned violence. [...]

[...] The meaning of the distinction between legitimate and illegitimate violence is not immediately obvious. The misunderstanding in natural law by which a distinction is drawn between violence used for just and unjust ends must be emphatically rejected. Rather, it has already been indicated that positive law demands of all violence a proof of its historical origin, which under certain conditions is declared legal, sanctioned. Since the acknowledgment of legal violence is most tangibly evident in a deliberate submission to its ends, a hypothetical distinction between kinds of violence must be based on the presence or absence of a general historical acknowledgment of its ends. Ends that lack such acknowledgment may be called natural ends, the other legal ends. The differing function of violence, depending on whether it serves natural or legal ends, can be most clearly traced against a background of specific legal conditions. For the sake of simplicity, the following discussion will relate to contemporary European conditions.

Characteristic of these, as far as the individual as legal subject is concerned, is the tendency not to admit the natural ends of such individuals in all those cases in which such ends could, in a given situation, be usefully pursued by violence. This means: this legal system tries to erect, in all areas where individual ends could be usefully pursued by violence, legal ends that can only be realized by legal power. [...]

[...] It can be formulated as a general maxim of present-day European legislation that all the natural ends of individuals must collide with legal ends if pursued with a greater or lesser degree of violence. (The contradiction between this and the right of self-defense will be resolved in what follows.) From this maxim it follows that law sees violence in the hands of individuals as a danger undermining the legal system. [...]

[...] [V]iolence confronts the law with the threat of declaring a new law, a threat that even today, despite its impotence, in important instances horrifies the public as it did in primeval times. The state, however, fears this violence simply for its lawmaking character. [...]

[...] [W]here the highest violence, that over life and death, occurs in the legal system, the origins of law jut manifestly and fearsomely into existence. In agreement with this is the fact that the death penalty in primitive legal systems is imposed even for such crimes as offenses against property, to which it seems quite out of "proportion." Its purpose is not to punish the infringement of law but to establish new law. For in the exercise of violence over life and death more than in any other legal act, law reaffirms itself. [...]

[...] [A] totally nonviolent resolution of conflicts can never lead to a legal contract. For the latter, however peacefully it may have been entered into by the parties, leads finally to possible violence. It confers on both parties the right to take recourse to violence in some form against the other, should he break the agreement. Not only that; like the outcome, the origin of every contract also points toward violence. It need not be directly present in it as lawmaking violence, but is represented in it insofar as the power that guarantees a legal contract is in turn of violent origin even if violence is not introduced into the contract itself. When the consciousness of the latent presence of violence in a legal institution disappears, the institution falls into decay. In our time, parliaments provide an example of this. They offer the familiar, woeful spectacle because they have not remained conscious of the revolutionary forces to which they owe their existence. [...] They lack the sense that a lawmaking violence is represented by themselves; no wonder that they cannot achieve decrees worthy of this violence, but cultivate in compromise a supposedly nonviolent manner of dealing with political affairs. This remains, however, a "product situated within the mentality of violence, no matter how it may disdain all open violence, because the effort toward compromise is motivated not internally but from outside, by the opposing effort, because no compromise, however freely accepted, is conceivable without a compulsive character. 'It would be better otherwise' is the underlying feeling in every compromise." [...]

[...] [H]owever desirable and gratifying a flourishing parliament might be by comparison, a discussion of means of political agreement that are in principle nonviolent cannot be concerned with parliamentarianism. For what parliament achieves in vital affairs can only be those legal decrees that in their origin and outcome are attended by violence. [...]

[...] Lawmaking is power making, and, to that extent, an immediate manifestation of violence. Justice is the principle of all divine end making, power the principle of all mythical lawmaking.

An application of the latter that has immense consequences is to be found in constitutional law. For in this sphere the establishing of frontiers, the task of "peace" after all the wars of the mythical age, is the primal phenomenon of all lawmaking violence. Here we see most clearly that power, more than the most extravagant gain in property, is what is guaranteed by all lawmaking violence. Where frontiers are decided the adversary is not simply annihilated; indeed, he is accorded rights even when the victor's superiority in power is complete. And these are, in a demonically ambiguous way, "equal" rights: for both parties to the treaty it is the same line that may not be crossed. Here appears, in a terribly primitive form, the same mythical ambiguity of laws that may not be "infringed" to which Anatole France refers satirically when he says, "Poor and rich are equally forbidden to spend the night under the bridges." [...]

3

Political crime
Louis Proal

[...] The law has been transformed by politics into an instrument of proscription and spoliation. Barbarous peoples make use of arms to kill and rob; people who think themselves civilised make use of laws. The law is as murderous as firearms, as potent an instrument of destruction as the axe, and depredations go on under cover of it as highway robbery under cover of a forest. Murder and robbery have been made part and parcel of the law; proscription and spoliation have been given legal Shape.

Legal proscription is more hateful than brutal violence, because upon iniquity it superimposes hypocrisy. The legists who lend persecution a legal guise are more depraved than those who butcher their fellow-men.

Politics have filled legislation with absurdities and hypocritical cruelties. Can anything be more monstrous, for example, than the English laws for the suppression of Catholicism in Ireland? The English legists devised a system of laws, of which Burke said that "it was the most cunning and powerful instrument of oppression that had ever been invented by the perverse genius of man to ruin, debase, and deprave a nation and to corrupt in it even the most unchangeable well-springs of human nature." These atrocious laws, said Canning again, seem to be the outcome of all the most cruel researches against human nature, of all the most atrocious combinations against men. In order to keep the Catholics in a state of destitution and ignorance, the law had forbidden them the acquisition of landed property and the exercise, of liberal professions. While not making Protestant instruction obligatory, the law banished the Catholic teachers; it did not forbid the Catholic form of worship, but it expelled the Catholic bishops and punished them with death in the event of their return, etc., etc.

These laws had for their object the despoilment of the Catholics as well as their persecution. "The English Parliament," says Walter Scott, "had arrogated to itself the right of making laws for Ireland, and exercised it in such a manner as to shackle the commerce of the kingdom as much as possible, to subordinate it to English commerce, and to keep it in a state of dependence." English legislation ruined the Irish wool manufacture. Ireland having protested against the law prohibiting the exportation of woollen goods, the House of Commons presented an address to the

Queen complaining "that although the wool manufacture was a branch of English commerce, which, the Legislature looked after with the utmost vigilance, yet Ireland, dependent upon and protected by England, not content with the liberty accorded it of having cotton manufactures, further claimed to devote its capital and credit to weaving woollens and manufacturing cloth to the detriment of England." Swift, indignant at English greed, urged the Irish in a pamphlet to make use of none but Irish products, and not to employ cloth stuffs imported from England. Criminal proceedings were instituted against the printer of the pamphlet.

I have cited the English laws against Ireland as an example of how persecution and spoliation are given hypocritically a legal shape. Analogous examples are to be found in the legislation of all peoples.

Politics, which are hostile to common law, tend towards the creation of privileges; they have instituted privileged classes, orders, and castes which did not pay taxes, and obtained the most important public posts. Undoing the work of God, who gave the same rights to all men, they have created inequality in the matter of civil and political rights, they have altered the true mutual relations of men, and they have established inequality even in respect to justice.[1]

The law ought to aim at the protection of the liberty and property of all citizens, but politics have always obtained the passing of laws favourable to the interests of those in power. When the power is in the hands of an aristocracy, the laws are framed in the interests of that aristocracy, and in the interests of the democracy when it is a democracy that wields the power. Under the old regime commoners were excluded in a general way from public functions; in several Italian republics, on the contrary, this exclusion was visited upon the nobles.

Laws ought to be general and impartial: politics makes them biassed and frames laws of exception.

Legislation has been corrupted to such an extent by polities, that Sir Thomas More, who, as Lord Chancellor, was well versed in legal matters, could not refrain from exclaiming: "When I reflect upon the laws and governments of our world, may I die if I find therein even the merest shadow of justice or equity! Good God! what equity, what justice is ours!"[2] The presence of unjust laws in the legislation of all peoples is to be attributed to political considerations. Laws of exception are always political laws, they are the arms to which parties have recourse to destroy their adversaries. In 1816 a Deputy cynically remarked in the Chamber: "Last year I voted measures of public safety, because they were to be employed against the opposite party; now that they may be employed against ourselves I will not hear of them."[3] When the law against the Emigrants was voted (it punished the crime of emigration with death) a speaker raised his voice in favour of the servants who had followed their masters abroad, but the Deputy who had charge of the Bill objected to him: "The law we propose is a law suggested by the circumstances; it is a weapon of offence; why occupy ourselves with any injustice it may involve?"[4] [...]

Notes

1 Under the old régime the nobleman guilty of a crime still enjoyed privileges. There were different penalties for the nobleman and the commoner.

2   Sir Thomas More, "Utopia," Bk. 11.
3   Berenger, "De la Justice Criminelle," p. 12.
4   Mortimer-Ternaux, op. cit., Vol. V., p. 164.

4

Eichmann in Jerusalem: a report on the banality of evil
Hannah Arendt

[...] The theory of the act of state is based on the argument that one sovereign state may not sit in judgment upon another, *par in parem non habet jurisdictionem*. Practically speaking, this argument had already been disposed of at Nuremberg; it stood no chance from the start, since, if it were accepted, even Hitler, the only one who was really responsible in the full sense, could not have been brought to account—a state of affairs which would have violated the most elementary sense of justice. However, an argument that stands no chance on the practical plane has not necessarily been demolished on the theoretical one. The usual evasions—that Germany at the time of the Third Reich was dominated by a gang of criminals to whom sovereignty and parity cannot very well be ascribed—were hardly useful. For on the one hand everyone knows that the analogy with a gang of criminals is applicable only to such a limited extent that it is not really applicable at all, and on the other hand these crimes undeniably took place within a "legal" order. That, indeed, was their out-standing characteristic.

Perhaps we can approach somewhat closer to the matter if we realize that back of the concept of act of state stands the theory of *raison d'état*. According to that theory, the actions of the state, which is responsible for the life of the country and thus also for the laws obtaining in it, are not subject to the same rules as the acts of the citizens of the country. Just as the rule of law, although devised to eliminate violence and the war of all against all, always stands in need of the instruments of violence in order to assure its own existence, so a government may find itself compelled to commit actions that are generally regarded as crimes in order to assure its own survival and the survival of lawfulness. Wars are frequently justified on these grounds, but criminal acts of state do not occur only in the field of international relations, and the history of civilized nations knows many examples of them—from Napoleon's assassination of the Due d'Enghien, to the murder of the Socialist leader Matteotti, for which Mussolini himself was presumably responsible.

Raison d'état appeals—rightly or wrongly, as the case may be—to *necessity*, and the state crimes committed in its name (which are fully criminal in terms of the dominant legal system of the country where they occur) are considered emergency measures, concessions made to the stringencies of *Realpolitik*, in order to preserve power and thus assure the continuance of the existing legal order as a whole. In a normal political and legal system, such crimes occur as an exception to the rule and are not subject to legal penalty (are *gerichtsfrei*, as German legal theory expresses it) because the existence of the state itself is at stake, and no outside political entity has the right to deny a state its existence or prescribe how it is to preserve it. However—as we may have learned from the history of Jewish policy in the Third Reich—in a state founded upon criminal principles, the situation is reversed. Then a non-criminal act (such as, for example, Himmler's order in the late summer of 1944 to halt the deportation of Jews) becomes a concession to necessity imposed by reality, in this case the impending defeat. Here the question arises: what is the nature of the sovereignty of such an entity? Has it not violated the parity (*par in parem non habet jurisdictionem*) which international law accords it? Does the "*par in parem*" signify no more than the paraphernalia of sovereignty? Or does it also imply a substantive equality or likeness? Can we apply the same principle that is applied to a governmental apparatus in which crime and violence are exceptions and borderline cases to a political order in which crime is legal and the rule? [...]

5

Sovereign police
Georgio Agamben

ONE OF the least ambiguous lessons learned from the Gulf War is that the concept of sovereignty has been finally introduced into the figure of the police. The nonchalance with which the exercise of a particularly devastating *ius belli* was disguised here as a mere "police operation" cannot be considered to be a cynical mystification (as it was indeed considered by some rightly indignant critics). The most *spectacular* characteristic of this war, perhaps, was that the reasons presented to justify it cannot be put aside as ideological superstructures used to conceal a hidden plan. On the contrary, ideology has in the meantime penetrated so deeply into reality that the declared reasons have to be taken in a rigorously literal sense—particularly those concerning the idea of a new world order. This does not mean, however, that the Gulf War constituted a healthy limitation of state sovereignties because they were forced to serve as policemen for a supranational organism (which is what apologists and extemporaneous jurists tried, in bad faith, to prove).

The point is that the police—contrary to public opinion—are not merely an administrative function of law enforcement; rather, the police are perhaps the place where the proximity and the almost constitutive exchange between violence and right that characterizes the figure of the sovereign is shown more nakedly and clearly than anywhere else. According to the ancient Roman custom, nobody could for any reason come between the consul, who was endowed with imperium, and the lictor closest to him, who carried the sacrificial ax (which was used to perform capital punishment). This contiguity is not coincidental. If the sovereign, in fact, is the one who marks the point of indistinction between violence and right by proclaiming the state of exception and suspending the validity of the law, the police are always operating within a similar state of exception. The rationales of "public order" and "security" on which the police have to decide on a case-by-case basis define an area of indistinction between violence and right that is exactly symmetrical to that of sovereignty. Benjamin rightly noted that:

The assertion that the ends of police violence are always identical or even connected to those of general law is entirely untrue. Rather, the "law" of the police really marks the point at which the state, whether from impotence or because of the immanent connections within any legal system, can no longer guarantee through the legal system the empirical ends that it desires at any price to attain.

Hence the display of weapons that characterizes the police in all eras. What is important here is not so much the threat to those who infringe on the right, but rather the display of that sovereign violence to which the bodily proximity between consul and lictor was witness. The display, in fact, happens in the most peaceful of public places and, in particular, during official ceremonies.

This embarrassing contiguity between sovereignty and police function is expressed in the intangible sacredness that, according to the ancient codes, the figure of the sovereign and the figure of the executioner have in common. This contiguity has never been so self-evident as it was on the occasion of a fortuitous encounter that took place on July 14, 1418: as we are told by a chronicler, the Duke of Burgundy had just entered Paris as a conqueror at the head of his troops when, on the street, he came across the executioner Coqueluche, who had been working very hard for him during those days. According to the story, the executioner, who was covered in blood, approached the sovereign and, while reaching for his hand, shouted: "Mon beau frère!"

The entrance of the concept of sovereignty in the figure of the police, therefore, is not at all reassuring. This is proven by a fact that still surprises historians of the Third Reich, namely, that the extermination of the Jews was conceived from the beginning to the end exclusively as a police operation. It is well known that not a single document has ever been found that recognizes the genocide as a decision made by a sovereign organ: the only document we have, in this regard, is the record of a conference that was held on January 20, 1942, at the Grosser Wannsee, and that gathered middle-level and lower-level police officers. Among them, only the name of Adolf Eichmann—head of division B-4 of the Fourth Section of the Gestapo—is noticeable. The extermination of the Jews could be so methodical and deadly only because it was conceived and carried out as a police operation; but, conversely, it is precisely because the genocide was a "police operation" that today it appears, in the eyes of civilized humanity, all the more barbaric and ignominious.

Furthermore, the investiture of the sovereign as policeman has another corollary: it makes it necessary to criminalize the adversary. Schmitt has shown how, according to European public law, the principle *par in parem non habet iurisdictionem* eliminated the possibility that sovereigns of enemy states could be judged as criminals. The declaration of war did not use to imply the suspension of either this principle or the conventions that guaranteed that a war against an enemy who was granted equal dignity would take place according to precise regulations (one of which was the sharp distinction between the army and the civilian population). What we have witnessed with our own eyes from the end of World War I onward is instead a process by which the enemy is first of all excluded from civil humanity and branded as a criminal; only in a second moment does it become possible and licit to eliminate the enemy by a "police operation." Such an operation is not obliged to respect any juridical rule and can thus make no distinctions between the civilian population and soldiers, as well as between the people and their criminal sovereign, thereby returning to the most archaic conditions of belligerence. Sovereignty's gradual slide toward the darkest areas of police law, however, has at least one positive aspect that is worthy of mention here. What the heads of state, who rushed to criminalize the enemy with such zeal, have not yet realized is that this criminalization can at any moment be turned against them. *There is no head of state on Earth today who, in this sense, is not virtually a criminal.* Today, those who should happen to wear the sad redingote of sovereignty know that they may be treated as criminals one day by their colleagues. And certainly we will not be the ones to pity them. The sovereigns who willingly agreed to present themselves as cops or executioners, in fact, now show in the end their original proximity to the criminal.

6

Unfinished business: state killings and the quest for truth

Bill Rolston

[...] Raising the issue of state killings while the war in Northern Ireland raged was [...] a difficult task because of a number of factors. First was the unquestioned belief that the state does not act as a terrorist, does not kill without reason or justification. Second was the presumption that 'there is no smoke without fire', that for all the protestations of innocence these victims had been somehow less than angelic. Third was the dissemination of these deep prejudices and presumptions by powerful institutions, especially the media. Fourth and finally was the deliberate misinformation and manipulation of the media by state forces, ensuring that a partial or downright false story was the first in the public domain and therefore the most likely to be believed and remembered.

Such was the power of this ideology that it was possible in the cases of state violence to override even the most obvious criterion of 'innocence'. Thus, it was usually presumed and often stated in official accounts that children killed by plastic bullets were involved in, or at least caught up in riots—the implication being that there was an element of contributory negligence involved.

Victims of state killings were often forgotten and ignored while the war was raging. To draw attention to them was to risk being labelled as 'soft on terrorism'. Criticising the state's human rights record was usually condemned on the grounds that it 'played into the hands of the terrorists'. It was even worse for relatives who dared to demand disclosure or prosecutions. To agitate was to draw down the wrath of the state forces on themselves, to become as marginalised and victimised as those for whom they fought. The vilification of the dead was echoed in the treatment of those who sought truth and justice. The fact that there were risks involved was undoubtedly one reason that agitation was less than might have been expected. Shock, powerlessness, marginalisation, harassment and fear were powerful deterrents. That powerlessness registered in different ways with different categories of victims. But it had a specific resonance in the case of relatives of members of paramilitary groups killed by state forces. Even if they believed that their relatives could have been arrested rather than killed, it was often difficult to find a sympathetic hearing for that view outside their own community, and sometimes even within. [...]

[...] It might be argued that it is elitist, perhaps even sectarian to focus only on state killings. Henry McDonald, *Observer* correspondent, has been a vocal proponent of such a criticism. For example, referring to the loyalist bombing of Dublin and Monaghan in 1974, and the Irish government's decision to hold an inquiry, he asks: 'Why was this atrocity any different to Bloody Friday, Enniskillen and Claudy?', all examples of mass killing by IRA bombs. He concludes: 'Either we draw a line under the past or we open up everything for examination' (*Observer* 8 August 1999).

[...] My focus is not on all victims, but solely on those killed by the state. There are two main reasons for this: first, they are qualitatively different from other killings because they have been carried out by an institution which, uniquely, claims to protect all citizens; and second, these victims have often been forgotten in the past, while those who have sought to keep the memory alive have been marginalised by the state and its institutions. None of this is to insinuate that the suffering of other victims and their relatives is necessarily any less than that of those killed by the state, even if in recent years some groups have had a more sympathetic hearing.

At the core of this issue is the question of equivalence. What truth is there about IRA massacres like Enniskillen and La Mon which needs to be uncovered and revealed? As a result of police investigations, court cases, etc. everything that can be known is known, except in some cases the names of the actual perpetrators. But there is no question of excessive force by a democratic state, no insinuation of state support or cover-up, no police or army harassment of those who demand justice in these cases. Moreover, in cases of killings by republicans it has been the presumption of the state, the media and large sections of public opinion that the victim is innocent, even if a uniformed and armed member of the security forces. Conversely, the victims of state violence have usually been presumed to be less than innocent, even if they were civilians. The state had the power to carry out these killings with impunity to block, legally and otherwise, any investigation, and to vilify and harass those who opposed its actions. To focus on these cases is to counterbalance the exclusion of such cases in the past. [...]

SECTION 2:

Partners in crime

The protection racket state

The first two articles in this section pick up directly from the discussion of the relationship between states, violence and crime developed in Section 1 and locate it in the historical context of the process of state formation.

Charles Tilly and Thomas Gallant are both concerned with the centrality of violence to the origins of the nation state system. Their studies of the process of early state formation both emphasise the centrality of direct violence to the process of state-making from the Middle Ages onwards. Their work, from different perspectives, shows clearly how the very foundations of the modern state are underpinned by military violence. For Tilly (1985: 170), the connection between state formation and violence is clearly exemplified by a continuum that '[b]anditry, piracy, gangland rivalry, policing and war making all belong to'. This continuum allows us to see how state violence is analogous to organised crime. From this perspective, states deploy organising principles similar to those deployed by private racketeers. Governments and the security apparatus of the state offer protection from the threat of external invasion, crime, anti-social behaviour, terrorism and so on. For Tilly (1985: 181), a protection racket is maintained by a process of 'extraction' – the economic means to pay for protection – which 'ranges from outright plunder to regular tribute to bureaucratised taxation'. In order to ensure that states have an ongoing capacity for state-making, war-making and protection, the state must maintain a violent process of 'extraction'. The ability of governments to run an efficient protection racket is therefore closely connected to their ability to legitimately monopolise violence and to fend off rivals. For states to enjoy unhindered and efficient means of 'extraction', 'outlaws' who continued to trade in and deliver violence, have to be brought 'inside' the state; they have to be incorporated into the state's regular military and police forces. This process is summed up by Tilly as follows: 'Robin Hood's conversion to royal archer may be a myth, but the myth records a practice. The distinctions between "legitimate" and "illegitimate" users of violence came clear only very slowly, in the process during which the state's armed forces became relatively unified and permanent' (extract: 173).

The relationship between violent 'outlaw' groups and the emerging nation states for Tilly was relatively passive and their function reduced to that of the outsider that needed to be brought fully 'inside' the state. The eradication of outlaws was therefore essentially a process of modernisation – the displacement of primitive violent groups by state-organised violence. But for Gallant (1999: 50–1), outlaws were much more centrally implicated in the process of state formation: 'rather than being archaic remnants of the pre-modern world, bandits and pirates were...both the products of and contributors to the advancement and consolidation of capitalism and modern states'. Gallant uses the term 'military entrepreneurs' to describe those same violent bands who took up arms and stood outside, often directly in opposition to, state forces. Those military entrepreneurs significantly contributed to the formation of states in the sense that they provided the basis for the penetration of markets into the most remote peripheral geographical areas: the borderlands and rural hinterlands. Thus, they had a range of uses to powerful elites, particularly in terms of their role in enclosing the land for new classes of property owners. They acted as border patrols; as guards to uphold property rights and protect property struggles between elites; they were deployed in remote areas on behalf of states and were used in wars between competing elites, particularly in the rural hinterlands and on the seas.

Just as military entrepreneurs were key to the penetration of the countryside by states, the markets in illegal goods they controlled, together with the proceeds of banditry, acted to elevate the level of marketisation in rural economies. Gallant therefore ascribes to military entrepreneurs a central and active role in the process of war-making and state-making. And he shows how this role was equally important whether they operated 'inside' or 'outside' of regular state forces. Sometimes military entrepreneurs were fully incorporated into the violent apparatuses of states and sometimes it suited the state to keep them at arm's length or at a formal distance when they were employed to do the state's dirty work. There are comparisons to be made here with the proliferation of private and para-security to support police and military forces in modern states, whereby those forces often fill a power vacuum, act in 'proxy' for states, or more simply supplement the coercive apparatuses of the state, enhancing capacities for imprisonment, policing, surveillance and militarised violence (Ryan and Ward, 1989; Whyte, 2003; O'Reilly and Ellison, 2006; Coleman, 2004). Some categories of military entrepreneurs were never fully incorporated into state mechanisms yet remained instrumental as allies or agents of the state. Just as we find and analogous relationship between 'private' security groups and regular government forces today, so there are contemporary similarities with the level of collusion that often exists between states and paramilitary groups – for example, in Colombia or Northern Ireland (Larkin, 2004; Stokes, 2004). And just as in the oft-cited example of the mujahidin alliance with the US in Afghanistan, some of Gallant's military entrepreneurs ended up switching sides in wars between elites.[1]

Gallant's article made another significant contribution in so far as it provided a modified history of the same phenomena that Eric Hobsbawm analysed in the book *Bandits* (1969). In this study, Hobsbawm argued that some groups of outlaws had an organic base in rural peasant communities and that they often led struggles and state bureaucracies. Hobsbawm therefore positioned many of the outlaw groups he documented as the class enemies of landowning and political elites, redefining them as 'social bandits'. Gallant recognises that his military entrepreneurs (of which Hobsbawm's social bandits can be though of as a subset) did play a role in popular insurrections and often had an organic link to, and enjoyed support from, rural peasant communities. However, his repositioning of bandits as, in some cases, the allies of elites and, in other cases, as intimately connected to struggles between elites meant that the picture was somewhat more complex than that offered by Hobsbawm, or indeed his critics (see also Blok, 1972; O'Malley, 1979).

Gallant therefore allows us to see how groups normally considered to be oppositional or existing 'outside' the state can simultaneously act as its 'partners' in crime, and therefore be considered as existing 'inside' the state. The remaining extracts in this section explore various aspects of how states form alliances and develop collusive relationships with institutions and groups for the purposes of committing acts of grand theft and violence.

Smedley Butler's extract here exposes a variation on this type of collusive relationship in a different historical context. It is a relationship that is character-ised in similar terms to those used by Tilly and Gallant. Butler, a relatively senior US military 'insider' at the turn of the twentieth century, became well known as a major critic of corporate power in the US of the 1930s and 1940s. Butler is an interesting character, not least because, at the time he decided to turn whistleblower, he was the most decorated marine in US history. The article from which the extract reproduced here comes, *In Time of Peace*, is essentially a shortened version of his famous pamphlet, *War is a Racket*, also published in 1935 (Butler, 2003). Picking up a theme reflected in Tilly's analogy of the protection racket, Butler notes his role in the US armed forces as a 'muscle man' or 'racketeer for capitalism'. In this extract, Butler raises important questions about US military and security state interventions on behalf of business at home and abroad, and points the finger at the private interests that benefit as 'partners' in war. It is a relationship that has been summed up more recently by neo-liberal commentator Thomas Friedman:

> The hidden hand of the market will never work without a hidden fist – McDonald's cannot flourish without McDonnell Douglas, the builder of the F-15. And the hidden fist that keeps the world safe for Silicon Valley's technologies is called the United States Army, Air Force, Navy and Marine Corps. (*New York Times Magazine*, 28 March 1999)

The similarities between Friedman and Butler's conclusions are telling, given that the former is one of capitalisms most dogmatic enthusiasts and the latter was one of its most trenchant 'muckrakers'. Both reveal an aspect of the relationship between states and corporations that is becoming more and more visible in the current era (for example, Klein, 2007).

Michael Woodiwiss is concerned with the systemic relationship between a range of different 'partners in crime', mediated by international political economy. His starting point in the book *Gangster Capitalism* is the rapid expansion of monopoly capital and the dawn of big finance at the start of the twentieth century in which, according to one commentator in the 1930s, 'the variety of rackets is endless' (2005: 21). The book characterises the restructuring of the international economy by the world's most powerful government in the past four decades as the creation of a 'crime-friendly world' (2005: 167). And, just like Butler's discussion of the war racket, Woodiwiss demonstrates how the state – in particular, the world's greatest superpower, the US – is less interested in crime control *per se* than in the concentration of power. In the text he shows how a network of powerful organised and state criminals is used instrumentally by the US state to strengthen its imperial reach on a global scale. And central to this is the very deliberate construction of an international financial and legal architecture that enables business transactions to remain relatively secret and anonymous, thus ensuring that criminal activities operate unhindered. The relationship between state and criminal interests is therefore at one level a marriage of convenience, and at another level is inscribed into the political economy of neo-liberalism.

William Chambliss notes at the start of his article *State-Organised Crime*:

> Twenty five years ago I began researching the relationship among organised crime, politics and law enforcement in Seattle, Washington...while continuing to research organised crime, I began a historical study of piracy and smuggling. In the process of analysing and beginning to write on these subjects, I came to realise that I was, in essence, studying the same thing in different time periods (1989: 183).

Chambliss details the routine involvement of state officials in piracy, smuggling, assassinations, criminal conspiracies, selling arms and supporting terrorism. More than a decade earlier, Frank Pearce (1976) outlined a closely interconnected and mutually reinforcing relationship that existed between politicians, corporate elites, and organised crime syndicates (see also Rawlinson, 1997; Beare, 2003; Ruggiero, 2000). A similar observation has latterly been made in an emergent literature on *political crime* (for example, Turk, 1982; Ross, 2003) that stands out from mainstream literature in both criminology and in political science. Whereas the literature in political science tends to rely upon individual explanations of corruption or tends to characterise political deviance as a pathological weakness (political crime is something that happens when the system does not work as it is supposed to work à *la* Proal), Pearce and Chambliss argued that the interconnections between organised crime, political factions and corporations are long-standing and ever-present characteristics of state power (see also Green and Ward, 2004: Chapter 6).

The evidence of state officials acting above and beyond the law in order to defend the integrity of the state that Chambliss documents here illustrates a fundamental contradiction at the heart of the rule of law, a contradiction that arises in the conflict between the legal prescriptions and the agreed goals of state agencies. It also brings a different dimension to debates on the 'state of exception' discussed in the previous section of this book. Chambliss identifies the arbitrary suspension of law by state officials without any open declaration of a 'state of emergency' This form of state crime, then, is an ongoing one that is organised by state officials, but is not made official by any decree or act of state authority. Chambliss's article has latterly influenced a growing body of literature on state-corporate crime (Aulette and Michalowski, 1993; Kauzlarich and Kramer, 1993; Kramer, 1992; Freidrichs, 1996; Michalowski and Kramer, 2006). In this literature state-corporate crime comes in two varieties: that approximating to Chambliss's formulation – 'state-organised' crime – and a rather different form, labelled 'state-facilitated' crime. Rather than a positive engagement or encouragement to commit crimes, the latter normally involves negative forms of complicity (failure to adequately regulate; wilful blindness; acts of omission rather than acts of commission). In other words, state-facilitated crimes are usually those that involve passive complicity rather than active collusion. The contradiction in the relationship between the state and its 'partners in crime' is therefore a much bigger one than that raised by Chambliss. For, as the extract by Nancy Wonders and Mona Danner shows, state-corporate crime also involves the weakening of womens' life chances in particular ways: their exposure to precarious and dangerous work; exposure to toxins, land degradation and deforestation and their massively disproportionate victimisation in war zones (see also Croall, 1995). This is a story not only of victimisation, but also of how corporate power and 'national interest' interact to facilitate displacement and violence against women both in the minority and majority worlds.

In the extract that brings this section to a close, Karl Marx shows how the British state strategically used illegal trade to undermine the economic position of a rival state. The strategy involved British merchant capitalists – encouraged and supported by the British government – acting very deliberately in breach of a Chinese government ban on opium importation. The interests of state and capital are so intertwined here that they are inseparable. British opium was grown in the Indian colony and exported to China by merchants and capitalists with the express intention of economically destabilising a rival empire. The Opium Wars were merely the latest in a long line of the British Empire's collaborative ventures with private profiteers. Throughout two and a half centuries, the English (latterly British) East India Company was implicated in countless atrocities against, and military suppression of, local peoples. Its colonial role of acting in proxy for the British government extended to the outlawing of many customs and religious rites of both Muslims and Hindus. The Company's private army also waged war against its French, Portuguese and Dutch counterparts to protect its access to raw materials and the factories and warehouses set up along the Indian coastline. The torture, decapitation and burning alive of corporate rivals was not unusual, in many cases merely for breaking mutual trade agreements. By the end of the company's reign, as Marx (1857) observed in his *New York Daily Tribune* column of the time, 'torture formed an organic institution of [British] financial policy'. Yet the torture and summary executions conducted by officers of the East India Company escaped criminal or even administrative punishment.

The British government set up other joint-stock corporations on a similar model at the end of the nineteenth century – notably the British Imperial East Africa Company and the British South Africa Company – to seize land, settle colonising forces and then plunder resources. Such companies were seen as the most expedient means of colonising Africa because they could administer trade, conduct military operations and run local police forces without overexposing the state. History showed that those companies had little moral compunction and embarked upon brutal campaigns of terror wherever they met local resistance. Indeed, they were key players in the imposition of regimes in southern Africa that Patrick Bond (1999) has called 'racist capitalist superexploitation'. This extract by Marx and the broader history that it reflects reveal to us a central dynamic in the development of imperialism: states facilitate strategies of capital accumulation that were supported by systematic violence and corruption (Litvin, 2004).

In some respects, the emergent literature on state-corporate crime marks a very early attempt to introduce into criminology fundamental questions about the nature and structure of states. And to delve further into those questions is something that lies outside the scope of this book. But it is important to look briefly at debates on the relationship between the 'public' and 'private' spheres in order to understand how crimes of the powerful are produced. The ways that governments, criminal enterprises and private corporations interact as 'partners in crime' raises the possibility that particular groups and institutions that are normally regarded as existing 'outside' the state can be used to project state power. Indeed, we can question the extent to which an institution or group might be considered to exist 'outside' the state if it is committing acts on the state's behalf, or if there exists a symbiotic relationship between 'public' and 'private' sectors. The distinction between the 'private sector' and the 'public sector' is a distinction that is defined in law. It is the formal definitions and powers prescribed in law and custom that decide which institutions are regarded as 'public' and which are regarded as 'private'. As Louis Althusser (2008: 18) put it, 'the State...is neither public nor private; on the contrary, it is the precondition for any distinction between public and private'.

So what exactly is the state? The prominent state theorist Bob Jessop (1990) argues that the state is not a 'thing' that possesses concentrated power but an *ensemble* of institutions and processes that provide a basis for the organisation of social forces. Schools, churches, business organisations, as well as government departments, police forces and armies, are part of the ensemble that projects state power. They contribute to a projection of state power by providing leadership and tutelage in the dominant morals and political ideas, or they contribute to the institutional ordering, of a society. The state mediates power relationships in society through key institutions (workplaces, the family, the market and so on), and as such the state can be more usefully thought of as a complex of mechanisms and apparatuses that mediates and organises social relations of power. And corporations play a crucial role in this process.

To say that private institutions can be defined as part of the state ensemble is not to say that they are under the spell of governments or that their interests always coincide with those of public institutions. Corporations enjoy some measure of real autonomy from governments – they have their own histories, customs and belief systems. Indeed, many of the largest corporations in the world today exist on the same scale – in economic terms – as some national governments and this makes them formidable power structures in their own right. So much so that we might argue that the concept of state-corporate crime might also include the categories of 'corporation-intiated' and 'corporation-facilitated' crime. The latter category might clearly be applied to cases where relatively powerful corporations fail to intervene, or act with wilful blindness, when private or government or bodies commit crime acting in close collaboration with corporations. Thus, for example, Coca Cola has faced widespread criticism and a high profile lawsuit following the assassination and torture by right-wing paramilitaries of trade unionists representing workers at its bottling plants in Colombia. It was alleged that paramilitary activities were carried out with the knowledge and complicity of plant management (see http://www.iradvocates.org/coke1case.html). Similarly, Human Rights Watch has raised concern about the human rights implications of BP's collaboration with Colombia's Defense Ministry in a context where disappearances and assassinations of opponents of the government and the oil company have been routine (http://www.hrw.org/advocacy/corporations/colombia/Oilpat-01.htm).

And there is a level of complicity that is not captured fully by the categories of 'corporation-initiated' and 'corporation-facilitated' crime. Often state crimes occur not because corporations actively encourage or even do anything to facilitate them, but merely because a mutual state–corporate interest exists. The Nigerian government's assassination of Ken Saro-Wiwa and the 'Ogoni 8' in 1995, for example, was a direct result of the close relationship with British/Dutch oil company Shell. This is not to say that Shell encouraged the Nigerian government to execute Saro-Wiwa, or even that the company had an interest in his killing. But Shell remained deeply involved in a crime that arose from its mutual interest with the Nigerian state in exploiting oil reserves of the Niger Data. In 2006, Shell's activities accounted for approximately 92% of Nigeria's foreign exchange earnings and 74% of government revenue (http://www.shell.com). The Nigerian state's ability to act with impunity cannot be separated from the strength it derives from its economic position. And Shell is a major contributor to the latter.

Together the readings in this section indicate that we should be wary of oversimplifying the relationship between governments and corporations as competing sources of power. States and corporations do not have a separate, autonomous existence outside each other and they do not stand in opposition to each other. Neither do they necessarily act in concert with each other. The relationship is far more complex than this. Corporations are given life by the state ensemble: they can only make profits and make investments because of the existence of a complex of rules and infrastructures that give them the ability to act. They are relatively autonomous in the sense that they make their own day-to-day business decisions, formulate their own strategies and project particular images of themselves to the outside world. But they also require the legal and market infrastructures created and maintained by governments. In this sense, we can say that private corporations exist both 'inside' and 'outside' the state. And we can say the same about powerful crime syndicates such as those described by Woodiwiss and Pearce. Rather than representing two separate and antagonistic elements of a society, the relationship between public and private spheres in capitalist societies can be understood as a complex and frequently contradictory institutional form through which state power is projected.

Neither does recognising that private institutions are part of a state ensemble mean that there are not important features that separate the 'public' from the 'private' sphere. For one thing, there are entirely different mechanisms of accountability applied to each and they can mean a great deal in terms of how we are able to observe or question those institutions. It is this point that brings us squarely back to the issue of state legitimacy. One of the reasons for the separation of powers as they exist in liberal democracies is to ensure that the political system is not corrupted by particular interests and to make sure that private interests are not used to wield political power. This is inscribed in the work of early liberal thinkers such as Montesquieu (1989) and Locke (1988) who proposed a clear separation of powers in the state and in the apparatuses of government. Thus, the political sphere is supposed to represent the will of the people, whereas the private sphere is where private individuals and institutions pursue their own private interests. But what this section has shown very clearly is that liberal democracies do not operate according to those principles. Moreover, it is not merely the fact that they do not operate according to their own principles that causes problems of legitimacy here, but the fact that the institutional structure of liberal democracies produces *criminal* relationships. This is a phenomenon that is not particular to Western liberal democracies or capitalist societies more generally. We can find forms of state-corporate crime in China or the former Soviet Union (Cheng Yang, 1995; Orland, 1986). But it is a phenomenon that – as we shall see in the next section – manifests itself in particular ways in capitalist societies.

Note

1 To the extent that those 'mujahidin' who affiliate themselves with Al Qaeda do exist in a recognisable organised form – and there are debates about the extent to which Al Qaeda can be said to exist in a conventional sense, with some form of internal coherence (Burke, 2004) – there are groups of armed fighters associated with Al Qaeda that in the past enjoyed a close relationship with the US state for many years, particularly when both had a common interest in fighting a war against the Soviet-controlled government in Afghanistan and latterly controlling the Afghan state.

References

Althusser, L. (2008) *On Ideology.* London: Verso.

Aulette, J. and Michalowski, R. (1993) 'Fire in Hamlet: A case study of state-corporate crime' in K. Tunnell (ed.) *Political Crime in Contemporary America: A critical approach.* New York: Garland.

Beare, M. (ed.) (2003) *Critical Reflections on Transnational Organised Crime, Money Laundering, and Corruption.* Toronto: University of Toronto Press.

Blok, A. (1972) 'The Peasant and the Brigand: social banditry reconsidered', *Comparative Studies in Society and History*, 14(4).

Bond, P. (1999) 'Political Reawakening in Zimbabwe', *Monthly Review*, 50(11).

Burke, J. (2004) *Al Qaeda: The true story of radical Islam*. London: IB Tauris.

Butler, S. (2003) *War is a Racket*. Los Angeles: Feral House.

Chambliss, W. (1989) 'State-organised Crime', *Criminology*, 27(2).

Cheng Yang, V. (1995) 'Corporate Crime: State owned enterprises in China', *Criminal Law Forum*, 6(1).

Coleman, R. (2004) *Reclaim the Streets*. Cullompton: Willan.

Croall, H. (1995) 'Target Women: Womens' victimization from white collar crime' in R. Dobash and L. Noakes (eds) *Gender and Crime*. Cardiff: Cardiff University Press.

Friedrichs, D. (1996) *Trusted Criminals: White collar crime in contemporary society*. Belmont, CA: Wadsworth.

Green, P. and Ward, T. (2004) *State Crime: Governments, violence and corruption*. London: Pluto.

Hobsbawm, E. (1969) *Bandits*. Harmondsworth: Penguin.

Jessop, B. (1990) *State Theory: Putting capitalist states in their place*. Cambridge: Polity.

Kauzlarich, D. and Kramer, R. (1993) 'State-corporate crime in the US nuclear weapons production complex', *Journal of Human Justice*, 5(4).

Klein, N. (2007) *The Shock Doctrine: The rise of disaster capitalism*. London: Allen Lane.

Kramer, R. (1992) 'The Space Shuttle Challenger explosion: A case study of state-corporate crime', in K. Schlegel and D. Weisburd (eds) *White-Collar Crime Reconsidered*. Boston: Northeastern University Press.

Larkin, P. (2004) *A Very British Jihad: Collusion, conspiracy and cover-up in Northern Ireland*. Belfast: Beyond the Pale.

Litvin, D. (2004) *Empires of Profit: Commerce, conquest and corporate responsibility*. Mason, OH: Thomson.

Locke, J. (1988) *Two Treatises on Government*. Cambridge: Cambridge University Press.

Marx, K. (1857) 'The Indian Revolt', *New York Daily Tribune*, 4 September.

Michalowski, R. and Kramer, R. (eds) (2006) *State-Corporate Crime: Wrongdoing at the intersection of business and government*. New Brunswick, NJ: Rutgers University Press.

Montesquieu, C. (1989) *The Spirit of the Laws*. Cambridge: Cambridge University Press.

O'Malley, P. (1979) 'Social bandits, Modern Capitalism and the Traditional Peasantry: A critique of Hobsbawm', *Journal of Peasant Studies*, 6(4).

O'Reilly, C. and Ellison, G. (2006) 'Eye Spy Private High: Reconceptualising high policing theory', *British Journal of Criminology*, 46(4).

Orland, L. (1986) 'Perspectives on Soviet Economic Crime', in S. Ioffe and M. Janis (eds) *Soviet Law and Economy*. Dordrecht: Martinus Nijhoff.

Pearce, F. (1976) *Crimes of the Powerful*. London: Pluto.

Rawlinson, P. (1997) 'Russian Organised Crime: A brief history', in P. Williams (ed.) *Russian Organised Crime: The new threat*. London: Frank Cass.

Ross, J. (2003) *The Dynamics of Political Crime*. London: Sage.

Ruggiero, V. (2000) *Crime and Markets: essays in anti-criminology*. Oxford: Oxford University Press.

Ryan, M. and Ward, T. (1989) *Privatisation and the Penal System*. Milton Keynes: Open University Press.

Stokes, D. (2004) *America's Other War: Terrorizing Colombia*. London: Zed.

Tilly, C. (1985) 'War Making and State Making as Organized Crime' in P. B. Evans, D. Rueschemeyer and T. Skocpol (eds) *Bringing the State Back In.* Cambridge: Cambridge University Press.

Turk, A. (1982) *Political Criminality.* London: Sage.

Whyte, D. (2003) 'Lethal Regulation: State-corporate crime and the UK government's new mercenaries', *Journal of Law and Society*, 30(4).

Woodiwiss, M. (2005) *Gangster Capitalism: The United States and the global rise of organised crime.* London: Constable.

7

War making and state making as organized crime
Charles Tilly

[...] What distinguished the violence produced by states from the violence delivered by anyone else? In the long run, enough to make the division between "legitimate" and "illegitimate" force credible. Eventually, the personnel of states purveyed violence on a larger scale, more effectively, more efficiently, with wider assent from their subject populations, and with readier collaboration from neighboring authorities than did the personnel of other organizations. But it took a long time for that series of distinctions to become established. Early in the state-making process, many parties shared the right to use violence, the practice of using it routinely to accomplish their ends, or both at once. The continuum ran from bandits and pirates to kings via tax collectors, regional power holders, and professional soldiers.

The uncertain, elastic line between "legitimate" and "illegitimate" violence appeared in the upper reaches of power. Early in the state-making process, many parties shared the right to use violence, its actual employment, or both at once. The long love–hate affair between aspiring state makers and pirates or bandits illustrates the division. "Behind piracy on the seas acted cities and city-states," writes Fernand Braudel of the sixteenth century. "Behind banditry, that terrestrial piracy, appeared the continual aid of lords."[1] In times of war, indeed, the managers of full-fledged states often commissioned privateers, hired sometime bandits to raid their enemies, and encouraged their regular troops to take booty. In royal service, soldiers and sailors were often expected to provide for themselves by preying on the civilian population: commandeering, raping, looting, taking prizes. When demobilized, they commonly continued the same practices, but without the same royal protection; demobilized ships became pirate vessels, demobilized troops bandits.

It also worked the other way: A king's best source of armed supporters was sometimes the world of outlaws. Robin Hood's conversion to royal archer may be a myth, but the myth records a practice. The distinctions between "legitimate" and "illegitimate" users of violence came clear only very slowly, in the process during which the state's armed forces became relatively unified and permanent.

Up to that point, as Braudel says, maritime cities and terrestrial lords commonly offered protection, or even sponsorship, to freebooters. Many lords who did not pretend to be kings, furthermore, successfully claimed the right to levy troops and maintain their own armed retainers. Without calling on some of those lords to bring their armies with them, no king could fight a war; yet the same armed lords constituted the king's rivals and opponents, his enemies' potential allies. For that reason, before the seventeenth century, regencies for child sovereigns reliably produced civil wars. For the same reason, disarming the great stood high on the agenda of every would-be state maker. [...]

[...] In retrospect, the pacification, cooptation, or elimination of fractious rivals to the sovereign seems an awesome, noble, prescient enterprise, destined to bring peace to a people; yet it followed almost ineluctably from the logic of expanding power. If a power holder was to gain from the provision of protection, his competitors had to yield. As economic historian Frederic Lane put it twenty-five years ago, governments are in the business of selling protection ... whether people want it or not. Lane argued that the very activity of producing and controlling violence favored monopoly, because competition within that realm generally raised costs, instead of lowering them. The production of violence, he suggested, enjoyed large economies of scale.

Working from there, Lane distinguished between (*a*) the monopoly profit, or *tribute,* coming to owners of the means of producing violence as a result of the difference between production costs and the price exacted from "customers" and (*b*) the *protection rent* accruing to those customers – for example, merchants – who drew effective protection against outside competitors. Lane, a superbly attentive historian of Venice, allowed specifically for the case of a government that generates protection rents for its merchants by deliberately attacking their competitors. In their adaptation of Lane's scheme, furthermore, Edward Ames and Richard Rapp substitute the apt word "extortion" for Lane's "tribute." In this model, predation, coercion, piracy, banditry, and racketeering share a home, with their upright cousins in responsible government. [...]

[...] To a larger degree, states that have come into being recently through decolonization or through reallocations of territory by dominant states have acquired their military organization from outside, without the same internal forging of mutual constraints between rulers and ruled. To the extent that outside states continue to supply military goods and expertise in return for commodities, military alliance or both, the new states harbor powerful, unconstrained organizations that easily overshadow all other organizations within their territories. To the extent that outside states guarantee their boundaries, the managers of those military organizations exercise extraordinary power within them. The advantages of military power become enormous, the incentives to seize power over the state as a whole by means of that advantage very strong. Despite the great place that war making occupied in the making of European states, the old national states of Europe almost never experienced the great disproportion between military organization and all other forms of organization that seems the fate of client states throughout the contemporary world. A century ago, Europeans might have congratulated themselves on the spread of civil government throughout the world.

In our own time, the analogy between war making and state making, on the one hand, and organized crime, on the other, is becoming tragically apt.

Note

1   Fernand Braudel, *La Méditerranée et le monde méditerranéan à l'époque de Philippe II* (Paris: Armand Colin, 1966), vol. 2, pp. 88–89.

8

Brigandage, piracy, capitalism, and state-formation: transnational crime from a historical world-systems perspective
Thomas W. Gallant

[...] Bandits and pirates stole. By definition, they expropriated goods and commodities illegally. Nevertheless, even this seemingly straightforward proposition is not without its difficulties once we move beyond the labels. Depending on the context and on which historical actor's viewpoint we adopt, the identical depredations by the same men could be and were considered legitimate by some and illegitimate by others. One state's pirate was another state's privateer. And when it came to opening their household larders to outsiders, it made little difference to peasants and rural laborers whether the open-palmed claimant was the taxman or an extortionist brigand. [...]

[...] In economic terms, the depredations of both bandits and pirates became at times quantitatively significant, but over the long term they often came to be considered as the almost predictable costs of doing business in many parts of the world. Nonetheless, the magnitude of their exactions could constitute a serious threat to a region's economy and would therefore justify the costs of a concerted state-level initiative to eradicate or at least to curtail brigand activity. There is, however, another, probably even more important, economic aspect of military entrepreneurship that has not been discussed in the literature, and that is the ways that banditry facilitated capitalist penetration of the peasant economy. [...]

[...] First, bandits elevated the level of marketization in the countryside. In most cases, brigands stole portable commodities of value: gold or bullion, spices, jewels, opium, and the like, depending on which part of the world we are talking about. In any event, with the exception of livestock, we can generally accept that bandits stole non-consumables. But even with livestock, it was frequently the case that the stolen meat and the hides in particular were destined for the market-place (Langer 1987: 177 and 122; Alexander 1985: 151). Perforce, therefore they had to purchase the basic foodstuffs they required for their subsistence, and they had to acquire these from the peasants and rural husbandmen among whom they lived and to whom they were often related (Hobsbawm 1981: 83–5). Granted, there are well-documented cases where armed gangs simply extorted food from villagers, but more often it appears that they purchased their supplies. After all, the gang's survival depended on the acquiescence or compliance of the peasants. Moreover, since most bandits were peasants or rural dwellers themselves, they were connected in a variety of ways with the local communities (Gallant 1988). Their relationship to rural society was more symbiotic than parasitic. As an old Chinese proverb expressed it: 'the rabbit never eats the grass around its own hole' (Perry 1980: 74). The market mechanism of exchange linked the brigand to the agriculturalist, and this led to the increased monetization of the rural economy.

Second, bandits also connected rural villages to outside markets. The stolen commodities injected into the local economy only had real value if they could be translated into other forms of wealth. In some cases, brigand gangs developed close working relationships with specific merchants. In Morocco, for example, each gang had attached to it a specific trader or *kamman* whose job it was to sell their booty (Hart 1987: 14–15). This type of arrangement is documented in India (Arnold 1979: 151), China (Antony 1990: 31; Perry 1980: 35), Africa (Kea 1986: 111), Mexico (Slatta 1987: 191–4), the Netherlands (Egmond 1986: 168–74), and the Balkans. The memoirs of the notorious thug Amir Ali in India are full of episodes in which he or members of his gang undertook delicate negotiations for the sale of their ill-gotten gain (P. Taylor 1985: 185–94).

In other situations, bandits themselves took on the role of merchants. A seventeenth-century observer concluded about the *uskoks* of Senj, for example, that 'these valorous warriors have become avaricious merchants of stolen goods, devoting themselves to nothing else than the sale of their plunder in Croatia, in Carniola, in Styria, in Hungary, even across the sea in Apulia and the Marches, and even in Venice itself, so that having abandoned the military arts they are applying themselves to one that is sweeter, that is, to profit' (Bracewell 1992: 111). Matija Danic, to cite a particularly apt example, left the life of the brigand and accumulated a vast fortune by acting as a broker for other *uskok* gangs (Bracewell 1992: 112). [...]

[...] The relationship between piracy and state formation resembles that of terrestrial brigandage. Frequently when states were unable to bear the considerable expense of mounting maritime naval expeditions against their foes, they would turn to private maritime military entrepreneurs. Privateers acting under commissions provided by a state carried out thousands of raids during the early modern period. Thomson (1994) shows how these depredations were part of proxy wars between the emerging European states. But as with those of their brethren on land, privateers' activities were always subject to definitional ambiguity. Sea dogs proved undiscriminating in their choice of prey and, even when they attacked vessels belonging to the states of their opponents, from somebody's perspective they were pirates. Because, like brigands on land, they presented authorities with a challenge to the state's claim to monopolize the legitimate means of violence, state consolidation of power had to come at the expense of maritime freebooters. In early modern Europe, state sovereignty was achieved partly through the curbing of maritime brigands' activities.

Like other military entrepreneurs, pirates could also become key players in the internal process of state formation or state consolidation. The best example comes from China during the late eighteenth century. Dian Murray in her examination of piracy in the South China Sea found that there was a close relationship between it and the Tay-san Rebellion. In their attempt to wrest power from the Emperor the Tay-san encouraged maritime predation. This politicization of piracy led to a dramatic increase in the numbers of men at arms. When the rebellion was put down, the seafaring warriors persisted in their piratical ways. If the Tay-san had been victorious then they would have been transformed into inlaws, and probably would have become the fleet of the new government. Since, however, they were clients of the losers, they stood once more outside the law, except that now their numbers were far greater than before. Unable to conquer them, the Chinese Emperor did what so many other rulers before and after him had done: he bestowed legitimate authority on some of the pirates, and ordered them to eradicate those who could not be accommodated. As we saw before, the politicization of brigandage led to an inflation of its magnitude.

Pirates acted both as economic agents and as informal warriors in facilitating European imperial expansion. V. G. Scammell has argued that European pirates and outlaws operating in Asia and Africa played an important role in the Asian maritime economy of the early modern period by sending goods and slaves to the American and Caribbean colonies. They also facilitated the extension of European power in Asia and Africa by keeping their countrymen informed of the local situation, by discovering new and important trade routes, and by enabling Westerners to enter new markets. Their activities in Asia and Africa only ended when European states institutionalized their military power over far-flung areas (Scammell 1992). [...]

[...] Military entrepreneurs literally and figuratively lived on the edge of society. When they operated without the sanction of the law as brigands rather than as enforcers, they often found themselves drawn and pushed into remote, inaccessible areas and frontier zones. Attracting them was the peculiar economic geography I discussed earlier and the fact that most of these men had their roots in rural society and, quite frequently, in that world's most marginal quarters. Compelling them to move to the margins was the need to seek protection from their pursuers in areas with rugged, difficult topographies and social environments open to them but inhospitable to outsiders. Another dynamic was at work as well. Newly emergent or developing nation-states and distant domains under the control of foreign empires were often forced to or found it cost-expedient to employ irregulars as the guardians of their frontiers. Almost invariably these border patrols were drawn from the same class of men who constituted brigand gangs. The dilemma of setting a thief to catch a thief arose again, and the interaction between outlaws and border patrols took on predictable forms. Brigandage flourished in the frontier zones and the security forces sent to control their depredations and guard the border were often indistinguishable from the outlaws. Nowhere, then, was the contest over control of the monopoly of coercive force more starkly evident than in the frontier zone.

The fledgling Kingdom of Greece after 1832, for example, proved incapable of controlling its hinter- and borderlands. In the absence of an effective rural police force, in the presence of a rural economy in flux, and in the midst of a crisis of national authority, military entrepreneurs flourished. Acting as estate guards and employed by the state to chase unauthorized brigands, men at arms operated pretty much as they had before independence. There was, however, a new dimension added: the border. The newly demarcated territorial boundary between Greece and Turkey needed to be guarded; and who better than the local bad men? But as before, they preyed on cross-border traffic. Moreover, since the border guards were drawn from the same class of military entrepreneurs, they would venture on bandit raids across the border. When they did this, they often had the unacknowledged approval of their government. The dilemma of labeling appears again. One side's border patrol was the other's bandit menace. It was, however, the activity of these men on the edges that elevated the role of the border zone to one of importance. Indeed it was through the activities of these men that the border actually took on real meaning and concrete form (Gallant 1997). [...]

9

In time of peace
Smedley D. Butler

[...] Our army and navy have only recently completed their largest and most ambitious peace-time maneuvers. Our National Guardsmen have done even better. In the past two years large National Guard forces have seen active service in 20 strikes in as many different states, from the Pacific Coast to New England, from Minnesota to Georgia. They have used gas, bullets, and tanks—the most lethal weapons of modern war—against striking workers. Casualty lists have been impressive. In one instance they erected barbed wire concentration camps in Georgia to "co-ordinate" striking workers with all the efficiency of the fascist repressive technique.

There isn't a trick in the racketeering bag that the military gang is blind to. It has its "finger men" (to point out enemies), its "muscle men" (to destroy enemies), its "brain guys," (to plan war preparations) and a "Big Boss," (super-nationalistic capitalism). [...]

[...] It may seem odd for me, a military man to adopt such a comparison [between the military and organised crime]. Truthfulness compels me to. I spent 33 years and 4 months in active service as a member of our country's most agile military force—the Marine Corps. I served in all commissioned ranks from a second lieutenant to Major-General. And during that period I spent most of my time being a high-class muscle man for Big Business, for Wall Street and for the bankers. In short, I was a racketeer for capitalism. [...]

[...] Thus I helped make Mexico and especially Tampico safe for American oil interests in 1914. I helped make Haiti and Cuba a decent place for the National City Bank boys to collect revenues in. I helped in the raping of half a dozen Central American republics for the benefit of Wall Street. The record of racketeering is long. I helped purify Nicaragua for the international banking house of Brown Brothers in 1909–12. I brought light to the Dominican Republic for American sugar interests in 1916. I helped make Honduras "right" for American fruit companies in 1903. In China in 1927 I helped see to it that Standard Oil went its way unmolested.

During those years, I had, as the boys in the back room would say, a swell racket. I was rewarded with honors, medals, promotion. Looking back on it, I feel

I might have given Al Capone a few hints. The best *he* could do was to operate his racket in three city districts. We Marines operated on three *continents*. [...]

[...] The import of these military intelligence reports can best be judged by the homework of military intelligence. The domestic brand of M. I. is mainly unadulterated Red-hunting. Hence intelligence officers cooperate more or less openly with such bulwarks of home defense as William Randolph Hearst, Ralph Easley, Harry Jung of Chicago, and such organizations as the National Security League, the American Vigilantes, and the Order of '76.

The intelligence men further justify their jobs by spy work on radical gatherings, by attending public forums in an attempt to detect political or economic [heresy], by keeping tabs on various suspects, and by smelling out what they consider to be subversive activities everywhere. In these extra-curricular activities whole-hearted cooperation from professional patrioteers and the Reserve Officers is received. In the New York area, for instance, the military intelligence officers are especially busy. With the 2nd Corps Area headquarters at Governor's Island off the Battery, and the Headquarters of the Communist party near Union Square, the intelligence men work like little beavers. Radical meetings are attended, notes taken, speakers listed, and as many of the audience identified as possible. It is well known in liberal and radical circles that the military intelligence units have been planting men within suspected organizations.[...]

[...] Now should the "finger" and "muscle" and "brain" men get the country all set for another war where would we get the supplies? Here is a question, the answer to which is very reassuring. Since the National Defense Act of 1920 the Procurement Planning division of the War Department has been busy surveying the industry of the country and its potential manufacturing capacity for war purposes. Thousands of factories have been visited and the manufacture of 2,500 articles in gigantic quantities for an army of several million men has been fully plotted. The diversity of the articles touches virtually every industry; from breakfast food to boiler plates. The amounts run, in estimated first costs, to several billions of dollars—sufficient to boom industry to new levels, to give impetus to a new war-time inflation and to create a new batch of millionaires equal to those of the past war.

But there is just one little flaw in this vast procurement plan of the army's. They haven't bothered to figure out any way to pay for all the thousands of tons of articles and raw materials needed. In their procurement work they have devised a dummy contract with all the various manufacturers ... but this contract does not specify price, payment or credit arrangements.

These contracts are of inestimable value to the War Department. Every manufacturer who has one, who has had his factory surveyed, his production capacity noted and his "M"-Day orders delivered, is a great big booster for the military. The fortunate industrialist! He knows that as soon as hostilities break out there will be nice fat orders to keep his factories running for some time. Indeed, he senses that a demand for more active war preparations would cause a good share of these contracts to be executed at once. The aircraft manufacturers and the shipbuilding industry, thanks to New Deal public works money have already learned this lesson. They wax fat—fatter than ever before in peace time. [...]

[...] Says the report of the Senate Committee on price control, page 4: "During the War the copper industry simply refused to produce at even the liberal prices first proposed by the government. The steel industry similarly refused to fill government orders until prices had been stabilized at levels satisfactory to the industry. The du Pont Company refused to build a great powder plant which it alone was qualified to build until it was assured of what is considered sufficient profits. Mr. Pierre du Pont wrote that "we cannot assent to allowing our patriotism to interfere with our duties as trustees." [...]

10

Gangster capitalism: the United States and the global rise of organized crime
Michael Woodiwiss

[…] Every nation has criminals but very few nations can create conditions that facilitate or even foster serious criminality internationally. Unfortunately, the United States, admittedly supported by most of the developed world, became one of these few and, as we shall see, has changed the nature and extent of organized crime in both legal and criminal markets throughout our now 'borderless' world.

The United States is by far the most powerful of all the states pulling the strings that move the limbs of international organizations that attempt to control legal markets, as Susan Strange rightly reminds us in her analysis of global finance.[1] The United States was the only country with a decisive power either to deregulate the international financial system and make it more conducive to organized criminal activities or to set rules that would govern financial transactions in the major international capital and money markets. Again, from the time of Nixon, it chose the first option. Globalization has been mismanaged in many other ways that have multiplied criminal opportunities and increased the destructive capacity of organized crime.

An international system has emerged of legal agreements that guarantee the global rights of capital, often at the expense of human rights. They also leave regulatory voids that lie not only beyond states but also beyond the interstate system.[2] A new breed of often murderous kleptocrats and sophisticated international business criminals emerged to exploit these regulatory voids to plunder. Suharto in Indonesia, Marcos in the Philippines, Mobutu in the Congo led the way by accumulating billions of dollars, essentially by robbing their peoples with the complicity of American and other western banks and financial institutions. In the 1980s the Bank of Credit and Commerce International (BCCI) helped not only kleptocrats escape with the profits of crime but also arms traffickers, drug traffickers and even terrorists. Since its exposure as a criminal bank in 1991, evidence has shown that the BCCI's banking practices were not unusual but instead merely reflected a more pervasive culture of corporate criminality.

Leading global financial institutions, notably the International Monetary Fund (IMF) and the World Bank, have done little to combat opportunities for serious organized criminality. In fact these institutions have served mainly to legitimize an international system open to widespread abuse. The IMF, for example, continued to lend and encourage other institutions to lend to Marcos, Suharto and Mobutu long after their pillage was common knowledge. And the World Bank's failure to notice or respond to BCCI's criminality over a long period of time may have been related to the large number of high-level personnel connections between the two institutions.[3]

More generally, as long as corporate and financial criminality is seen as being secondary to Mafia-type organized crime and as long as political criminality throughout the world is defended in terms of *realpolitik,* the global political economy is endlessly vulnerable to criminal activity. While the global media focused on the criminality of Gotti in America, Totò Riina in Italy, Pablo Escobar in Colombia and their equivalents throughout the world during the 1980s and 1990s, far too little attention was paid to the witting, systematic role of foreign banks in the kleptocrats' ascents, and the specific role of the global haven banking system, which fostered the accumulation of massive, public, foreign debts side by side with the accumulation of massive, illicit, foreign private assets.[4]

The culture of corporate criminality is not of course restricted to American corporations, as BCCI and the Parmalat collapse and scandal in Italy in January 2004 show. Parmalat, like many other big companies, had interests in offshore havens, mainly to avoid or perhaps evade paying tax. The low reporting requirements in many of these havens allow them to mask the transactions, profits and even the ownership structure of their offshore subsidiaries. An environment has emerged that encourages secrecy, and for those inclined to cook the books this has obviously been too tempting an opportunity to resist. In the case of Parmalat, large-scale fraud was clearly involved in the company's bankruptcy and the threat to the livelihood of its 36,000 staff in 30 countries.[5]

Kleptocrat plunder and corporate fraud has contributed to making the world we live in less equal, with millions mired in poverty and many of these desperate to flee towards a better life. Every day of the year thousands of people from poor countries are desperate enough to fill the pockets of people traffickers in the hope of finding work in rich countries. They make this decision largely because life in their own countries has become intolerable. Many had been pushed from the land in rural areas by economic adjustment programmes imposed on their governments by international loan agencies, such as the IMF and the World Bank. They then had to fight for their survival in the rapidly increasing and expanding slums around the 'mega-cities' of the developing world, where the infrastructure to support decent communities is almost non-existent and where young people are more likely to join predatory gangs than to find meaningful work.[6] It is not surprising that those who can afford it pay traffickers for the privilege of risking death in transit or capture by home government border agents followed by a forced return to the woeful conditions in the country of their origins. If they succeed in getting into North America or European countries where there is a demand for their cheap labour, they risk exploitation and often their health and safety. In 1996, for example, it was revealed that more than a hundred illegal immigrants from Asia and South America were forced to live and work like slaves in sweatshops surrounded by barbed wire and razor wire near Los Angeles.[7]

Drug traffickers, arms traffickers, corporate fraudsters, kleptocrats, people traffickers, sweatshop operators and a host of other networked criminals have all profited by changes that accompanied globalization. They have been allowed to do so because national and international organized-crime-control policies are woefully inadequate and the rights of people to be protected from crime have been subordinated to the rights of property. The situation now is best described as a global fix. This type of fix is not synonymous with bribery and corruption but it does, of course, involve both of these. The fix in this case involves world-wide networks of alliances, commitments and obligations, all mutually reinforcing, of such a nature as to move much of the world towards a condition of almost complete paralysis of law enforcement and observance. Crucial to this paralysis are the patterns of understanding that define the limits of debate about criminality and the meaning of terms like 'organized crime'. Precisely those things that need to be addressed become either inaccessible to thought or else are understood to be 'inevitable' – that is, beyond politics, unfortunate facts of human nature. So, for example, IMF and World Bank policies are considered almost exclusively as belonging to the realm of economics and therefore cannot be connected in anything like a meaningful way with the discussion of organized crime. This despite the fact that their interventions in the developing world have often led to orgies of theft, violence and institutional madness. [...]

Notes

1   Susan Strange, *Casino Capitalism* (Manchester: Manchester University Press. 1997) 171.
2   These issues are discussed in Anthony Woodiwiss, *Making Human Rights Work Globally* (London: Glasshouse, 2003); Saskia Sassen, *Globalization and its Discontents* (New York: New Press, 1998; and Robert Tillman, *Global Pirates: Fraud in the Offshore Insurance Industry* (Boston: Northeastern University Press, 2002).
3   Journalists Peter Truell and Larry Gurwin name some of those who were associated with both the World Bank and BCCI in *False Profits: The Inside Story of BCCI, the World's Most Corrupt Financial Empire* (Boston: Houghton Mifflin, 1992) 97–8.
4   See James S. Henry, *The Blood bankers: Tales from the Global Underground Economy* (New Yor: Four Walls Eight Windows, 2003) 52, for this point applied to the Marcos regime in particular.
5   Conal Walsh and Oliver Morgan, 'Parmalat: Could it Happen Here?', *Observer*, Business, 11 January 2004; Sophie Arie, 'Parmalet Admits Real Debt is £14 Billion'. *Guardian*, 27 January 2004.
6   See UN-Habitat, *The Challenge of the slums: Global Report on Human Settlements* (London: United Nations, 2003) and Mike Davis' discussion of the report in 'Planet of slums', *New Left Review*, vol. 26, March/April 2004, 5–34.
7   Alan Block, 'Bad Business: A Commentary ob the Criminology of Organized Crime in the United States', in Tom Farer (ed.), *Transnational Crime in the Americas* (London: Routledge, 1999) 230–1.

11

State-organized crime
William Chambliss

[...] Why would government officials from the NSC, the Defense Department, the State Department, and the CIA become involved in smuggling arms and narcotics, money laundering, assassinations, and other criminal activities? The answer lies in the structural contradictions that inhere in nation-states (Chambliss, 1980).

As Weber, Marx, and Gramsci pointed out, no state can survive without establishing legitimacy. The law is a fundamental cornerstone in creating legitimacy and an illusion (at least) of social order. It claims universal principles that demand some behaviors and prohibit others. The protection of property and personal security are obligations assumed by states everywhere both as a means of legitimizing the state's franchise on violence and as a means of protecting commercial interests (Chambliss and Seidman, 1982).

The threat posed by smuggling to both personal security and property interests makes laws prohibiting smuggling essential. Under some circumstances, however, such laws contradict other interests of the state. This contradiction prepares the ground for state-organized crime as a solution to the conflicts and dilemmas posed by the simultaneous existence of contradictory "legitimate" goals. [...]

[...] Contradictions inherent in the formation of states create conditions under which there will be a tendency for state officials to violate the criminal law. State officials inherit from the past laws that were not of their making and that were the result of earlier efforts to resolve conflicts wrought by structural contradictions (Chambliss, 1980; Chambliss and Seidman, 1982). The inherited laws nonetheless represent the foundation on which the legitimacy of the state's authority depends. These laws also provide a basis for attempts by the state to control the acts of others and to justify the use of violence to that end.

For England in the sixteenth century, passing laws to legitimize piracy for English pirates while condemning as criminal the piracy of others against England would have been an untenable solution, just as it would undermine the legitimacy of America's ideological and political position to pass legislation allowing for terrorist acts on the part of U.S. officials while condemning and punishing the terrorism of others.

Law is a two-edged sword; it creates one set of conflicts while it attempts to resolve another. The passage of a particular law or set of laws may resolve conflicts and enhance state control, but it also limits the legal activities of the state. State officials are thus often caught between conflicting demands as they find themselves constrained by laws that interfere with other goals demanded of them by their roles or their perception of what is in the interests of the state. There is a contradiction, then, between the legal prescriptions and the agreed goals of state agencies. Not everyone caught in this dilemma will opt for violating the law, but some will. Those who do are the perpetrators, but not the cause, of the persistence of state-organized crime.

When Spain and Portugal began exploiting the labor and natural resources of the Americas and Asia, other European nations were quick to realize the implications for their own power and sovereignty. France, England, and Holland were powerful nations, but not powerful enough at the time to challenge Spain and Portugal directly. The dilemma for those nations was how to share in the wealth and curtail the power of Spain and Portugal without going to war. A resolution to the dilemma was forged through cooperation with pirates. Cooperating with pirates, however, required violating their own laws as well as the laws of other countries. In this way, the states organized criminality for their own ends without undermining their claim to legitimacy or their ability to condemn and punish piracy committed against them.

It should be noted that some monarchs in the sixteenth and seventeenth centuries (James I of England, for example) refused to cooperate with pirates no matter how profitable it would have been for the Crown. So, too, not all CIA or NSC personnel organize criminal activities in pursuit of state goals.

The impetus for the criminality of European states that engaged in piracy was the need to accumulate capital in the early stages of capitalist formation. State-organized criminality did not disappear, however, with the emergence of capitalism as the dominant economic system of the world. Rather, contemporary state-organized crime also has its roots in the ongoing need for capital accumulation of modern nation-states, whether the states be socialist, capitalist, or mixed economies.

Sociologically, then, the most important characteristics of state-organized crime in the modern world are at one with characteristics of state-organized crime in the early stages of capitalist development. Today, states organize smuggling, assassinations, covert operations, and conspiracies to criminally assault citizens, political activists, and political leaders perceived to be a threat. These acts are as criminal in the laws of the nations perpetrating them as were the acts of piracy in which European nations were complicitous.

At the most general level, the contradictions that are the force behind state-organized crime today are the same as those that were the impetus for piracy in sixteenth-century Europe. The accumulation of capital determines a nation's power, wealth, and survival today, as it did 300 years ago. The state must provide a climate and a set of international relations that facilitate this accumulation if it is to succeed. State officials will be judged in accordance with their ability to create these conditions.

But contradictory ideologies and demands are the very essence of state formations. The laws of every nation-state inhibit officials from maximizing conditions conducive to capital accumulation at the same time that they facilitate the process. Laws prohibiting assassination and arms smuggling enable a government to control such acts when they are inimical to their interests. When such acts serve the interests of the state, however, then there are pressures that lead some officials to behave criminally. Speaking of the relationship among the NSC, the CIA, and drug trafficking, Senator John Kerry, chairman of the Senate Foreign Relations Subcommittee on Terrorism, Narcotics and International Operations, pinpointed the dilemma when he said "stopping drug trafficking to the United States has been a secondary U.S. foreign policy objective. It has been sacrificed repeatedly for other political goals" (Senate Hearings, 1986). He might have added that engaging in drug trafficking and arms smuggling has been a price government agencies have been willing to pay "for other political goals."

These contradictions create conflicts between nation-states as well as internally among the branches of government. Today, we see nations such as Turkey, Bolivia, Colombia, Peru, Panama, and the Bahamas encouraging the export of illegal drugs while condemning them publicly. At the same time, other government agencies cooperate in the export and import of illegal arms and drugs to finance subversive and terrorist activities. Governments plot and carry out assassinations and illegal acts against their own citizens in order to "preserve democracy" while supporting the most undemocratic institutions imaginable. In the process, the contradictions that create the conflicts and dilemmas remain untouched and the process goes on indefinitely. [...]

12

Globalization, state-corporate crime and women
Nancy Wonders and Mona Danner

[...] As Friedrichs (1996a:154) notes, "the premise for the concept of state-corporate crime is that modern states and corporations are profoundly interdependent." He goes on to say that "above all, the concept of state-corporate crime compels us to recognize that some major forms of organizational crime cannot be easily classified as either corporate or governmental, and that the interorganizational forms of crime that bring together corporations and government entities may be especially potent and pernicious" (156).

In employing the concept of state-corporate crime, we are not arguing that corporations and governments necessarily bear equal responsibility for the harms generated by certain capitalist practices. In the modern world, the power of transnationals frequently exceeds state power, particularly in developing countries where international commercial, financial, and regulatory organizations exert strong influence over national policy decisions. At the same time, it has been argued elsewhere (see Caulfield and Wonders 1993) that many harms against women can be viewed as political crimes, predominantly characterized as crimes of omission, since the state tacitly supports these harms by failing to protect women's basic human rights. In this chapter we extend this argument by illustrating the way that many corporate harms fostered by globalization can only occur because nation-states collaborate with or ignore the perils associated with corporate practices in their country. In making this argument we recognize that nation-states are frequently bullied, threatened, and/or punished into compliance with corporate desires. [...]

[...] One of the central features of globalization is the mass movement of people within countries and across borders (Wonders and Michalowski 2000). As transnational corporations seek to dominate the economic landscape of every country, people engaged in traditional survival practices, particularly agricultural production, are displaced. By now it is well established that this displacement has disproportionately affected women (Lorentzen and Turpin 1996; Schoepf, Schoepf, and Millen 2000). Women have historically served as the primary workforce in agricultural production in developing countries (Steady 1996). As global corporations leverage land in developing countries, whether for purposes of agribusiness, cash crops, or natural resource exploitation, traditional agricultural workers, overwhelmingly women, are driven from the land. Privatization of the land occurs through several strategies, but most commonly requires collaboration between developing nations and large corporate or private interests. Governments "sell" land that, though not necessarily "owned" by indigenous people, had been under their control for generations. Although this land is frequently (but not always) purchased by corporations, the economic displacement caused by corporate control of indigenous lands is clearly not figured into the price paid to developing countries.

Corporate control of land in developing countries has a decidedly gendered character. Lorentzen and Turpin (1996:4) note that this control "often means the transfer of resources into men's hands, even where women do the bulk of the labor. In much of Africa, colonial laws and development policies generally allocate land only to men. Women have lost their traditional rights to the land, even though they do up to three quarters of the agricultural labor." In other words, economic displacement has also had political ramifications, reducing the real power of women to control their lives or to make decisions over the geographic space within which they reside. In countries where women are structurally or practically restricted from political influence, this loss of economic power further weakens their ability to exert control over their own life chances.

This economic displacement has led numerous scholars to note that women's migration far exceeds men's in the current period (International Labor Organization 1996; Kempadoo and Dozema 1997). Women migrate to cities and, increasingly, to other countries, to sell their labor for a paycheck, a radical change from the relative self-sufficiency offered by agricultural production. This displacement serves corporate power and national interests in another way by creating a large pool of available, even desperate, workers for industrial production. In this way women have become the new industrial workforce for the global economy. As numerous authors have noted, women constitute a significant industrial army for the New World Order (Sassen 1998). But unlike the parallel labor position that was once occupied by men working in industrial production in the West, women rarely have any legal protections from the harsh realities of corporate capitalism: no unions, no family wage, no workplace regulations. [...]

[...] In many developing countries, it is not uncommon for women to be recruited for factory work before the age of fourteen (Millen and Holtz 2000; United Nations Development Programme 1996). Labor practices approach indentured servitude as families send young daughters off to work in the nearest factory, sometimes paying the factory back a portion of wages earned to cover lunches or housing (United Nations Development Programme 1996). In developing countries, there are few restrictions on the hours that can be worked, and wages are uniformly low. The poverty wages paid to women workers have consequences not only for their health and welfare but for their children as well, since women are frequently the primary providers for their families (Steady 1996). Peterson and Runyan (1999:135) note that "by the early 1990's, one-third of the households in the world were headed by women, and the highest numbers of these were in the

Third World (reaching more than 40% in parts of Africa and the Caribbean)." Despite the fact that many women bear primary responsibility for the economic well-being of their families, it is typical for women to earn less than men. In the free trade zones established by some countries to attract transnational corporations, women's wages are 20 to 50 percent lower than men's (Millen and Holtz 2000). In most developing countries, nation-states collude with corporations by forbidding unions or labor organizing, and in some cases have used internal military force to violently crush unionizing efforts (Millen and Holtz 2000).

In addition, working conditions in many factories are hazardous and, in too many cases, even deadly. The lack of governmental regulation over workplace safety creates an important incentive for global corporations to locate in a particular country. In the electronics industry, women frequently work with hazardous chemicals without the benefit of protective gear or adequate ventilation. Steady (1996) reviews a range of research that supports this point, including one study that found that one-third of all women in Taiwan were harmed by exposure to environmental toxins in the workplace. She also notes additional studies that report similar damage to women workers in the *maquiladora* industry in Mexico and in factories in the Caribbean.

Some corporate practices violate women's basic right to control their own bodies. Some factories in Honduras require that women and girls take birth control injections or pills so that they do not become pregnant; similarly, mandatory pregnancy tests are given to women working in the *maquiladoras* in Mexican free trade zones (Human Rights Watch 2000a; Millen and Holtz 2000). In the U.S. commonwealth of Northern Mariana Islands, there are even reports that some pregnant women workers have been forced by transnational apparel companies to have abortions (Millen and Holtz 2000).

The lack of governmental regulation or minimum standards of protection is best characterized as a crime of omission rather than commission, but the effects are no less dangerous for women. The impact of many of these harmful labor practices in developing countries has been exacerbated by Structural Adjustment Programs. Although global corporate culture creates the pressure for counties to accept SAPs, it is the collusion between corporations and nation-states that leads directly to economic displacement and the consequent hyperdependence of women on wage labor to survive. At the same time, SAPs have all but eliminated basic social welfare programs, guaranteeing that women must accept the conditions associated with paid employment, however dangerous or harmful they might be. [...]

[...] Environmental harm takes many forms and many of these cause increased risk, danger, and sometimes death to women.

The most obvious form of environmental harm is pollution caused by the toxins associated with industrialization. In developed countries, women and children, particularly those of color or those who belong to immigrant groups, are disproportionately poor and are, therefore, less able to escape the hazards associated with housing near industrial centers, landfills, or hazardous waste sites (Bullard 1993; Seager 1993; Steady 1996). Pollutants of all kind pose particularly serious dangers for women in their childbearing years, who are more likely to suffer miscarriages and problem pregnancies and to have children with birth defects. For women in developing countries, the impact of corporate pillage of the environment is even more damaging. In many of these countries, environmental degradation has a more visible face than buried toxins or groundwater pollution; more often the corporate practices in these countries, including clear cutting, strip mining, the use of toxic pesticides that would be illegal in the West, strip the land permanently of the natural resources necessary to sustain life (Madeley 1999; Millen and Holz 2000). Typically these practices are sanctioned or ignored by the government as a way to encourage corporate investment.

Corporate agribusiness has had particularly devastating effects in some developing countries. Governmental collaboration with agribusiness has been a common feature of the "Green Revolution." Viewed as another strategy designed to make developing countries global players, the Green Revolution has been characterized by the shift from farming practices designed to feed local populations to the production of luxury crops for sale on the global market. Despite promises of greater wealth and economic stability for indigenous populations, this practice can better be characterized as a form of state-corporate crime, given the harm it has caused to indigenous populations, particularly women.

The harmful consequences of this strategy are well documented and include reductions in biodiversity, permanent damage to the land because of the mechanization of farming practices, pesticide poisoning, and malnutrition and hunger among indigenous peoples who cannot eat coffee beans, flowers, tobacco, or other luxury crops and survive (Madeley 1999). One example of this shift from the production of indigenous crops to luxury crops is provided by many Latin American countries now growing flowers for export. "Persistent exposure to highly toxic chemicals is now causing serious health problems in a number of Latin American countries, especially for women engaged in flower production, who suffer high miscarriage rates, and recurrent headaches and dizzy spells" (Madeley 1999:46).

Land degradation is another consequence of the over-farming practices commonly employed by agribusiness, since paying for new land is sometimes cheaper than employing environmentally sensitive farming practices. As Lorentzen and Turpin (1996:3) explain, "ecological degradation affects women disproportionately. The increased burden placed on women is not from environmental deterioration per se, but rather from a sexual division of labor that considers family sustenance to be women's work. Thus, fuel gathering, food preparing, water collecting, and subsistence farming are generally considered women's tasks. In much of Africa women produce 80 percent of the food. Women comprise 60 percent of the farmers in India, 64 percent in Zaire, and 98 percent in Nepal."

Deforestation by agribusiness has created near deserts in some parts of the world where water and firewood were already scarce. This has caused local populations, but particularly women, to travel farther and work longer hours in search of water and firewood (Lorentzen and Turpin 1996; Madeley 1999). The seriousness and extent of this problem are hard to appreciate for those who live in the West. Yet research has established that the struggle to obtain water and firewood has been exacerbated as a result of corporate agribusiness in countries as distant from each other as Bangladesh and El Salvador; in some cases this means that women must devote more than seven hours a day to this activity alone (Turpin and Lorentzen 1996; Rodda 1991)[...]

Another consequence of globalization is the heightened role militarism plays as an ordinary strategy to ensure stability for corporations, to "free" markets, and to quell nationalist or ethnic resistance to globalized change. [...]

[...] A hidden feature of the apparently male face of militarism is the disproportionate cost of militarism to women's bodies. Indeed, Lorentzen and Turpin (1996:6) point out that women are "more likely than men to become war's casualties or refugees"; in the 1990s, 90 percent of all casualties during war were civilians, and the majority of these were women and children. These authors go on to say that other harmful consequences of war also fall disproportionately on women; for example, "more than four-fifths of war refugees are women and young girls, who often experience additional violence during their flight" (Lorentzen and Turpin 1996:6).

Militarism also has other adverse consequences, including the diversion of resources away from basic health and welfare to armaments and environmental damage and pollution. Thus militarism creates other casualties among the citizenry beyond the immediate dangers associated with guns and bombs. The diversion of national resources to militarism is a highly political decision with little direct benefit to women, whose participation rates in state militaries is uniformly low worldwide. As Peterson and Runyan (1999:121) note, "women are not direct recipients of military spending." But to the extent that militarism has costs, it is clear that these costs are disproportionately borne by women (Nikolić-Ristanović 1996). These costs include the direct harm caused to women by geographical displacement, physical violence and injury as war casualties, and the sexual assault of women during wartime; they also include the indirect costs associated with state-corporate policies to foster weapons production and militarism at the expense of other social and economic goals more beneficial to women's lives. [...]

13

Free trade and monopoly
Karl Marx

[...] In 1837 the Chinese Government had at last arrived at a point where decisive action could no longer be delayed. The continuous drain of silver, caused by the opium importations, had begun to derange the exchequer, as well as the moneyed circulation of the Celestial Empire. Heu Nailzi, one of the most distinguished Chinese statesmen, proposed to legalize the opium trade and make money out of it; but after a full deliberation, in which all the high officers of the Empire shared, and which extended over a period of more than a year's duration, the Chinese Government decided that, "On account of the injuries it inflicted on the people, the nefarious traffic should not be legalized." As early as 1830, a duty of 25 per cent would have yielded a revenue of $3,850,000. In 1837, it would have yielded double that sum, but then the Celestial barbarian declined, laying a tax sure to rise in proportion to the degradation of his people. In 1853, Hien Fang, the present Emperor, under still more distressed circumstances, and with the full knowledge of the futility of all efforts at stopping the increasing import of opium, persevered in the stern policy of his ancestors. Let me remark, en passant, that by persecuting the opium consumption as a heresy the Emperor gave its traffic all the advantages of a religious propaganda. The extraordinary measures of the Chinese Government during the years 1837, 1838 and 1839, which culminated in Commissioner Lin's arrival at Canton, and the confiscation and destruction, by his orders, of the smuggled opium, afforded the pretext for the first Anglo-Chinese war, the results of which developed themselves in the Chinese rebellion, the utter exhaustion of the Imperial exchequer, the successful encroachment of Russia from the North, and the gigantic dimensions assumed by the opium trade in the South. Although proscribed in the treaty with which England terminated a war, commenced and carried on in its defence, the opium trade has practically enjoyed perfect impunity since 1843. The importation was estimated, in 1856, at about $35,000,000, while in the same year, the Anglo-Indian Government drew a revenue of $25,000,000, just the sixth part of its total State income, from the opium monopoly. The pretexts on which the second opium war has been undertaken are of too recent date to need any commentary.

We cannot leave this part of the subject without singling out one flagrant self-contradiction of the Christianity-canting and civilization-mongering British

Government. In its imperial capacity it affects to be a thorough stranger to the contraband opium trade, and even to enter into treaties proscribing it. Yet, in its Indian capacity, it forces the opium cultivation upon Bengal, to the great damage of the productive resources of that country; compels one part of the Indian ryots to engage in the poppy culture; entices another part into the same by dint of money advances; keeps the wholesale manufacture of the deleterious drug a close monopoly in its hands; watches by a whole army of official spies its growth, its delivery at appointed places, its inspissation and preparation for the taste of the Chinese consumers, its formation into packages especially adapted to the conveniency of smuggling, and finally its conveyance to Calcutta, where it is put up at auction at the Government sales, and made over by the State officers to the speculators, thence to pass into the hands of the contrabandists who land it in China. The chest costing the British Government about 250 rupees is sold at the Calcutta auction mart at a price ranging from 1,210 to 1,600 rupees. But, not yet satisfied with this matter-of-fact complicity, the same Government, to this hour, enters into express profit and loss accounts with the merchants and shippers, who embark in the hazardous operation of poisoning an empire.

The Indian finances of the British Government have, in fact, been made to depend not only on the opium trade with China, but on the contraband character of that trade. Were the Chinese Government to legalize the opium trade simultaneously with tolerating the cultivation of the poppy in China, the Anglo-Indian exchequer would experience a serious catastrophe. While openly preaching free trade in poison, it secretly defends the monopoly of its manufacture.

SECTION 3:

Capitalism and crimes of the powerful

The slow sacrifice of humanity

This section introduces the reader to accounts of crimes of the powerful that are located in capitalist relations of production and consumption. The first four readings are drawn from analyses of the phase of rapid industrial development in the late nineteenth and early twentieth century. Those readings are then followed by two, more contemporary, accounts. Together the readings in this section broaden our understanding of the criminogenic character of capitalist social orders.

The first extract, by Karl Marx, is an account of the brutal conditions experienced by factory workers in nineteenth-century Britain and led to the enactment of some of the first laws protecting workers, the Factory Acts. In this account, the British working class were quite literally being worked to death in the factories. The government's own reports to the Children's Employment Commissioners on the occupational health of workers in the potteries, match-making and paper industries document in gruesome detail the physically and morally degenerating conditions of work: vulnerability to disease; low life expectancy; and the mutilation of children, many suffering stunted growth and premature ageing. The conditions of the British factory, Marx argues, surpassed even the worst horrors conjured up by Dante's *Inferno*.

Half a century on, Roger Casement's work as a commissioner for the British government documented the horrors of the rubber plantations of the Amazonian Putumayo. Casement, having in 1903 exposed the atrocities committed in the Belgian Congo Free State by the rubber industry, was commissioned to investigate allegations of similar atrocities made against a British rubber corporation, the Peruvian Amazon Company. He was subsequently to become more famous for his efforts in support of an Irish Free State and his execution by the British government for those efforts. And this aspect of his life has overshadowed his remarkable work as a 'corporate crime investigator' for the British government. His descriptions of the Putumayo rubber industry are extracted here from diaries reporting his 1910 visit to the Amazon. His subsequent reports to the British government made visible the murder and terror imposed on indigenous peoples who were forced to work for the Peruvian Amazon Company. The *New York Times* on 14 July 1912 reported Casement's findings, noting that the crimes he discovered

> included innumerable murders and torture of defenseless Indians, pouring kerosene oil on men and then setting fire to them, burning them at the stake, dashing out the brains of children, and again cutting off the arms and legs of Indians and leaving them to speedy death in their agony.

For Casement, the crimes of the Peruvian Amazon Company arose directly as a result of the form that capitalist development assumed. He saw how a ruthless drive for profits created a structure of reward for unspeakable brutality and inhumanity. And he saw how the structure of capitalist institutions created a means of extracting profits 'at a distance', both physically and emotionally, from the torture and human suffering he witnessed. After the House of Commons Select Committee had considered Casement's evidence, it concluded that although the directors of the company knew little of the atrocities in the Amazon, they were guilty of 'culpable negligence'. Reporting the Select Committee's response, *The Economist* of 20 July 1912 commented:

> The lightheartedness and indifference with which men are ready to undertake directorships is the most reprehensible feature of modern commercial life. It cannot be too strongly emphasised that there is no position that carries with it graver responsibilities than that of a company director.

This recognition that the position of director allows its incumbent to act from a safe moral distance is an important theme that is developed further in Section 5 of this text.

Casement's account has been the subject of some debate about the nature of the relationship between the torture in the Putumayo and the rationalities of business capitalism and 'civilisation' in recent years (Taussig, 1984). There is too little space here to get into the intricacies of those debates (though see also Ward, 2005), but Casement's position is concisely set out in his summary report written on the journey back to London in December 1910.

> To get rich quick...by the crushing enslavement of a hapless subject people – this is the explanation of the longest and, most sordid and assuredly most appalling tragedy of the contact of Christian civilization with weaker peoples. ...Has our Christian civilization itself no share in the blame? Has our modern commercialization, our latter-day company promoting – whose motto would seem to be that a Director may pocket the proceeds without perceiving the process – no part in this enterprise of horror and shame?... . And they found English men and English finance prepared to without question accept their Putumayo 'estates' and their numerous native 'labourers' at a glance, a glance at the annually increasing output of rubber. Nothing beyond that was

needed. The rubber was there. How it was produced, out of what a hell of human suffering no one knew, no one asked, so one suspected. Can it be no one cared? (Casement, 1997: 504)

Written a few years before Casement's trip to the Amazon, Ross's *Sin and Society* is generally regarded as a classic account of the 'criminaloid'. But rarely is it fully acknowledged for its insights into the criminogenic structure of capitalism. Neither Ross's focus on the *corporation* nor his attention to the criminogenic structure of capitalism have been adequately recognised in academic criminology. Pick up any criminology book, and if it mentions Ross's work on the crimes of the powerful at all, it is invariably to introduce the figure of the 'criminaloid' who uses his/her position of privilege to 'counterfeit the good citizen'. In *Sin and Society* it is Ross's moralising, religio-sentimental appeals to a 'good' society led by 'good' men (as opposed to criminaloids) that are remembered rather than his forensic assault upon capitalist social orders and capitalist institutions for their systematic production of criminality.

The extract reproduced in this section contains some of Ross's most trenchant observations of American capitalism and the the rise to dominance of the corporation. His emotive observations are directed against business leaders and the corporation. Thus, he castigates the railroad and mining companies and their owners for committing 'manslaughter in the name of business' (extract: 17). And in the extract reproduced here Ross describes how corporations provide a motivational structure for offending that is relatively unconstrained. We also find in the discussion of 'remote evil' (Ross, 1973: 56) an early development of a concept of victim/offender proximity whereby Ross – just as Roger Casement did – notes how corporate crimes are often committed from a relatively safe 'space' that enables the high status offender to remain remote from the victim.

Ross, who was as opposed to a socialist transformation of society as he was to enduring capitalist exploitation, used *Sin and Society* to document how the central evils of capitalism legitimise militant opposition to corporate power. The concentration of capital and the influence of the powerful over the form that the law takes threaten angry resistance and even class warfare (see Ross, 1973: 145–52). By 'murdering representative government' (Ross, 1973: 13) capital undermines its own conditions of existence. Rather than hasten this process to its conclusion (which, in Ross's analysis just as in Marx's, means socialist revolution), he appeals for a *just* capitalist society. Ross's work is located in the Roosevelt-influenced tradition of advocating a more humane capitalist order rather than social transformation (see also the Conclusion to Woodiwiss, 2005). But at the same time, in the very act of raising this problem, Ross questions whether a humane society is reconcilable with capitalism. His discussion of law enforcement in the final chapter of the book reveals that the key concern of this work is a paradox familiar to latter-day students of corporate crime: the conflict between the socially protective role of states and their role in encouraging and promoting profitable business. It is a paradox that is present somewhere in all of the excerpts in this section. This paradox is well illustrated by the socially protective role played by environmental or health and safety regulation. Such regulatory interventions have two connected effects: on the one hand, they limit the harms created by corporations, and, on the other, they enable those same corporations to continue being harmful in a more controlled manner (Tombs and Whyte, 2008).

Marx had earlier argued that the impulse to place legal restrictions upon capital is not simply the result of a consensual or philanthropic decision to make humane progress, but that the conditions of the factory threatened to eradicate the source of its profits by threatening the sustainability and the compliance of the labour force. His analysis of the emergence of the Factory Acts proposed that the carnage in the factories had created an urgent need for the state to use the law to control the excesses of industrial capitalism, personified by factory owners who demonstrated little respect for the rule of law. The social order was threatened by the intensification of class conflict between the ruling class and those that worked in the factories. It therefore became clear that the industrial system of production could not regulate its own rampant physical abuse of labour, and thus threatened the long-term viability of the factory system. Identifying this growing problem of legitimacy, Frederick Engels (1850) noted that 'measures had to be taken by the state to curb the manufacturers' utterly ruthless frenzy for exploitation, which was trampling all the requirements of civilised society underfoot'.

Josephson's dense history of the 'robber barons', a term first used by Mark Twain to describe the aggressive generation of early industrialists in the US who accumulated wealth and power by routinely breaking the law, provides a deeper insight into capitalism's ruthless frenzy for exploitation. In a text first published in 1899, *The Theory of the Leisure Class*, Thorstein Veblen (1994) argued that the robber barons were no different from barbarians – they used brute force, cunning and competitive skills to profit from the spoils of conquests, and their profits came not from socially productive, but from socially destructive, activities. Jay Gould (railways), JP Morgan (banking), Andrew Carnegie (steel) and John Rockefeller (oil) all accumulated huge fortunes by plundering new markets, price-fixing, and then using their immense industrial wealth to circumnavigate trust laws, to drive out competitors, to smash trade union organisations and to impose brutal conditions on their workforces. *The Robber Barons* shows how new social and moral values of capital accumulation and 'free enterprise' promoted by the ruling business and political classes were used to legitimise their barbarism. Government regulations and laws aimed at protecting consumers and workers were – just as we saw in Marx's account of the British factories – viewed by the most powerful members of the ruling elite as obstacles standing in the way of industrial progress. In the capitalist frontiers of the United States, just as in Victorian Britain, a rising class of industrialists felt little compunction to obey the few laws that existed to control the violent excesses of profit accumulation. The shipping magnet Cornelius Vanderbilt summed up the spirit of the robber barons when he famously declared: 'What do I care about the law. Ain't I got the power?' (Josephson, 1962: 15).

The extract from *The Robber Barons* reproduced here documents the birth of mass production of meat in the Chicago process and packing industry. It traces precisely how anti-competition offences (forming cartel 'conspiracies' and price-fixing) are not merely crimes that impose a financial penalty upon consumers, but also produce a risk of death or serious illness, since there was 'none to say nay' if they used diseased or rotting animals in the new processed foods.

Upton Sinclair's fictional account of the same industry in *The Jungle*, published in January 1906, had reported the virtually unparalleled rates of injury in the Chicago slaughterhouses that literally butchered workers, albeit at a slightly slower rate than livestock. And Sinclair showed how the same conditions that brutalised workers and tortured livestock were inseparable.

> [Descriptions of] the animals which came to this place would have been worthwhile for a Dante or a Zola. It seemed that they must have agencies all over the country, to hunt out old and crippled and diseased cattle to be canned. There were cattle which had been fed on 'whisky malt', the refuse of the breweries, and had become what the men called 'steerly' – which means covered with boils. It was a nasty job killing these, for when you plunged your knife into them they would burst and splash foul-smelling stuff into your face; and when a man's sleeves were smeared with blood, and his hands steeped in it, how was he ever to wipe his face, or to clear his eyes so he could see? It was stuff such as this that had killed several times as many United States soldiers as all the bullets of the Spaniards; only the army beef, besides, was not fresh canned, it was old stuff that had been lying for years in the cellars. (Sinclair, 1986: 117)

> There were the men who worked in the cooking rooms, in the midst of steam and sickening odours, by artificial light; in these rooms the germs of tuberculosis might live for two years, but the supply was renewed every hour ... . There were the wool-pluckers whose hands went to pieces even sooner than the hands of the pickle men; for the pelts of sheep had to be painted with acid to loosen the wool, and then the pluckers had to pull this wool out with their bare hands, till the acid had eaten their fingers off ... . Some worked at the stamping machines and it was seldom that one could work long there at the pace that was set, and not give out and forget himself, and have part of his hand chopped off...and as for the other men, who worked in tank rooms full of steam, and in some of which there were open vats near the level of the floor, their peculiar trouble was that they fell into the vats; and when they were fished out, there was never enough of them to be worth exhibiting – sometimes they would be overlooked for days, till all but the bones of them had gone out to the world as Durham's Pure Leaf Lard! (Sinclair, 1986: 119–20)[1]

A fictional account this may have been, but it was based upon Sinclair's meticulous research. So powerful were his accounts of the industry that the book contributed significantly to public scandal around the production of food that led to a Congressional Inquiry and in June 1906, the introduction of the US Pure Food and Drug Act. So just as in Marx's and Engel's accounts of the Victorian factories, limits had to be placed upon the ruthless frenzy of the robber barons.

The extract from George Robb's text returns us to the period of intense industrial development in Victorian Britain and to a rather different story of widespread criminality amongst capitalist elites. In this case, a range of new types of fraud emerged as investment opportunities grew rapidly following the rise of the joint-stock corporation. By the end of the nineteenth century around two-thirds of British national wealth was invested in shares. Those shareholdings absorbed the new wealth of industrialisation accumulated in the industrial bourgeoisie and the growing middle class. It was the huge surplus profits derived from what Marx called 'the slow sacrifice of humanity' in the factories that bred new forms of venal and predatory criminality. False accounting, embezzlement of funds held in trust, false share issues and so on were rife in the boardrooms of late Victorian Britain. Robb is keen to point out that, widespread though this criminality was in nineteenth-century British capitalism, the majority of companies remained within the rules. Yet a key point worth noting for the purposes of the discussion here is that those criminal opportunities were produced by structural and ideological factors that were intrinsic to the development of capitalism. Several factors identified by Robb combined to create a climate favourable to corporate fraud in nineteenth-century Britain. And the most significant of these factors were connected to the restructuring of industrial capitalism. First, the separation in capitalist enterprises of the functions of ownership from control increased the distance between shareholders and directors and reduced the accountability of directors who were trusted with very large amounts of shareholder's funds. Second, accounting and auditing controls were not developed at the same rate as new forms of investments and financial transactions emerged, making fraud difficult to discover and act on. Third, the entrepreneurial culture of Victorian Britain that emerged during this period bred aggressive businessmen impatient with ethical codes and preoccupied with material success. Fourth, the dominance of 'laissez-faire' (or 'free market') ideology and emphasis on individual responsibility discouraged state intervention and ensured that some forms of corporate and financial regulation remained off the political agenda.

The final two readings in this section show how capitalist corporations, left to exist relatively free from social controls, systematically produce outcomes that are financially attractive to them, but in human terms are morally unthinkable. Braithwaite's description of Big Pharma reproduced here shows how the profits of the drug companies are kept high through the invention and exaggeration of medical conditions (see also Ebeling, 2008) and overblown – often untested – evidence of the ameliorating effects of their products. It is an industry that not infrequently releases products onto the market that kill in their thousands. Cases documented elsewhere (Abraham, 1995; Adams, 1984; Mintz, 1985; Sjöstöm and Nilsson, 1972) confirm the accuracy of his analysis. Elsewhere in his book, *Corporate Crime in the Pharmaceutical Industry*, he identifies an almost unfathomable array of profligate crimes and harms produced by the industry. These include dumping of dangerous pharmaceuticals on relatively weak economies, systematic avoidance of regulatory standards protecting workers and consumers, price-fixing, illegal transfer pricing and medicare fraud. Indeed, Braithwaite (1984: 274) notes in this dense and comprehensive study that '[p]harmaceutical companes are forever keen to point out that they always abide by the laws of the country in which they operate. I am not aware of any pharmaceutical transnational for which that would be true.'

The excerpt from Frank Pearce and Steve Tombs' *Toxic Capitalism* identify similar features of a criminogenic political economy in the catastrophe that occurred at Bhopal, India. As the authors point out, the incident can be partly explained by a racist imperialism that allowed particular forms of hazardous production to be exported as well as by the downward pressure exerted on regulatory standards in the host country. But, as the authors point out here, we cannot take this relationship of structural weakness for granted, since India in many respects has a relatively developed chemical industry. We must therefore look to other conditions, including the relative balance of class forces, trends in the commercial value of markets, and factors driving levels of investment. In the case of Bhopal, more immediate causes of the disaster are to be found in a corporate structure that imposed tough conditions of production from above and forced the Indian plant to operate under highly volatile market conditions.

The tens of thousands of people who were killed or permanently injured – and the future generations of injured and ill – at Bhopal did not result from deliberate or intended mass murder. But they did result from conditions of production that were intensified to an unbearable level. In the chemical production industry, everyone at a senior management level is aware of the potential for catastrophe. Yet there was never any danger that the chief executives of Union Carbide Corporation would be properly held to account for their complicity in what has frequently been described as one of the crimes of the century. In the aftermath of the September 2001 attacks on New York and Washington, Arundhati Roy noted the 'dead or alive' manhunt for Osama bin Laden and asked:

> can India put in a side request for the extradition of Warren Anderson of the US? He was chairman of Union Carbide, responsible for the gas leak…[w]e have collated the necessary evidence. It's all in the files. Could we have him, please?

Other than standing trial in an Indian court, it is difficult to see how the senior management of Union Carbide Corporation might be made accountable for their actions. In the aftermath of the event, there was no acknowledgment of their culpability. Indeed, as Pearce and Tombs note elsewhere in their text:

> there is evidence that UCC executives used racist rationalisations to justify their carelessness and unusual level of risk taking – life is not valued in Third World countries, Indians are technologically unsophisticated, do not comprehend the purpose of safety procedures, and accidents are generally due to worker incompetence…which allowed the actor [senior management of UCC] to ignore the effects of their actions on other people. (Pearce and Tombs, 1998: 207)

Alternative (racist, individualising, patronising) explanations are typically privileged above systemic explanations in order to preserve the legitimacy of managements, even when they have palpably and spectacularly failed. In any other type of criminal event, the lack of remorse and victim blaming displayed by the culprits would most probably be scandalised.

The readings in this section together show that what Engels called a 'frenzy for exploitation' is supported by a value system or moral code that we find in the ideology of the emerging ruling class of industrialists. The moral indifference to human suffering (Pemberton, 2004) displayed in equal measure by the British factory owners, Amazon rubber producers pharmaceutical company executives and American robber barons is supported by a belief system that elevates capitalist values (economic success and profiteering) above social values (equality, shared success, social protection).

It is in the process of commodification – the reduction of the value of a human being to his or her surplus value as a worker (as little more than an input in the production process) or to his or her value as a consumer – that capitalism's belief system is created. The suppression of human and social values occurs when the economic system itself transforms human beings into units of economic value. And we find the suppression of human and social values built into the very architecture of capital's institutional forms (the factory, the market and the corporation). In Robb's account we see the beginnings of a structure of financialisation in which the owners of capital know next to nothing about how their profits are actually produced; they are only concerned with knowing about the most successful investment strategies. In The Peruvian Amazon Company and in Union Carbide, dividends, were paid to those who most likely could not have pointed to the Putumayo or to Bhopal on a map.

But the process of eradicating humanity through moral and physical distancing has never eradicated resistance or opposition. The inhumanity of capitalism has historically been met with resistance from the social class it exploits and from within its own class. It is this resistance that causes problems for maintaining the order and stability of capitalist societies. And just as was the case in the Victorian factories and banks and in turn-of-the-century food production, early twenty-first-century capitalism is posed with a dilemma: how to preserve a value system that is fundamentally inhumane and dehumanising, whilst at the same time ensuring that the system is stable enough to reproduce itself. For this role – as the extracts at various points in this book show (in particular, Sections 4 and 7), a quest for stability means establishing a system of law that is capable of preserving the viability and legitimacy of the economic system and at the same time is capable of preserving the primacy and autonomy of the economically powerful. In Section 5 we will return to the question of how moral distance is organised in the context of state crimes and corporate crimes. But in the following section we will explore the way that the law structures the legal and moral responsibilities of capitalist corporations and explore some of the deeper (legal) questions raised by capitalism's slow sacrifice of humanity.

Note

1 An equally powerful, up-to-date, non-fiction account of the US meat processing industry can be found in Eric Schlosser's excellent *Fast Food Nation* (2002).

References

Abraham, J. (1995) *Science, Politics and the Pharmaceutical Industry*. London: UCL Press.

Adams, S. (1984) *Roche versus Adams*. London: Jonathan Cape.

Braithwaite, J. (1984) *Corporate Crime in the Pharmaceutical Industry*. London: Routledge, Kegan & Paul.

Casement, R. (1997) *The Amazon Journal of Roger Casement* (ed. A. Mitchell). Dublin: Lillyput.

Ebeling, M. (2008) *Beyond Advertising: The pharmaceutical industry's hidden marketing tactics*. Madison Wisconsin: Centre for Media Democracy (www.prwatch.org/node/7026, accessed 10 May 2008)

Engels, F. (1850) The Ten Hours Bill, *Neue Rheinische Zeitung: Politisch-Ökonomische Revue*, No. 4.

Josephson, M. (1962) *The Robber Barons*. New York: Harcourt, Brace and World.

Mintz, M. (1985) *At Any Cost: Corporate greed, women and the Dalkon Shield*. New York: Pantheon.

Pearce, F. and Tombs, S. (1998) *Toxic Capitalism and the Chemical Industry*. Aldershot: Ashgate.

Pemberton, S. (2004) 'A Theory of Moral Indifference: Understanding the production of harm by capitalist society' in P. Hillyard, C. Pantazis, S. Tombs and D. Gordon (eds) *Beyond Criminology: Taking harm seriously*. London: Pluto.

Ross, E.A. (1973) *Sin and Society: An analysis of latter-day iniquity*. New York: Harper & Row.

Roy, A. (2001) 'The Algebra of Infinite Injustice', *The Guardian*, 29 September.

Schlosser, E (2002) *Fast Food Nation: What the all American meal is doing to the world*. Harmondsworth: Penguin.

Sinclair, U. (1986) *The Jungle*. Harmondsworth: Penguin.

Sjöstöm, H. and Nilsson, R. (1972) *Thalidomide and the Power of Drug Companies*. Harmondsworth: Penguin.

Taussig, M. (1984) 'Culture of Terror – Space of Death: Roger Casement's Putumayo report and the explanation of torture', *Contemporary Studies in Society and History*, 26: 467–97.

Tombs, S. and Whyte, D. (2008) 'The State and Corporate Crime' in R. Coleman, J. Sim, S. Tombs and D. Whyte (eds) *State, Power, Crime*. London: Sage.

Veblen, T. (1994) *The Theory of the Leisure Class*. London: Penguin.

Ward, T. (2005) 'State Crimes in the Heart of Darkness', *British Journal of Criminology*, 45(4).

Woodiwiss, M. (2005) *Gangster Capitalism: The United States and the global rise of organised crime*. London: Constable.

14

Capital: a critical analysis of capitalist production, Volume 1
Karl Marx

[...] The years 1846–47 are epoch-making in the economic history of England. The Repeal of the Corn Laws, and of the duties on cotton and other raw material; Free-trade proclaimed as the guiding star of legislation; in a word, the arrival of the millennium. On the other hand, in the same years, the Chartist movement and the 10 hours' agitation reached their highest point. They found allies in the Tories panting for revenge. Despite the fanatical opposition of the army of perjured Free-traders, with Bright and Cobden at their head, the Ten Hours' Bill, struggled for so long, went through Parliament.

The new Factory Act of June 8th, 1847, enacted that on July 1st, 1847, there should be a preliminary shortening of the working-day for "young persons" (from 13 to 18), and all females to 11 hours, but that on May 1st, 1848, there should be a definite limitation of the working-day to 10 hours. In other respects, the Act only amended and completed the Acts of 1833 and 1844.

Capital now entered upon a preliminary campaign in order to hinder the Act from coming into full force on May 1st, 1848. And the workers themselves, under the pretence that they had been taught by experience, were to help in the destruction of their own work. The moment was cleverly chosen. "It must be remembered, too, that there has been more than two years of great suffering (in consequence of the terrible crisis of 1846–47) among the factory operatives, from many mills having worked short time, and many being altogether closed. A considerable number of the operatives must therefore be in very narrow circumstances; many, it is to be feared, in debt; so that it might fairly have been presumed that at the present time they would prefer working the longer time, in order to make up for past losses, perhaps to pay off debts, or get their furniture out of pawn, or replace that sold, or to get a new supply of clothes for themselves and their families."[1]

The manufacturers tried to aggravate the natural effect of these circumstances by a general reduction of wages by 10%. This was done, so to say, to celebrate the inauguration of the new Free-trade era. Then followed a further reduction of $8\frac{1}{3}$% as soon as the working-day was shortened to 11, and a reduction of double that amount as soon as it was finally shortened to 10 hours. Wherever, therefore, circumstances allowed it, a reduction of wages of at least 25% took place. Under such favourably prepared conditions the agitation among the factory workers for the repeal of the Act of 1847 was begun. Neither lies, bribery, nor threats were spared in this attempt. But all was in vain. Concerning the half-dozen petitions in which workpeople were made to complain of "their oppression by the Act," the petitioners themselves declared under oral examination, that their signatures had been extorted from them. "They felt themselves oppressed, but not exactly by the Factory Act." But if the manufacturers did not succeed in making the workpeople speak as they wished, they themselves shrieked all the louder in press and Parliament in the name of the workpeople.

They denounced the Factory Inspectors as a kind of revolutionary commissioners like those of the French National Convention ruthlessly sacrificing the unhappy factory workers to their humanitarian crotchet. This manœuvre also failed. Factory Inspector Leonard Horner conducted in his own person, and through his sub-inspectors, many examinations of witnesses in the factories of Lancashire. About 70% of the workpeople examined declared in favour of 10 hours, a much smaller percentage in favour of 11, and an altogether insignificant minority for the old 12 hours.[2]

Another "friendly" dodge was to make the adult males work 12 to 15 hours, and then to blazon abroad this fact as the best proof of what the proletariat desired in its heart of hearts. But the "ruthless" Factory Inspector Leonard Horner was again to the fore. The majority of the "over-timers" declared: "They would much prefer working ten hours for less wages, but that they had no choice; that so many were out of employment (so many spinners getting very low wages by having to work as piecers, being unable to do better), that if they refused to work the longer time, others would immediately get their places, so that it was a question with them of agreeing to work the long time, or of being thrown out of employment altogether."[3] [...]

[...] The masters began their revolt with the simple declaration that the sections of the Act of 1844 which prohibited the *ad libitum* use of young persons and women in such short fractions of the day of 15 hours as the employer chose, were "comparatively harmless" so long as the work-time was fixed at 12 hours. But under the Ten Hours' Act they were a "grievous hardship."[4] They informed the inspectors in the coolest manner that they should place themselves above the letter of the law, and re-introduce the old system on their own account.[5] They were acting in the interests of the ill-advised operatives themselves, "in order to be able to pay them higher wages." "This was the only possible plan by which to maintain, under the Ten Hours' Act, the industrial supremacy of Great Britain." "Perhaps it may be a little difficult to detect irregularities under the relay system; but what of that? Is the great manufacturing interest of this country to be treated as a secondary matter in order to save some little trouble to Inspectors and Sub-Inspectors of Factories?"[6]

All these shifts naturally were of no avail. The Factory Inspectors appealed to the Law Courts. But soon such a cloud of dust in the way of petitions from the masters overwhelmed the Home Secretary, Sir George Grey, that in a circular of

August 5th, 1848, he recommends the inspectors not "to lay informations against mill-owners for a breach of the letter of the Act, or for employment of young persons by relays in cases in which there is no reason to believe that such young persons have been actually employed for a longer period than that sanctioned by law." Hereupon, Factory Inspector J. Stuart allowed the so-called relay system during the 15 hours of the factory day throughout Scotland, where it soon flourished again as of old. The English Factory Inspectors, on the other hand, declared that the Home Secretary had no power dictatorially to suspend the law, and continued their legal proceedings against the pro-slavery rebellion.

But what was the good of summoning the capitalists when the Courts, in this case the country magistrates—Cobbett's "Great Unpaid"—acquitted them? In these tribunals, the masters sat in judgment on themselves. An example. One Eskrigge, cotton-spinner, of the firm of Kershaw, Leese, & Co., had laid before the Factory Inspector of his district the scheme of a relay system intended for his mill. Receiving a refusal, he at first kept quiet. A few months later, an individual named Robinson, also a cotton-spinner, and if not his Man Friday, at all events related to Eskrigge, appeared before the borough magistrates of Stockport on a charge of introducing the identical plan of relays invented by Eskrigge. Four Justices sat, among them three cotton-spinners, at their head this same inevitable Eskrigge. Eskrigge acquitted Robinson, and now was of opinion that what was right for Robinson was fair for Eskrigge. Supported by his own legal decision, he introduced the system at once into his own factory.[7] Of course, the composition of this tribunal was in itself a violations of the law.[8] These judicial farces, exclaims Inspector Howell, "urgently call for a remedy—either that the law should be so altered as to be made to conform to these decisions, or that it should be administered by a less fallible tribunal, whose decisions would conform to the law ... when these cases are brought forward. I long for a stipendiary magistrate."[9]

The crown lawyers declared the masters' interpretation of the Act of 1848 absurd. But the Saviours of Society would not allow themselves to be turned from their purpose. Leonard Horner reports, "Having endeavoured to enforce the Act ... by ten prosecutions in seven magisterial divisions, and having been supported by the magistrates in one case only. ... I considered it useless to prosecute more for this evasion of the law. [...]

Notes

1 "Rep. of Insp. of Fact.," 31st Oct., 1848, p. 16.
2 p. 17, l. c. In Mr Horner's district 10,270 adult male labourers were thus examined in 101 factories. Their evidence is to be found in the appendix to the Factory Reports for the half-year ending October 1848. These examinations furnish valuable material in other connexions also.
3 l. c. See the evidence collected by Leonard Horner himself, Nos. 69, 70, 71, 72, 92, 93, and that collected by Sub-Inspector A., Nos. 51, 52, 58, 59, 62, 70, of the Appendix. One manufacturer, too, tells the plain truth. See No. 14, and No. 265, l. c.

4   Reports, &c., for 30th April, 1848, p. 28.
5   Thus, among others, Philanthropist Ashworth to Leonard Horner, in a disgusting Quaker letter. (Reports, &c., April, 1849, p. 4.)
6   l. c., p. 140.
7   Reports, &c., for 30th April, 1849, pp. 21, 22. Cf. like examples ibid. pp. 4, 5.
8   By I. and II. Will. IV., ch. 24, s. 10, known as Sir John Hobhouse's Factory Act, it was forbidden to any owner of a cotton-spinning or weaving mill, or the father, son, or brother of such owner, to act as Justice of the Peace in any inquiries that concerned the Factory Act.
9   l. c.

15

The Amazon journal of Roger Casement
Roger Casement

[...] There are doubtless 530 Indians inscribed, whose duty is to bring in every three months some 30 kilogs of rubber against battle, murder and sudden death if they don't [...] Let us see how that works. Say 30 kilogs per man per quarter gives 120 kilogs per annum plus 530 "labourers", gives 63,600 kilogs. The actual quantity collected per man must, therefore, be less than 30 kilogs per quarter. Yet in the Store today I weighed one of the one-man loads lying there, and it comes to 33½ kilogs, and I was told it did not represent the full amount for a *fabrico*, or rubber term. The *cepo*, or stocks, are also in this rubber store. There is nothing else. It is the whole ground floor of the big house, and is lined round the two long sides with shelves on which the rubber lies, according as each Indian "labourer" brings it in every ten days or fifteen days. To be accurate he does not bring it in, I am told. Although a collector, he is himself collected when the rubber is "due". [...] They are marched down to the Station here, each man (or family) with his or their load of rubber, which is here weighed. If correct, the man escapes back to his forest home to begin almost immediately collecting afresh. If not up to weight he gets flogged or put in *cepo*. Such is mildly, the system. At the end of the fabrico, which is five of these collections, he receives not payment on the 30 kilogs, or whatever the exact amount may be he has gathered, but an "advance" against the next fabrico, that is to say, he is kept on "the books of this commercial establishment as a debtor to the firm. He is not asked if he wants an advance, or what he would like, he is only too happy to escape with a whole skin, or with his wife and daughter. [...]

[...] This Putumayo Slavery is, indeed, as Hardenburg said, and as I laughed at when I read it a year ago in *Truth*, a bigger crime than that of the Congo, although committed on a far smaller stage and affecting only a few thousands of human beings, whereas the other affected millions.[1]

The other was Slavery under Law, with judges, Army, Police and Officers, often men of birth and breeding even, carrying out an iniquitous system invested with monarchical authority, and in some sense directed to public, or so-called public ends. It was bad, exceedingly bad, and, with all its so-called safeguards, it has been condemned and is in process, thank God, of passing or being swept away.

But this thing I find here is slavery without law, where the slavers are personally cowardly ruffians, jail birds, and there is not authority within 1200 miles, and no means of punishing any offence, however vile. Sometimes Congolese "justice intervened, and an extra red-handed ruffian was sentenced, but here there is no jail, no judges, no Law. Every Chief of Section is judge and law in one, and every Section itself is only a big jail with the Indians on the treadmill, and the criminals as the jailers." [...]

[...] These men came here not as settlers "to trade" with the Indians, but to appropriate the Indians. It is not the rubber trees so much as the Indians they wanted and want. The trees are valueless without the Indians, who, besides getting rubber for them, do everything else these creatures need — feed them, build for them, run for them and carry for them and supply them with wives and concubines.

They couldn't get this done by persuasion, so they slew and massacred and enslaved by terror, and that is the whole foundation. What we see today is merely the logical sequence of events — the cowed and entirely subdued Indians, reduced in numbers, hopelessly obedient, with no refuge and no retreat, and no redress. Here, this very year, is this very man, Jiménez, heading a large armed band of the "Company's servants" far into the Republic of Colombia, many days beyond the Caquetá, the indisputed frontier of that State, and putting three Colombians in Stocks for 21 days on their own soil, and bringing them and 21 Indians down here as prisoners. These 21 Indians had fled many days' journey to escape from this regime, and they are not saved by flight, even into another so-called civilised country. The whole thing from top to bottom is slavery without law — the most lawless state of things imaginable in this stage of human progress, for these Agents are not savages, but are the highly paid servants of a great English Company — citizens of a civilised state and amenable, so we are told, to an "efficient administration of justice." [...]

[...] But the Company objects to the habits and customs of the Indians. They are not civilised — moreover, they would not produce rubber. So the woman of the Indian household is kept at Entre Rios, or Occidente, or Atenas as the case may be, for a space of from a week to ten days to cultivate the fields of the Company, so that its staff may have cheap food, while her husband, under the "directions" of a half breed much more ignorant of agriculture than the wildest Indian in the world, is forced to plant and hoe yucca in order that his body may be fortified against the next *fabrico*, which begins right away. If this uncongenial task is not performed to the satisfaction of the *Empleado Racionale* sent to his village to chase and hunt him to it, he will not receive his "payment" (or "advance" — the terms are synonymous and transposable) for the last *fabrico* of 40 or 50 or 60 or 70 kilogrammes of rubber he has delivered to the Company — not until he has satisfied this agricultural expert. This seems to me almost the chief refinement of cruelty of this truly devilish system of cruelty. The whole thing is hard to beat, and it has been going on for years — longer than I like to think of, and will go on, I fear, until the last Indian had delivered up his last *puesta*, and, with it, his poor, starved, beflagellated ghost to the God that sent the *veracucha* to be his moral guide and friend. Alas! poor Peruvian, poor South American Indian! The world thinks the slave trade was killed a century ago! The worst form of slave trade and of slavery — worse in many of its aspects, as I shall show — than anything African savagery gave birth to, has been in full swing here for 300 years until the dwindling remnant of a population once numbering millions, is now perishing at the doors of an English Company, under the lash, the chains, the bullet, the machete to give its shareholders a dividend.[2] [...]

[...] Moreover it must always be borne in mind that the Indian is no party to the contract. He is compelled by brutal and wholly uncontrolled force — by being hunted and caught — by floggings, by chaining up, by long periods of imprisonment and starvation, to agree to "work" for the Company and then when released from this taming process and this 5/- worth of absolute trash given to him he is hunted and hounded and guarded and flogged and his food robbed and his womenfolk ravished until he brings in from 200 to perhaps 300 times the value of the goods he has been forced to accept.

If he attempts to escape from this commercial obligation, he and his family as defaulting debtors are hunted for days and weeks, the frontier of a neighbouring state being no protection and when found are lucky if they escape with life. The least he can expect is to be flogged until raw, to be again chained up and starved, to be confined in the stocks, in a position of torture for days, weeks and even months. Many Indians have been so kept for months.

When he has acquitted himself of the commercial obligation and has carried in at great fatigue and physical deprivation of many kinds the quantity of rubber assessed upon his unhappy shoulders there is no escape. An enormous load of this, often, as I have seen, in excess of 50 kilos. has to be carried for distances of 40 to 70 miles to the nearest "port" on the Igara-paraná, over roads that even a mule cannot traverse — more fit for monkeys to scramble over than for men — and this without food save such as this wife and children can bring along with the heavy loads of rubber laid upon them also. Death on their road often attends them — death from hunger, from exposure, from fever and from sheer physical and mental break up.

Notes

1 As with any genocide, exact figures are hard to pin down but recent estimates suggest that around three million Africans died under Leopold II's regime in the Congo Free State. Figures regarding extermination of Amazon tribal people during the rubber boom are even harder to calculate. In the Putumayo around 40,000 indians were exterminated from the time of first contact with *Caucheros* to the end of the boom. It seems likely that death figures rise well into the hundreds of thousands, possibly millions when all the vast rubber districts of Amazonia are considered. But the details of the Indian slave hunts and killings are largely unrecorded.

2 Here Casement unequivocally lays the blame for this long process of genocide at the feet of the white man and latterly targets the British trading interests involved with the exploitation of wild rubber resources. Casement's resent-

ment and anger regarding British involvement in financing the slave-kingdoms of the Amazon went deeper as his investigation continued. It was a matter, however, that he could ony express in private.

16

Sin and society: an analysis of latter-day iniquity
E.A. Ross

[...] The sinful heart is ever the same, but sin changes its quality as society develops. Modern sin takes its character from the mutualism of our time. Under our present manner of living, how many of my vital interests I must intrust to others! Nowadays the water main is my well, the trolley car my carriage, the banker's safe my old stocking, the policeman's billy my fist. My own eyes and nose and judgment defer to the inspector of food, or drugs, or gas, or factories, or tenements, or insurance companies. I rely upon others to look after my drains, invest my savings, nurse my sick, and teach my children. I let the meat trust butcher my pig, the oil trust mould my candles, the sugar trust boil my sorghum, the coal trust chop my wood, the barb wire company split my rails.

But this spread-out manner of life lays snares for the weak and opens doors to the wicked. Interdependence puts us, as it were, at one another's mercy, and so ushers in a multitude of new forms of wrongdoing. The practice of mutualism has always worked this way. Most sin is preying, and every new social relation begets its cannibalism. No one will "make the ephah small" or "falsify the balances" until there is buying and selling, "withhold the pledge" until there is loaning, "keep back the hire of the laborers" until there is a wage system, "justify the wicked for a reward" until men submit their disputes to a judge. The rise of the state makes possible counterfeiting, smuggling, peculation, and treason. Commerce tempts the pirate, the forger, and the embezzler. Every new fiduciary relation is a fresh opportunity for breach of trust. To-day the factory system makes it possible to work children to death on the double-quick, speculative building gives the jerry-builder his chance, long-range investment spawns the get-rich-quick concern, and the trust movement opens the door to the bubble promoter.[...]

[...] The sinister opportunities presented in this webbed social life have been seized unhesitatingly, because such treasons have not yet become infamous. The man who picks pockets with a railway rebate, murders with an adulterant instead of a bludgeon, burglarizes with a "rake-off" instead of a jimmy, cheats with a company prospectus instead of a deck of cards, or scuttles his town instead of his ship, does not feel on his brow the brand of a malefactor. The shedder of blood, the oppressor of the widow and the fatherless, long ago became odious, but latter-day treacheries fly no skull-and-crossbones flag at the mast-head. [...]

[...] There is a special cause for the condoning of sins committed in the way of business and without personal malice. Business men, as a rule, insist upon a free hand in their dealings, and, since they are conspicuous and influential in the community, they carry with them a considerable part of the non-business world. The leisured, the non-industrial employees, the bulk of professional men, and many public servants, hold to the unmitigated maxim of *caveat emptor*, and accept the chicane of trade as reasonable and legitimate. In England till 1487 any one who knew how to read might commit murder with impunity by claiming "benefit of clergy." There is something like this in the way we have granted quack and fakir and mine operator and railroad company indulgence to commit manslaughter in the name of business. [...]

[...] The corporation, to be sure, has certain good points. The corporate owner — of course we are not speaking of one-man corporations, or of those whose officers follow their own sweet will — is not warped by race antipathy or religious prejudice or caste pride. Unlike the individual business man, its course is never shaped by political ambitions or social aspirations or the personal feuds of its wife. It does not exact personal subservience, does not indulge itself in petty tyranny, is not held back from negotiation with its employees by aristocratic haughtiness. It does not feel anger or hold a grudge. If it ruins any one, it does so not from malice, but simply because he stands in the way. Let him meekly creep into the ditch, and it honks by unnoticing. The business man may be swerved by vindictiveness or by generosity, by passion or by conscience, but the genuine corporation responds to but one motive. Toward gain it gravitates with the ruthlessness of a lava stream.

Nevertheless, if the corporate owner is free from the weakness of the individual, it escapes also his wholesome limitations. It feels not the restraints that conscience and public sentiment lay on the business man. It fears the law no more, and public indignation far less, than does the individual. You can hiss the bad man, egg him, lampoon him, caricature him, ostracize him and his. Not so with the bad corporation. The corporation, moreover, is not in dread of hell fire. You cannot Christianize it. You may convert its stockholders, animate them with patriotism or public spirit or love of social service; but this will have little or no effect on the tenor of their corporation. In short, it is an entity that transmits the greed of investors, but not their conscience; that returns them profits, but not unpopularity.

In view of the psychology of the corporation, the fact that in a lifetime it has risen to the captaincy of more than half the active wealth of this country cannot be without a bearing on our moral situation. A current manual describes 6700 companies (not including banking and insurance companies) with a capitalization of thirty-six billions of dollars, and an actual property estimated to be worth twenty-seven billions or sixty per cent of all the wealth of the United States outside of farm values and of city values in residences and in private businesses. Surely the misconduct of this giant race of artificial persons deserves consideration by itself. [...]

[…] Now, the stockholders for whom all these iniquitous things are done do not consciously stand for them. They do not will that children should be worn out, workmen maimed, consumers defrauded, the ballot polluted, or public men debauched. They seem to demand such conduct only because they fail to realize what they are doing when they exact the utmost penny. However harmless their intentions, their clamor for fat dividends inevitably throws the management of quasi-public — and some other — businesses into the hands of the domineering-arrogant or the suave-unscrupulous type. The manager represents just one side of the shareholders, namely, their avarice. In other respects he is no more typical of them than the company doctor is typical of physicians or the corporation attorney is typical of lawyers. […]

[…] Now, the corporation cannot mend itself. More and more it is impersonal and non-moral. More and more the far-away manager is rated as a profit conveyer, and the conduit with the bigger flow is always preferred. It has become a machine, and Mammon is its master. Reform, therefore, will not come from the inside. Those who supply the capital cannot mould it to their better will. But they can change its spirit if they will join with their fellow citizens in restraining the corporation by public opinion and by statute. If the reaction of organized society upon the Gradgrind type of manager is so severe that he cannot make so much money for his stockholders as a more reasonable and representative type, he will give way to the better man, and one cause of the needless alienation of classes will be removed. […]

[…] In the corporation the men who give orders, but do not take them, are the directors. They enjoy economic freedom. If their scruples cost them a reelection, their livelihood is not jeopardized. In the will of these men lies the fountain-head of righteousness or iniquity in the policies of the corporation. Here is the moral laboratory where the lust of an additional quarter of a per cent of dividend, on the part of men already comfortable in goods, is mysteriously transmuted into deeds of wrong and lawlessness by remote, obscure employees in terror of losing their livelihood. […]

[…] In enforcing the rules of the game the chief problem is how to restrain corporations. The threat to withdraw the charter alarms no one, for corporations know they are here to stay. Fine the law-breaking officers, and the board of directors by indemnifying them encourages them to do it again. Fine the corporation, and, if its sinning is lucrative, it heeds the fine no more than a flea-bite. Never will the brake of the law grip these slippery wheels until prison doors yawn for the convicted officers of lawless corporations. Even then you cannot fasten upon the officers legal responsibility for much of the iniquity they instigate. For example, to deceive the state insurance commissioners the president of a culpable insurance company directs the actuary to make up a report of such and such a character. He hands it to the treasurer and the auditor who, as required by law, swear that "to the best of their knowledge and belief" it is true. The high officials who screen their mismanagement with this false report have not been obliged to perjure themselves by swearing to it. The law has no hold upon them.

Again, a rich corporation desires legislation favorable to its own interests. The president engages an eminent attorney to draft a bill to that effect. He then takes it to a great law firm versed in practice of a legislative character. "I want you gentlemen to use all proper and legitimate means to secure the passage of this measure. Send the bill to me." The firm gets the measure introduced and then engages the service of a great lobbyist. The lobbyist seeks to influence men who are under obligations to him for financial aid in getting elected. If some needed legislators stand out demanding money, he engages the services of small lobbyists, or sends an intermediary with a bribe. Thus the chief offenders protect themselves by working through accomplices, in many cases so remote from them that they are not even aware of the accomplices' existence.

Until the courts recast their definitions of legal evidence and legal responsibility, much of the control of corporations must devolve upon some agent free from the pedantries and Byzantism of the law. [...]

[...] Corporations are necessary, yet, through nobody's fault, they tend to become soulless and lawless. By all means let them reap where they have sown. But why let them declare dividends not only on their capital, but also on their power to starve out labor, to wear out litigants, to beat down small competitors, to master the market, to evade taxes, to get the free use of public property? Nothing but the curb of organized society can confine them to their own grist and keep them from grinding into dividends the stamina of children, the health of women, the lives of men, the purity of the ballot, the honor of public servants, and the supremacy of the laws.

17

The robber barons
Matthew Josephson

[...] The most successful of the early industrial pools was formed toward 1880 by the slaughterhouses of Chicago. Here at the natural transshipment center where numerous great railroad trunk lines converged, the grain, produce, cattle and swine of the West seemed to flow toward the world markets as through a bottle-neck held in the hands of packing-houses, elevators and millers.

"I like to turn bristles, blood, and the inside and outside of pigs and bullocks into revenue ..." said the astute Philip D. Armour. This puritanical and grasping dealer in pigs was among the first to note the enormous waste of labor and material in his trade. Both he and Nelson Morris had soon ceased to sell cattle "on the hoof," and had begun to systematize the work of despatching, dressing, smoking and canning steers in their stockyards by large-scale methods. After the Civil War, Morris had begun shipping frozen beef during the winter to points as far distant as Boston; and in 1874, the Cape Cod Yankee Gustavus Swift had revolutionized the industry by introducing the refrigerator car, under the Tiffany patents, with its bunkers and tanks for ice, and its heat-proof doors. So instead of shipping merely smoked or frozen meat in winter, it became possible suddenly to sell at all seasons of the year to every corner of the globe. By dint of further technical advance contributed as well by the firms of Cudahy, Hammond (later Wilson & Company) and others, the stockyards of Chicago became the home of a gigantic and rhythmically functioning industry, which was soon famous throughout the world for the "mass production" of animal food. By an ingenious arrangement of the yards, and division of the labor, the droves of cattle which poured into Chicago were disassembled with amazing rapidity. Passing swiftly through winding viaducts into pens they would be suddenly stunned, dropped through trap-doors into slaughtering rooms, then killed. Thereafter laborers hung the carcasses by wire around the legs to a moving trolley-line, cut up, bled, dressed, and classified them. The operations of the laborers, chiefly Negroes and Slav immigrants, gathered in mighty armies, was thoroughly and shrewdly regimented and driven at top speed throughout the process. Finally every by-product, every spectes of animal raw material, was put to use, so that tremendous economies were gained on every hand in a hundred different ways.

The opportunity for large-scale management of the slaughtering trade, after the coming of the refrigerator car, had brought quickly a movement of consolidation among the numerous firms. The little houses were bought up by bigger ones; distributing agencies or large packing-houses were set up in strategic centers such as Omaha, St. Louis and Kansas City, and fleets of refrigerator cars were formed to carry the dressed-meat and vegetable traffic which now proceeded to boom magnificently.

Armour, Morris and the other packers who used to give each other "a wallop with a smile," at length arrived at a complete "gentlemen's agreement" which ended all competition between them. Thus unified, the Big Four of meat, as distributors, faced the consumers with their compact organization and fixed price system. On the other hand, as refiners (or "processors") of raw material, they confronted the disorganized producers, that is, the farmers, with the same concealed unanimity. At the stockyards, ever since 1880, according to Charles Edward Russell's lively account in his "The Greatest Trust in the World," only four buyers would come to bid on the cattle offered each morning:

The first offers a low price, the second is not interested, the third is not interested, nor is the fourth in a hurry to make a purchase. The next day the buyer for another one of the Big Four sets a price, and the other three refuse to buy.

The price is low, but there is no other buyer. No "conspiracy" is perceptible; there is only an accidental harmony of minds.

These overlords of beef now had their hands over the market in live cattle. Cooperating with each other firmly and using the utmost secrecy, they were also able to fight with remarkable effect against the rulership which the great railroads held over them in turn. During the '80's the beef pool soon forced down rates on their shipments, obtained rebates like the oil-refiners, and set up refrigerator car companies through which all perishable food and vegetables must be handled solely, receiving indirect toll from farms of the South, the Middle West and the Pacific Coast. Moreover their combination was able to force the railroads to pay them a "mileage fee of three-fourths of a cent per mile for the use of their refrigerator cars. Where a railroad seemed tardy in complying with such orders, as in the case of the New York Central, it was punished almost at once, according to Russell, by the diversion of as much as 150 cars of freight per week. Thus, empty or laden, the refrigerator cars brought a perpetual ransom from the railroads to the barons of the packing-houses, who ruled unchallenged over a mighty national traffic in food.

Neither from adjacent industries, such as railroads, nor from would-be invaders of their field, nor farmers nor middlemen nor consumers, would the packers brook interference. Resistance in every direction was met with an implacable force, now operating through financial and now through political "influences". Widespread and violent strikes of the workers were broken in 1886, in 1894 and again in 1904 by the united front of the stockyard firms and a system of uniform blacklisting carried out by them with perfect discipline. This aroused the admiration of captains of industry in all other fields, and gave Chicago long ago its atmosphere of violence.

The power of the kings of animal food was supreme, grandiose and feudal; and sad to relate, like many earlier dynasts they abused it. There was none to say nay if they used diseased swine, goats, or cows in making their famous sausages or hams or tinned beef. For thirty years, although millions of persons patronized them, the four or five overlords in Chicago alone decided what sanitary measures of inspection or approval should be taken. They themselves did not eat this dressed food which they disseminated so widely to an invisible public, toward whom their moral attitude was strictly detached and impersonal. Overwhelmingly bent on pecuniary gains to be derived from the handling of the animal carcasses, and also prone to utilize with ingenious technology a steadily inferior product, they were universally believed guilty of many lapses which did small honor to the American table. Yet none oversaw their activities, and few protested even when frequent cases of sickness or even death were traced directly to their merchandise. [...]

18

White collar crime in modern England: financial fraud and business morality 1845–1929

George Robb

[…] Victorian England witnessed the birth of a new, industrial economy and a financial structure characterized by individual shareholdings in joint-stock corporations. By the end of the nineteenth century, the British had invested several billion pounds in company shares, or roughly two-fifths of total national wealth. This level of shareholding had no parallel in the world, amounting to more than twice the sum of French and German company investment combined.[1] Corporate organization fecilitated British domination of the world economy and enriched many members of the investing public; yet this novel and peculiar form of economic arrangement also proved vulnerable to abuse. White-collar crime was the soft underbelly of the modern British economy, robbing the public of millions of pounds, undermining trust in commercial integrity and depressing the level of investment in new industries.

A number of structural and ideological factors combined to create a climate favorable to corporate fraud in nineteenth-century England. The divorce of ownership from control in large companies increased the distance between shareholders and directors and heightened the impersonality of the relationship. Directors held vast sums of money in trust for investors, and the temptation to misappropriate or misapply that money was at times irresistible. The primitive nature of accountancy and auditing made fraud difficult to discover and the complexity of modern finance blurred the boundaries between crime and misadventure. The entrepreneurial culture of Victorian England bred aggressive businessmen who were impatient with ethical codes and whose preoccupation with material success led them to fear failure more than fraud. A *laissez-faire* mentality and an emphasis on individual responsibility discouraged state intervention to protect shareholders. Victorian class prejudice permeated the criminal justice system, which directed its greatest wrath against the lower classes and treated upper-class criminal capitalists with relative leniency.

White-collar crime actually posed a far greater threat to property than did the thefts of burglars, shoplifters and pickpockets. In 1894 the journalist A.R. Barnett observed: "there seems to be more danger from the trusted officer and the employee than from the burglar … now it is the skilled financier or bank clerk who coolly and quietly abstracts or misapplies the funds, falsifies the accounts, and makes away with millions where the burglar got thousands."[2] To give but one example, in *London Labour and the London Poor*, Henry Mayhew recorded that the property stolen by London's thieves amounted to £71,000 for the year 1860.[3] A substantial sum to be sure, but one that pales in comparison to the £260,000 embezzlement of a single London bank clerk, W.G. Pullinger, also in 1860.[4] Unlike the burglars who made off with the family silver, frauds and embezzlers could deprive people of their capital, or of their life's savings. In commenting on the embezzlements of the bankers Strahan, Paul and Bates, the London *Times* listed the levels of crime from pickpocket to highwayman, but awarded the highest criminal "honors" to financiers who scatter "ruin over hundreds of quiet, respectable, and virtuous households, the scene of sacred economy and the sweet charities of domestic life." *The Times* went on to lament:

> How many girls will go portionless! how many young ladies become governesses! how many young men go to Australia, or behind counters, instead of to College or the Guards, in consequence of this bankruptcy! How many hearts will be broken! how many constitutions undermined by trudging and drudging, that have hitherto known nothing worse than a headache after an evening party or the shaking of an ill-hung carriage.[5]

Although the financial frauds of middle-class bankers, brokers and company directors dwarfed the thefts of the Victorian underworld, it was Mayhew's rag-tag pickpockets and audacious burglars (or their literary equivalents, the Artful Dodger and Bill Sikes) that dominated popular images of criminality. Contemporary historians have inherited the class prejudices of the last century, and have for the most part accepted uncritically the assumption that "crime" was a working-class phenomenon. This study rejects such an idea through its emphasis on the criminal "upperworld." [...]

[...] Individual losses from fraud or embezzement could be considerable. After the Financial Crisis of 1866, the Master of Rolls, Lord Romilly, informed Parliament:

> Very few days pass without my receiving letters from contributories in the country, who say that they are entirely ruined by being called upon to pay a contribution, and that they had no conception what the company was which they joined. They are persons, perhaps, who have saved after along life of industry, £200 or £300, to live upon in their old age, and they have been induced to join a company, and they are utterly ruined.[6]

A specific example from the period involved the three thousand shareholders of the Alliance Building Society who lost between £300,000 and £400,000 when that firm failed in 1866. The Alliance had been recklessly managed, though it drew in shareholders from temperance circles by falsely implying a connection between itself and the United Kingdom Alliance, the principal temperance organization in England. Shareholders included many widows and spinsters who had invested all their savings, and the newspapers noted the suicides of several victims.[7]

The City of Glasgow debacle in 1878 resulted in the loss of almost £6 million of shareholders' and depositors' money. According to the *Contemporary Review*:

> In almost every town and hamlet of our land, however far from the centre of the explosion, there stands some home unroofed and torn open to the hard gaze of public curiosity and public compassion. It is true that the sufferers have in public and in private, shown resignation to God and constancy before men, even beyond belief; but how many lives, maimed and all but cut in two, have crept away beyond our ken into a seclusion where hope and energy are slowly ebbing from the wounded spirit.

Nor was this mere rhetoric. Over one thousand shareholders were bankrupted by demands to meet their unlimited liability and an army of small investors lost their all. So profound was the resulting distress that a charitable relief fund was organized to assist the victims.[8] [...]

[...] Those investors most vulnerable to fraud were persons of slender means, such as the elderly, widows, spinsters, clergymen, half-pay officers, small tradesmen and domestic servants. Possessed of relatively small savings, modest investors were unable to diversify, and tended to place all their funds into a single investment, very often a bank, building society or insurance company. As early as 1844, the Parliamentary Committee on Joint-Stock Companies realized that humble investors were the greatest sufferers from company fraud:

> The extent of the evil is to be measured rather by the circumstances of the victims than the amount of plunder. They are usually persons of very limited means, who invest their savings in order to obtain the tempting returns which are offered. Annuity Companies have proved the most dangerous in this respect. Old people, governesses, servants, and persons of that description, are tempted to invest their little all, and when the concern stops, they are ruined.[9]

The insurance company frauds and savings bank embezzlements of the 1840s had sent a number of small depositors to the workhouse.[10] This particular class of investor continued to be most adversely affected by the frauds and·failures of Victorian and Edwardian England.

The more affluent investor, of course, could afford a greater margin of error than his *petit bourgeois* counterpart. Wealthy investors also lessened their risks by diversifying their stock portfolios. Corporations were especially well placed to offset losses from fraud. In 1860, for example, the Union Bank of London was able to cover the £260,000 embezzlement of its chief cashier by transferring £220,000 from its reserve fund along with £40,000 from the yearly profits. Despite the enormity of the loss, the Union Bank was still able to pay a respectable 5%

dividend that year.[11] With the growth of investment trusts and institutional shareholdings during the twentieth century, individual losses from white-collar crime have been minimized even further.

Even more profound than shareholders' losses was fraud's impact on the economy as a whole – both in undermining commercial trust and depressing levels of investment. As the *National Review* put the case in 1898: "this is not merely a question as is often urged of a few credulous investors or speculators losing their money. Other and larger issues are involved, such as the lowering of hitherto accepted standards of commercial integrity."[12] The commercial world was bound together by stocks, bonds, contracts, bills of exchange, letters of credit and promissory notes. Fraud was seen as a "canker at the heart of this complicated system"[13] because it threatened the inviolability of contracts and the integrity of financial instruments. According to D.M. Evans: "In a commercial country such as England, no crime can be more heinous against society, as constituted, than a breach of mercantile trust. To tolerate it, or to pass it over with ill-judged sympathy, or equally ill-timed mercy, would be to sap the foundations of mercantile prosperity."[14] By late century, some critics of the City believed that fraud was sapping the vitality of the entire nation:

> There is something disagreeably un-English about the new financial methods and the vulgar trickery and chicane which characterize them; and in these days when finance and politics are connected by the closest ties their demoralizing influence is especially to be deplored ... there are still a few who believe that the national character is one of the main foundations of our greatness both at home and abroad, and that anything which tends to impair it is a source of national weakness. As a commercial people our credit rests on our good name, and as a nation with an imperial mission we can ill afford to play fast and loose with it ... It is not merely rectitude, unctuous or otherwise, it is plain common sense – "good business," in fact – to recognize that this good name and this national character are things worth preserving, and that the beginnings of pecuniary corruption may also, whatever our new Machiavellians may say, be the seeds of a nation's decadence.[15] [...]

Notes

1 See above, chapter 1.

2 A.R. Barnett, "Era of Fraud and Embezzlement: Its Causes and Remedies, " *Arena* 14 (October 1894): 196.

3 Henry Mayhew, *London Labour and the London Poor,* 4 vols. (1861; reprint, New York: Dover Publications, 1968), vol. 4, 276.

4 See above, chapter 6.

5 *The Times* (London), 22 June 1855.

6 Select Committee on Limited Liabilty Acts, *Parliamentary Papers,* 1867, x, Minutes, 81.

7 *Westminster Popular* No. 5, 3–7.

8   Alexandra Taylor Innes, "The Personal Responsibility of Bank Directors," *Contemporary Review* 34 (January 1879): 322.
9   Select Committee Report on Joint Stock Companies, *Parliamentary Papers,* 1844, VII, 363.
10 See Scratchley, *On Savings Banks, 54–55, and Francis, Chronicles and Characters of the Stock Exchange, 355–56.*
11 Union Bank, *Minute Books, vol. 13, 157–61, National Westminster Bank Archives,* London.
12 Stutfield, "The Higher Rascality," 77.
13 "Commercial Frauds," *Irish Quarterly Review 9 (April 1859): 193.*
14 Evans, *Facts, Failures and Frauds, 123.*
15 Stutfield, "The Higher Rascality," 84–85. See also Stutfield, "The Company Scandal: A City View," 575–83.

19

Corporate crime in the pharmaceutical industry
John Braithwaite

The overmedicated society

> The subcommittee heard that one out of every two hospitalized Americans who receives antibiotics this year will be taking a drug that is irrationally prescribed and which may result in an adverse drug reaction. As an overall class, adverse drug reactions already account for $2 billion in medical and hospital costs and 30,000 deaths each year. Eighty percent of these reactions are thought to be preventable (Senator Edward Kennedy, Subcommittee on Health, 1974: 719).

The number of deaths from adverse drug reactions in the United States each year has been a hotly disputed question, with some researchers claiming that the number could be as high as 130,000 for hospital-induced reactions alone (e.g. Shapiro et al., 1971). Irrespective of whether a more accurate figure is 30,000 or 130,000, it is certain that America pays a heavy price for being an overmedicated society. Invariably, drugs which are powerful enough to control a disease are also capable of causing severe injury to patients. As one corporate medical director explained: 'Prescription drugs are no more than tamed poisons.'

The diseases for which a drug is recommended are called its indications, and the diseases for which it would be particularly dangerous to use the drug are its contra-indications. Pharmaceutical companies naturally have an interest in expanding markets by promoting wide indications and limiting contra-indications.

> The extent of a drug's indications is no academic question. If, for example, a drug is recommended and used for a disease against which it is not effective, then the disease, perhaps serious, will be left untreated. In addition, and despite the ineffectiveness of the drug, the person using it still runs the risk of its toxic effects. Even if the drug is effective, the person may be subjected to unnecessary risks if a less toxic drug would do the job as well (Ledogar, 1975: 7).

Pharmaceutical compapanies even manage to invent new diseases as indications. Madison Avenue is able to respond creatively when the pharmaceutical company says: 'Here's the cure, find the disease.' An example of such creativity was the promotion of Lilly's Aventyl for a new disease called 'behavioral drift'. Behavioral drift, according to the medical journal advertisements, is defined as:

> 1st visit ... and then I start crying for no real reason; 2nd visit ... I can't sit still. It makes me nervous to stay in one place; 3rd visit ... I seem to have lost my powers of concentration; 4th visit ... The least noise and I'm ready to climb the walls; 5th visit ... Maybe it's silly, but I think I have cancer; 6th visit ... I feel so worthless all the time; 7th visit ... I can't fall asleep, so I roam through the house; 8th visit ... Doctor, are you *sure* it's not cancer?

Then there is the more basic strategy of defining indications such as depression as widely as possible. Dr Richard Crout, Director of the FDA's Bureau of Drugs, gives the example of a Pfizer videotape distributed to hospitals. The tape begins by asserting that 4 to 8 million Americans suffer from depression, bet later we are told that under a definition of depression as 'absence of joy' the figure would be 20 million. Crout concludes that Pfizer were attempting to create the impression that depression was 'everywhere and being under-diagnosed'.

Valium has been the drug which has been most heavily and successfully promoted in this kind of way. The overuse of Valium has brought a frightful cost. For a twelve-month period in 1976–77, one study found that 54,400 sought hospital emergency room treatment in the United States concerning the use, overuse, or abuse of Valium (Hughes and Brewin, 1979: 8–9). During the same period, the study, conducted by the National Institute of Drug Abuse, found at least 900 deaths attributable to Valium use, plus another 200 deaths linked to its chemical predecessor, Librium. Many of the deaths were due to either accidental or intentional overdose. Hence the conclusion of Dr Edward Tocus, chief of the Drug Abuse Staff at the FDA that 'We are developing a population dependent on this drug equal to the number of alcoholics in this country. We are in a situation now where we see at least as many people being hurt by this drug as are being helped by it' (Hughes and Brewin, 1979: 24).

The National Institute of Drug Abuse concludes from its study that Lilly's Darvon is an even bigger danger than Valium. It was linked to 1,100 deaths during the year. Darvon has been the subject of a concerted public-interest campaign for withdrawal from the market. Lilly defends its product by pointing out that if used properly and cautiously, it has therapeutic value. The public-interest movement, in turn, replies that the product is not being used cautiously precisely because of the advertising hype of Lilly's promotion of Darvon in the years following its release.

The most wanton example of the overuse of a drug causing social harm because of promotion for excessive indications is that of chloramphenicol by Parke-Davis (now a subsidiary of Warner-Lambert). Chloramphenicol is a remarkably effective antibiotic in the treatment of a limited range of infections – typhoid fever, haemophilus influenza, and a few others. But it was promoted as a broad-spectrum antibiotic, and prescribed by doctors for everything from sore throats to acne. In its first year on the market, 1951, Parke-Davis sold $52 million worth of chloramphenicol (brand name Chloromycetin), to put the company at the top of drug-company earnings for that year.

Unfortunately, chloramphenicol was associated with a number of serious side-effects, the worst being aplastic anaemia. Aplastic anaemia causes a terrible death, especially in children. The probability of the side-effect appearing was not high, so in the treatment of a serious disease like typhoid, it was a risk worth taking. But for the treatment of common cold and other trivial complaints the risk is unconscionable. The FDA was concerned, and in 1952 issued an official warning that chloramphenicol 'should not be used indiscriminately for minor infections'. Parke-Davis misrepresented the FDA warning to its own sales representatives in a 'President's Letter' which read: 'Chloromycetin [chloramphenicol] has been officially cleared by the FDA and the National Research Council with no restrictions on the number or the range of diseases for which Chloromycetin may be administered.' The Nelson Subcommittee discovered in November 1967 that 3.5 to 4 million Americans were being dosed with Parke-Davis Chloromycetin each year. If the drug had been prescribed only for conditions for which it was truly indicated, it was estimated that only 10,000 persons at most would have received it (US Senate, 1968; Part 6: 2566). [...]

20

Toxic capitalism: corporate crime and the chemical industry
Frank Pearce and Steve Tombs

[...] In Bhopal, India, a chemical plant, operated by Union Carbide of India Limited (UCIL), a subsidiary of Union Carbide Corporation (UCC), used the highly toxic chemicals, carbon monoxide, chlorine, phosgene ('Mustard Gas'), monomethylamine and methyl iso-cyanate (MIC) to produce carbamate pesticides. On the night of Sunday, December 2, 1984 water entered an MIC storage tank setting in process an exothermic reaction. Soon a cocktail of poisonous gases, vapours and liquids — including up to forty tons of MIC and unknown quantities of hydrogen cyanide, nitrous oxide, and carbon monoxide — was spewed into the atmosphere. Between 200,0000 and 450,000 local people were exposed to the toxic fumes, some 60,000 were seriously affected, more than 20,000 were permanently injured, and at least 1700 and as many as 10,000 people may have died as an immediate result of the tragedy.

UCC immediately responded to the disaster with a series of defensive claims: that the disaster was totally unprecedented and unanticipated so it was not surprising that an 'evacuation or safety plan had never been developed'; that they had not located the MIC plant at Bhopal 'for reasons of economy or to avoid safety standards'; that they had the same safety standards in their American and overseas operations — 'in India or Brazil or someplace else ... same equipment, same design, same everything' (Everest 1986: 47–8). In short, UCC claimed that although the Bhopal plant was managed exclusively by Indian nationals, its safety standards were identical to the standards at Institute, West Virginia.

Subsequently, UCC has taken every opportunity to deny its own responsibility for the gas leak by claiming that: it had an excellent safety record, and the design of the plant's Standard Operating Procedures (SOPs) — UCC's responsibility — was basically sound; the production of MIC in India, the siting of the plant and the quality of the materials used, were all the responsibility of UCIL and the Indian State; UCIL was an independent company responsible for its own affairs; India's cultural backwardness was responsible for the poor maintenance and management, poor planning procedures and the inadequate enforcement of safety regulations; the accident was due to sabotage. [...]

Let us first address the last contention — for the 'sabotage theory' plays a key role in UCC's 'definitive version' of the sequence of events that led to the leak at the plant. According to this 'theory', on the night of the accident a disgruntled employee, who was not on duty, removed a pressure gauge and then used a hose to put water into an MIC tank; his intention was to spoil a batch of chemicals rather than create a disaster. This version of events, circulated to the media and to UCC personnel, was most fully articulated when it formed the basis of a paper presented by 'independent consultant' Dr. Ashok Kalelkar at a London conference in May 1988 (Kalelkar 1988). Kalelkar had in fact been a member of the team organized by UCC in March 1985 which even then had mooted the possibility of sabotage, although a lack of evidence meant, it claimed, that 'it was unable to develop this theory further at the time' (ibid.; Pearce and Tombs 1993).

Yet, this 'definitive version' was only the last in a series of such 'theories' involving alleged saboteurs. First, it had been claimed that the disaster itself was the result of the actions of careless or malicious employees who had placed a water line where a nitrogen line should have been used. The *New York Times* on 26 March 1985 pointed out that neither an accidental nor a deliberate incorrect coupling were possible since the relevant nitrogen and water lines were of a different colour and the nozzles were of different sizes. That same day Union Carbide Chairman, Warren Anderson, had to withdraw the accusation at Congressional Hearings when he admitted that he had no evidence of sabotage. Then, between 31 July 1985 and 3 January 1986, UCC claimed that a group of Sikh extremists called the Black June Movement were responsible. But no such group was ever identified in any context other than allegedly putting up posters about Union Carbide; moreover, it was virtually impossible for anybody to actually plan a disaster of this kind. Not surprisingly, this claim was also quietly abandoned. In August 1986 a specific but unnamed employee was blamed — but it was not until May 1988 that all references to nitrogen lines were dropped and a pressure meter was mentioned.

The legal reasoning behind UCC's strategy of using the sabotage argument is clear:

> Union Carbide and UCIL are hoping, first, to avoid vicarious liability on the ground that the employee would have been acting without authority and outside the course of his employment, and, secondly, to avoid liability under Rylands v. Fletcher, on the ground that an employee who comes onto his employers' premises without authority and causes the escape of a dangerous thing is a 'stranger' for whose acts the occupier is not responsible.
>
> (Muchlinski 1987: 575)

What should be immediately clear is that even if we were to accept that the accident *was* caused by sabotage, then this only serves to demonstrate how unsafe the actual plant was. That is, any sabotage theory itself only serves to underline UCC's responsibility for the accident. Acceptance of such a theory raises two key questions about plant organisation. First, why was it possible to remove a pressure dial by hand when this was connected to such a toxic and volatile chemical? And, second, why was there water in the area? As a leading specialist on safety in chemical plants has written, if water is not there, 'it cannot leak in, no matter how many valves leak or how many errors are made' (Kletz 1988: 86).

Whether or not sabotage occurred, a more fundamental issue is the ease with which a disaster of almost unprecedented scale could occur. The focus on sabotage only serves to detract attention from UCC's well documented responsibility for many key factors — for example, the poor design of the Bhopal plant, its inappropriate siting, its inadequate safety systems, the lack of a proper emergency plan, and its generally run-down condition. In other words, the plant itself — the way in which it had been designed and managed — was one in which accidents and crimes were likely to be produced, and, if realised, likely to have catastrophic potential. As a crime, the Bhopal disaster was produced by a corporate structure and a corporate *modus operandi*. Let us explore these contentions in more detail. [...]

Let us focus, in more detail, on the circumstances of the accident. At Bhopal enormous amounts of MIC were stored in three 15,000 gallon tanks. The temperatures and pressures of these were routinely too high — they should have been kept at 0–5 degrees Celsius but were in fact between 15 and 20 degrees Celsius. Furthermore, these temperatures and pressures were not rigorously logged. Because plant instrumentation was inadequate to monitor normal plant processes, leaks were detected by smell (only possible at levels 20 times higher than its Threshold Limit Value), although this was certainly not the case at the Institute, West Virginia plant which, in this and many other respects, had superior technology. On the night of 2 December, workers reported smelling MIC but could not locate its source, and so informed a supervisor of the leak, who postponed investigating its source until after a tea break. Before that was over, a tank, tank 610, was rumbling, concrete cracking, and the tank's temperature was about 200 Celsius, the pressure at over 180 psi, 140 psi in excess of the tank's rupture disk limit. Gases, vapours and liquids burst past the rupture disk, shot through the relief valve vent header, then the vent gas scrubber, and into the atmosphere. The vent gas scrubber was on standby, and although it was eventually turned on, it probably never worked. The flare tower was inoperative, and an attempt to douse the gas with water was unsuccessful because the hoses had insufficient water pressure to reach the stack from which the gas was escaping. The operators could not dilute the MIC in tank 610 since it was already overly full and the emergency dump tank had a defective gauge which indicated that it was also 22 per cent full. Although the tanks should have been refrigerated, the refrigeration unit had been turned off — to save $50 per week. There is no doubt that badly maintained equipment, lack of spare parts, inadequate SOPs and untrained staff all contributed to the accident. But equally important were *ad hoc* modifications to the plant designs, such as a jumper line that may well have been the means by which water entered the MIC tank.

There are also serious questions that need to be addressed regarding the plant design itself. Plant instrumentation was inadequate to monitor normal plant processes. Furthermore, whilst large amounts of MIC were also stored at Institute, it had larger dump tanks and an additional dedicated sump system with a capacity of 42,000 gallons. It is possible that the Bhopal storage tanks had originally been used at Institute, since they were of a type unsuitable for Indian climatic conditions. The refrigeration plant at Bhopal, *even when working*, was not powerful enough to cool all of the MIC stored there, and the vent gas scrubber and flare tower were only designed to deal with single phase (that is, gas not liquid, or gas *and* liquid) emissions. At Institute, moreover, there was an additional and more powerful emergency back-up system. *Bhopal was demonstrably inadequate and inferior to Institute.* Nevertheless, even with this inferior technology, far fewer people would have died if: the plant had not been sited near shanty towns; there had been adequate risk assessment, modelling and monitoring of discharges and emergency planning and management; the plant personnel, local medical services and the state and national government had known more about the nature and effects of the deadly gaseous emissions.

Thus it appears, *contra* the claims of Anderson and others, that the Bhopal plant was an inferior plant to the UCC plant at Institute, West Virginia. But this should not be taken as an indication that the Bhopal plant was a maverick operation of an essentially law-abiding and socially responsible corporation, nor that the Institute plant was safe. In fact, in March 1985 an acetone/mesityl oxide mixture had been accidentally released from Institute; and in August of the same year, there was a leak of aldicarb oxime, a chemical of definite but unquantified toxicity. Evidence emerged that alarm systems were either shut off or not working, staff were inadequately trained, the SOPs were imprecise and management slipshod (Jones 1988: 163–186). Subsequently, OSHA sent several teams of inspectors to conduct a 'wall-to-wall' inspection. This led to 221 charges of violations, 130 of which were 'wilful', and proposed fines totalling $1.4 million — though OSHA and UCC eventually reached a settlement of just over $4400 for five serious violations on the agreement that the others would be corrected. It is important to note that on the basis of an apparently good safety record — determined using data which UCC had itself collected and provided — UCC's Institute plant had been exempted from OSHA inspections. Of particular interest is the fact that US Labour Secretary Brock revealed that had UCC actually kept *accurate* records (that is, rather than those on the basis of which they were exempt from inspection), then their accident record would have been 'substantially higher' than the US chemical industry average (Jones 1988: 163–186; Pearce 1990). One hundred and twenty-nine of the charges originally laid by OSHA were for failings to meet legal requirements to record accidents or ill-health (Jones 1988: 176). In February 1990, there were two more leaks at the plant, one injuring seven workers, the other resulting in 15,000 people confined to their homes. In March, the Seadrift, Texas plant exploded killing one worker and injuring thirty-two others in addition to injuring another six people outside of the plant. Carbide was originally fined $2.8 million by OSHA for 115 violations, 112 of which were described as wilful (the fine was contested by Carbide).

More generally, UCC has long been a prime example of 'toxic capital' — from the Gauley Bridge disaster in West Virginia where 476 deaths from silicosis were recorded, through its role in the development and use of the carcinogen, vinyl chloride, through its nuclear weapons manufacturing plant in Oak Ridge, Tennessee, its dangerous graphite electrodes production facilities in Yabucoa, Puerto Rico

(Agarwal et al. 1985: 14–23) and its plant in Alloy, West Virginia which alone puts 'out more pollution annually than the total emitted in New York City in a year' (*New York Times*, 10 September 1989). Clearly, Union Carbide's slogan of 'Safety at any Cost' portrays a corporate image that is not borne out by reality. [...]

[...] UCC had a significant degree of 'control' over UCIL. UCIL's production and marketing strategies were dictated by the corporate strategies of UCC (Morehouse and Subramaniam 1986: 17). Moreover, the continued existence of the Bhopal plant was UCC's decision: it had commissioned a preliminary study of the cost of dismantling the MIC unit and other pesticide production facilities at Bhopal (Dinham et al. 1986: 27). Despite such a threat to its existence, UCIL was not in a position to 'go to a competitor of Union Carbide and buy a pesticide plant' ready-made; and it would be prohibitively expensive to develop a 'pesticides plant from scratch' (Muchlinski 1987: 582).

UCC, to a large extent, 'possessed' the Bhopal plant. It had always dictated how and which chemicals were produced and stored. In the 1970s, it had 'insisted that large amounts of MIC be stored in Bhopal over UCIL's objections ... (T)he UCIL position [was] that only token storage [of the chemical at Bhopal] was necessary' (Everest 1986 : 31). It monitored safety procedures and UCIL was forced to rely upon UCC for technological assistance and updates (ibid. 167–171). Indeed, at Bhopal, UCC received significant revenues from its licensing, managerial, monitoring and marketing activities, a not atypical arrangement when TNCs engage in joint ventures in less developed countries (Kolko 1988: 165). UCC had the right to intervene in day-to-day matters if safety was affected. A UCC safety team had monitored the plant in May 1982, and found 61 hazards, 30 of them considered major, of which 11 were in the phosgene/MIC unit, and areas of concern were 'procedures training and enforcement together with attention to the equipment and mechanical deficiencies' (Everest 1986: 56). Nevertheless, production was allowed and expected to continue.

Detailed reports on safety and related matters were sent to UCC every three to six months (ibid.: 171). This included decisions on plant expenditure — on investment and cutbacks, on staffing levels, on refrigeration and so on. All of these had certainly been cut back: for example, there were fewer operatives, and amongst these, fewer first class BSc graduates; theoretical and practical training had been reduced or abolished; maintenance procedures were dangerously abbreviated (Sandberg 1985: 17).

In short, then, even though it is clear that the actual social relations in the individual enterprises were 'lived' and fulfilled by specific Indian managerial personnel (and individual workers), UCC 'possessed' the enterprise. [...]

[...] UCIL's production of the pesticides Temik and Sevin took place under commodified conditions — i.e., they were supposed to be produced and sold in such a way that subdivisions of the company showed a normal profitable return on investment. It is questionable whether it was possible for UCIL to safely make and sell these pesticides at a profit. If not, either the company could have engaged in safe but 'uneconomic' production, or it could have produced less safely and more 'economically'. It is clear that UCC's SOPs were both inadequate and (to some extent) ignored, this with the collaboration of certain of UCC's personnel. Which of these organizational models is appropriate, and how much control was — or could be — exercised by UCC must ultimately remain a moot point. *What is clear, however, is that the top management of UCC had represented itself to its shareholders as effectively controlling the different subsections of its organisation and had received the rewards and privileges commensurate with such control, and were thus responsible for, if not in fact totally in control of, the organization's actions.* [...]

[...] It should also be noted that following two decades of huge growth — encouraged by government 'subsidies, tax breaks, low-cost loans and lax safety regulations' (Shrivastava 1993: 260) — the pesticides market in India had become extremely competitive by the end of the 1970s. Indeed, by the beginning of the 1980s, 'pesticide demand in India had collapsed' (ibid.: 258). This was partly structural, due to the influx of agrochemical capital. But other, contingent factors, exacerbated these new conditions of intense competition: agricultural production in India declined severely in 1980, and only recovered mildly in the next three years; and weather conditions in 1982 and 1983 caused many farmers to abandon temporarily their use of pesticides. Thus, the industry became characterised by harsher and increasing levels of competition (Shrivastava 1992: 30–5). These factors partially explain why Union Carbide had decided to 'backward integrate' and begin (in 1979) the domestic manufacture of MIC and other pesticide components at the Bhopal plant (Shriastava 1992: 33–4). The general context of multinational-host government relations, and the particular context of the local pesticides market, are crucial contextual factors in understanding the disaster. [...]

[...] As we (and others) have shown, a major cause of the Bhopal disaster was a severe cutback in investment which resulted in an inappropriate use of technology, non-replacement of defective parts, and inadequate maintenance and monitoring of the production process. Whilst there was an overall decline in the pesticide market, there were also fluctuations in demand. The subsequent problem of supplying the market during production bottlenecks contributed to the dangerous practice of storing large quantities of MIC. Moreover, whilst such factors associated with particular 'scrimping and saving' during the plant's operation are likely to contribute to chemical disasters, so does the general need for 'economy' and the pressure of time during the design, manufacture and erection of plants.

It is, thus, not surprising to find that at Bhopal on 14 May 1983 the following 'agreement' was signed by UCIL (Agricultural Products Division) and the hourly-paid plant operatives:

> The selection, placement, distribution, transfer, promotion of personnel, fixing of working hours and laying down of working programmes, planning and control of factory operations, introduction of new or improved production methods, expansion of production facilities, establishment of quality standards, determination and assignment of workload, evaluation and classification of jobs and establishment of standards, maintenance of efficiency, maintenance of discipline in the factory ... are *exclusively* rights and responsibilities of the Management.

(cited in Union Research Group 1985a: 1–2) [...]

SECTION 4:

Law and the corporation

Structures of irresponsibility

In the previous two sections we saw how in capitalist societies, corporations are routinely involved in killing, maiming, stealing from and defrauding their workers, customers and the wider public. And we saw how very often those crimes of the powerful are produced as a result of the close relationship between the state and the economy. This section develops an understanding of the role the law plays in reproducing this criminogenic relationship.

The creation of a particular form of political/economic citizenship with its origins in the 'North-Atlantic seaboard community' (the European nations and the settlers in North America) is, for Thorstein Veblen, the key to understanding how powerful actors in capitalist societies are able to escape legal scrutiny and accountability. He locates the structure of legal inequality in the emergence of the doctrine of individual right and liberty, and the form that it took as 'freedom of contract' between two, formally free, individuals. He argued that whereas in pre-industrial societies the idea of freedom of contract guarded against pecuniary (economic) or other forms of coercion between individuals, this same notion of freedom of contract has the effect of reinforcing coercion in industrial societies. A contract between two parties in industrial societies cannot guarantee freedom since it does not take account of 'the pecuniary pressure of price or subsistence' that arises from 'concatenation of industrial processes' (excerpt: 276). In other words, he argues that the freedom to make a legally binding contract, originally created in law to apply to relatively straightforward relationships between individuals – making payments for goods or services – becomes distorted by the complex of interdependent relationships and the growth of new organisational forms that emerged out of the process of industrialisation. The processes that Veblen is alluding to were developing at a fearsome pace at the turn of the nineteenth century, a period that witnessed the rise of the modern corporation as a key unit of economic organisation and power. Those new forms of industrial organisation enhanced the ability of the economically powerful to set the price of goods, to hire and fire workers, to organise factory production and so on. And in an economy of growing complexity, those relationships could combine to produce ravaging effects for the most vulnerable. Contractual relations between employers and employed, landlord and tenant, for example, appear to be guided by principles of 'liberty' and individual 'right', but in reality are mediated by a complexity of economic and social conditions. In the new industrial system, for example, changes in the price of goods, housing or other basics could coerce workers into accepting degrading or dangerous work. Risk to life and livelihood is the price that is often exacted from workers and consumers. The socially oppressive effects of the complexity of social and economic relations in industrial societies that Veblen described are well illustrated by Barbara Ehrenreich's book *Nickled and Dimed* (2001). Her investigation into the working poor of America showed clearly how workers who appear free to leave the worst-paid and most exhausting work are unable to do so – even in states where work is plentiful – because the loss of even a week's wages risks their eviction or leaves them without money to buy food. Thus, the 'freedom' inscribed in law in industrial societies reinforces the 'discrepancy between law and fact' (Veblen excerpt: 278).

Veblen's conclusion is that the 'assault and battery' arising in the structures of industrial societies – and here he is referring to deaths and injuries at work caused by employers – do not count as crime, since they arise from a relationship governed by 'free contract' and are therefore 'not repugnant to the principles of natural liberty' (excerpt: 277). And that this is why employers and their organisations rarely find themselves in the courtroom, or if they do, are rarely punished. The fundamental purpose of the law then is not to protect us from harm, but to enact a highly circumscribed set of 'freedoms' that both mask and reinforce gross inequalities, and reproduce human relationships based upon the domination of one social class over the other.

Following Veblen's analysis, and in order to further our understanding of the social relationships that law imposes in industrial societies, it is necessary to understand how law allows powerful institutions to function in particular ways. For Joel Bakan this means developing an understanding of the legal structure of corporations, and in particular how legal impunity was realised through the device of *limited liability*. The extract from Bakan's *The Corporation* therefore allows us to understand the centrality of the corporation to the process of social ordering set out by Veblen. It also allows us to see more clearly how the corruption of the Victorian economy described by Ross in the previous section was given force by the *legal* order of things. For what Bakan is describing is how the concept of limited liability allowed a space to be opened up between the 'owners' of or investors in the corporation and the social costs of its harmful activities. Since the former are only responsible for the nominal value of capital that they invested in the first place (Parkinson, 1993), they are exempt from the full economic and social costs produced by the corporations they invest in. By avoiding those costs, the principle of limited liability ensures that they are absorbed not by owners but by other, more vulnerable, sections of the population. In the Enron case, huge losses were incurred by pension fund holders and creditors which led to a major loss of social protection for some and of jobs for others. Those costs were born by the victims rather than the owners of Enron (Blackburn, 2002) – and the same point can be made about the major UK financial frauds of the 1990s (Fooks,

2003a, 2003b). The rule is simple: in law, the financial benefits that accrue to the owners of corporations are unlimited, whilst at the same time their losses are limited.

In order to protect investors, the law creates a shell of limited liability by conjuring up a separate 'personality' for the corporation. The law creates this fictional personality to give the corporation a status as a single entity, disconnected from its human elements (owners, manager, workers and so on). The law therefore takes the real elements of the corporation (the human and other material resources that it is comprised of, the differential power held by different groups within the corporation and so on) and creates a fictional entity so that when the law intervenes to control or regulate its target is the abstract fiction of the corporation, it normally intervenes against the fictional entity of the coporation, rather than the people that comprise the corporation.

This is not to say that the corporation, as a legal entity, can be dismissed as merely a 'fiction'. Corporations do 'act out' the part given to them by law. It is therefore possible to observe, as Frank Pearce does, that corporations do share some of the attributes of human beings. Just as individuals can engage in actions that result in the realisation of a particular goal, so can corporations. However, they lack the emotional capacities and non-teleological attributes of individuals (autonomy of their actions, responsibility, human ethics and so on). As we saw in the introduction to the previous section, as the dominant institutional form taken by capital, corporations *can* be said to possess particular sets of ethical values, particular responsibilities to client groups and publics. And as we saw, those values are the antithesis of human values. For Pearce, as for Veblen, Bakan, and Wells, corporate value systems are always linked to the realisation of the goals of the corporation (the maximisation of profits, growth and survival), and it is those separate value systems that encourage corporations and their managers to operate in a 'criminogenic arena' (Punch, 1996).

The corporate value system is shaped by the formal organisation of the corporation (its autocratic and strictly hierarchical command structure, its tightly constructed goals, the fiduciary duties of directors to maximise profits for a distant constituency of shareholders, and the rules of incorporation that grant it limited liability) combine to produce "structures of irresponsibility". The same features of the formal organisation of the corporation make it virtually impossible to attribute the normal rules of criminal liability to individuals within the corporation or to the corporation itself. The corporate structure enables managers to remain distant from the real conditions of production, to blur lines of accountability for decisions, and ultimately to eradicate the incentives necessary to remain law-abiding. Given this combination of incentives, legal impunity, and fractured division of function, it is indeed difficult to see how corporations could ever act responsibly.

The extract from Celia Wells's *Corporations and Criminal Responsibility* develops our understanding of how the law developed a distinctive set of logics to deal with the corporation. It also brings a more nuanced understanding of the impunity employers enjoy in the courts described by Veblen at the beginning of this section. Wells points to how contractual obligations, as they developed in law, gave rise to new forms of *corporation* liability; or, to be more precise, how the law of contract prevented the legal fiction of the corporation becoming abstract to the point that it could be absolved of liability entirely. Wells notes how following the industrial revolution, corporations were frequently the cause of damage and injury to property and to the person, and that precisely because of the complexity of those structures, it was more advantageous for both the harmed individual and for the senior managers and directors of those corporations 'to treat the corporation as the actor'. This enabled the harmed individual to get over the problem of identifying one person in the company responsible for the harm (even if they managed to do so, they might not gain much compensation by suing another individual). For the senior manager and director, the advantages were perhaps more obvious.

The particular forms of liability Wells identifies here (on 'strict' and 'vicarious' liability, see also Gobert and Punch, 2003; on the former, see also Section 7) allowed the *corporation* to be prosecuted or sued. The consequence of this was that corporate liability shielded masters, directors or senior managers from liability because the corporation would take the rap. And, as Wells notes at the end of this extract, this created further procedural problems of accountability since corporations were not amenable to the usual form of punishment available to the courts. When corporations are punished the sentence is usually in the form of a fine – a punishment from which their owners are also shielded because the fine is rarely large enough to affect the value of large corporations, and because the fine can normally be offset against operating costs, rather than being levied against assets or equity (Coffee, 1981). The fictional personality of the corporation has therefore created a corporate veil that protects the owners of the corporation from *criminal* as well as *civil* liability. Managers are very rarely prosecuted for corporate crimes. In the UK, the conviction of directors occurs in less than 2% of all prosecutions for health and safety crimes, and this tends to be applied in only the smallest of corporations where the lines of accountability are clearest (Tombs and Whyte, 2007).

Harry Glasbeek analyses how the concept of *mens rea* creates problems for conceptualising corporate crime. In criminal cases, the Latin phrase *mens rea* is used to describe one of the most basic elements of a crime that must be present for liability to be established. The literal translation of *mens rea* is 'knowing mind'. The term is used in a legal sense to mean that intent or knowledge on the part of the offender is required before a crime can be said to have occurred. The enduring importance of *mens rea* originates in the development of a body of criminal law that was designed to deal with the crimes committed by relatively powerless individuals, rather than institutions or organisations. Whereas individuals can be shown clearly to have knowing mind, it is a little more tricky to demonstrate the knowing mind of a corporation or other organisation. The criminalisation of corporate offences highlights a further problem caused by the enduring presence of *mens rea* in criminal law. Rather than resulting from a positive intention to harm a worker, safety crimes or crimes against the environment may often be the result of management failure to do something they should have done to protect workers and the public. They are more likely to result from indifference, and the failure or refusal to comply with the law or provide adequate protection from harm. Now, this does not make employers any less culpable when it comes to corporate crimes, but it does mean that *mens rea* is often not applicable in such cases.

Nonetheless, a form of corporate *mens rea* began to develop in the twentieth century after it became obvious that industrial societies had a problem on their hands. For the process of industrialisation had created a monster with the capacity to produce a great deal of harm. At the same time, this monster remained almost wholly unaccountable for its crimes. As we saw earlier in the extract by Wells, criminal liability was initially created in the forms of strict and vicarious liability to fit corporate crimes. It took many more years to do so, but in a series of decisions that spanned the twentieth century (see Slapper and Tombs, 1999: 28–30) the courts also devised a particular form of *mens rea* to apply to the corporation. The formula for corporate *mens rea* was developed perhaps most significantly by Lord Denning's formulation in English case law:

> A company may in many ways be likened to a human body. It has a brain and nerve centre which controls what it does. It also has hands which hold the tools and act in accordance with directions from the centre. Some of the people in the company are mere servants and agents who are nothing more than hands to do the work ... . Others are directors and managers who represent the directing mind and will of the company and control what it does. The state of mind of these managers is the state of mind of the company and it is treated by the law as such.[1]

Yet few cases have been able to apply this formulation of corporate criminal liability in any meaningful way. The difficulties faced by the courts in applying corporate manslaughter cases brought against large companies in England and Wales (Slapper, 1999) and in Scotland (Whyte, 2006) in the 1990s and 2000s, revealed the difficulties of applying this formulation (for a discussion of the concept as it applies in the US see Schlegel, 1990). Corporate *mens rea* has not closed the gap in criminalisation, and because it has never been applied except in a handful of token cases, it has done little else other than preserve corporations as structures of irresponsibility. As Glasbeek makes clear, this is because the structure of the corporation has remained pretty much unaltered by a series of juridical attempts to develop corporate criminal liability. In other words, whilst the courts reserve the power to develop legal concepts to apply to corporations, those concepts do not interfere with the basic structure of corporate personality and the corporate veil from which corporations' socio-economic power is derived (Spencer, 2004).

The legal regulation of corporations, then, as this section notes, is guided by the general social ordering impetus of the legal system, that configures the 'ebb and flow', as Wells puts it, of complex and often perplexing contingencies. The law does not simply 'create' the corporation and then leave it to its own devices. As we have seen throughout this text, law plays an important role in supporting the legitimacy of the social order by creating and adapting the boundaries of corporate power. As in Section 1, where we noted that state crime and state violence cause problems for the legitimacy of states, so the corporation causes legitimacy problems for capitalist social orders. What this means is that the law also has an important role to play in preventing some of the harms produced by corporations.

However, this section has described a structure of law that both encourages corporate criminality and provides a basis for corporate immunity. The process by which corporate criminality/immunity is created can be summarised as follows: the law abstracts the real conditions of coercion and violence that allow corporations to thrive (Veblen); the corporation itself is granted in law a personality that provides impunity to owners (Bakan); the law at the same time creates a split corporate personality which encourages it to act as a 'structure of irresponsibility' (Pearce); the personality is then used to create a new legal subject that can be prosecuted and regulated in a way that does not disrupt the basic order of things (Wells and Glasbeek).

This strange and artificial notion of personality, then, is a useful concept for understanding the contradictory relationship between the law and the corporation. If, as this section has demonstrated, an understanding of corporations as 'structures of irresponsibility' is crucial for understanding the formative conditions in which corporate crime is produced and reproduced, the following section of this book explores a range of key perspectives that develop explanations of the causation of state crime and corporate crime.

Note

1. *H.L. Bolton (Engineering) Co. Ltd* v *T.J. Graham & Sons* [1957] I QB 159, at 172.

References

Blackburn, R. (2002) 'The Enron Debacle and the Pension Crisis', *New Left Review*, no. 14, March/April.
Coffee, J. (1981) 'No Soul to Damn, no Body to Kick', *Michigan Law Review*, 79(3).
Ehrenreich, B. (2001) *Nickled and Dimed: On (not) getting by in America.* London: Metropolitan Books.
Fooks, G. (2003a) 'In the Valley of the Blind the One Eyed Man is King: Corporate crime and the myopia of financial regulation' in S. Tombs and D. Whyte (eds) *Unmasking the Crimes of the Powerful: Scrutinising states and corporations.* New York: Peter Lang.
Fooks, G. (2003b) 'Contrasts in Tolerance: The curious politics of financial regulation', *Journal of Contemporary Politics*, 9(3).
Gobert, J. and Punch, M. (2003) *Rethinking Corporate Crime.* London: Butterworths.
Parkinson, J. (1993) *Corporate Power and Responsibility.* Oxford: Oxford University Press.
Punch, M. (1996) *Dirty Business: Exploring corporate misconduct.* London: Sage.
Schlegel, K. (1990) *Just Deserts for Corporate Criminals.* Boston: Northeastern University Press.
Spencer, R. (2004) *Corporate Law and Structures: Exposing the roots of the problem.* Oxford: Corporate Watch.

Slapper, G. (1999) *Blood in the Bank: Social and legal aspects of death at work*. Aldershot: Ashgate.

Slapper, D. and Tombs, S. (1999) *Corporate Crime*. Harlow: Longman.

Tombs, S. and Whyte, D. (2007) *Safety Crimes*. Cullompton: Willan.

Whyte, D. (2006) 'Corporate Homicide', *SCOLAG Legal Journal*, no. 347, September.

21

The corporation: the pathological pursuit of profit and power
Joel Bakan

[...] Long before Enron's scandalous collapse, the corporation, a fledgling institution, was engulfed in corruption and fraud. Throughout the late seventeenth and early eighteenth centuries, stockbrokers, known as "jobbers," prowled the infamous coffee shops of London's Exchange Alley, a maze of lanes between Lombard Street, Cornhill, and Birchin Lane, in search of credulous investors to whom they could sell shares in bogus companies. Such companies flourished briefly, nourished by speculation, and then quickly collapsed. Ninety-three of them traded between 1690 and 1695. By 1698, only twenty were left. In 1696 the commissioners of trade for England reported that the corporate form had been "wholly perverted" by the sale of company stock "to ignorant men, drawn in by the reputation, falsely raised and artfully spread, concerning the thriving state of [the] stock."[1] Though the commissioners were appalled, they likely were not surprised.

Businessmen and politicians had been suspicious of the corporation from the time it first emerged in the late sixteenth century. Unlike the prevailing partnership form, in which relatively small groups of men, bonded together by personal loyalties and mutual trust, pooled their resources to set up businesses they ran as well as owned, the corporation separated ownership from management—one group of people, directors and managers, ran the firm, while another group, shareholders, owned it. That unique design was believed by many to be a recipe for corruption and scandal. Adam Smith warned in *The Wealth of Nations* that because managers could not be trusted to steward "other people's money," "negligence and profusion" would inevitably result when businesses organized as corporations. Indeed, by the time he wrote those words in 1776, the corporation had been banned in England for more than fifty years. In 1720, the English Parliament, fed up with the epidemic of corporate high jinks plaguing Exchange Alley, had outlawed the corporation (though with some exceptions). It was the notorious collapse of the South Sea Company that had prompted it to act.

Formed in 1710 to carry on exclusive trade, including trade in slaves, with the Spanish colonies of South America, the South Sea Company was a scam from the very start. Its directors, some of the leading lights of political society, knew little about South America, had only the scantiest connection to the continent (apparently, one of them had a cousin who lived in Buenos Aires), and must have known that the King of Spain would refuse to grant them the necessary rights to trade in his South American colonies. As one director conceded, "unless the Spaniards are to be divested of common sense ... abandoning their own commerce, throwing away the only valuable stake they have left in the world, and, in short, bent on their own ruin," they would never part with the exclusive power to trade in their own colonies. Yet the directors of the South Sea Company promised potential investors "fabulous profits" and mountains of gold and silver in exchange for common British exports, such as Cheshire cheese, sealing wax, and pickles.[2]

Investors flocked to buy the company's stock, which rose dramatically, by sixfold in one year, and then quickly plummeted as shareholders, realizing that the company was worthless, panicked and sold. In 1720—the year a major plague hit Europe, public anxiety about which "was heightened," according to one historian, "by a superstitious fear that it had been sent as a judgment on human material ism"[3]—the South Sea Company collapsed. Fortunes were lost, lives were ruined, one of the company's directors, John Blunt, was shot by an angry shareholder, mobs crowded Westminster, and the king hastened back to London from his country retreat to deal with the crisis.[4] The directors of the South Sea Company were called before Parliament, where they were fined, and some of them jailed, for "notorious fraud and breach of trust."[5] Though one parliamentarian demanded they be sewn up in sacks, along with snakes and monies, and then drowned, they were, for the most part, spared harsh punishment.[6] As for the corporation itself, in 1720 Parliament passed the Bubble Act, which made it a criminal offense to create a company "presuming to be a corporate body," and to issue "transferable stocks without legal authority."

Today, in the wake of corporate scandals similar to and every bit as nefarious as the South Sea bubble, it is unthinkable that a government would ban the corporate form. Even modest reforms—such as, for example, a law requiring companies to list employee stock options as expenses in their financial reports, which might avoid the kind of misleadingly rosy financial statements that have fueled recent scandals[7]—seem unlikely from a U.S. federal government that has failed to match its strong words at the time of the scandals with equally strong actions. Though the Sarbanes-Oxley Act, signed into law in 2002 to redress some of the more blatant problems of corporate governance and accounting, provides welcome remedies, at least on paper,[8] the federal government's general response to corporate scandals has been sluggish and timid at best. What is revealed by comparing that response to the English Parliament's swift and draconian measures of 1720 is the fact that, over the last three hundred years, corporations have amassed such great power as to weaken government's ability to control them. A fledgling institution that could be banned with the stroke of a legislative pen in 1720, the corporation now dominates society and government.

How did it become so powerful?

The genius of the corporation as a business form, and the reason for its remarkable rise over the last three centuries, was—and is—its capacity to combine the capital, and thus the economic power, of unlimited numbers of people. Joint-stock companies emerged in the sixteenth century, by which time it was clear that partnerships, limited to drawing capital from the relatively few people who could practicably run a business together, were inadequate for financing the new, though still rare, large-scale enterprises of nascent industrialization. In 1564 the Company of the Mines Royal was created as a joint-stock company, financed by twenty-four shares sold for £1,200 each; in 1565, the Company of Mineral and Battery Works raised its capital by making calls on thirty-six shares it had previously issued. The New River Company was formed as a joint-stock company in 1606 to transport fresh water to London, as were number of other utilities.[9] Fifteen joint-stock companies were operating in England in 1688, though none with more than a few hundred members. Corporations began to proliferate during the final decade of the seventeenth century, and the total amount of investment joint-stock companies doubled as the business form became a popular vehicle for financing colonial enterprises. The partnership still remained the dominant form for organizing businesses, however, though the corporation would steadily gain on it and then overtake it.

In 1712, Thomas Newcomen invented a steam-driven machine to pump water out of a coal mine and unwittingly started the industrial revolution. Over the next century, steam power fueled the development of large-scale industry in England and the United States, expanding the scope of operations in mines, textiles (and the associated trades of bleaching, calico printing, dyeing, and calendaring), mills, breweries, and distilleries.[10] Corporations multiplied as these new larger-scale undertakings demanded significantly more capital investment than partnerships could raise. In postrevolutionary America, between 1781 and 1790, the number of corporations grew tenfold, from 33 to 328.[11] [...]

[...] America's nineteenth-century railroad barons, men lionized by some and vilified by others, were the true creators of the modern corporate era. Because railways were mammoth undertakings requiring huge amounts of capital investment—to lay track, manufacture rolling stock, and operate and maintain systems—the industry quickly came to rely on the corporate form for financing its operations. In the United States, railway construction boomed during the 1850s and then exploded again after the Civil War, with more than one hundred thousand miles of track laid between 1865 and 1885. As the industry grew, so did the number of corporations.[12] The same was true in England, where, between 1825 and 1849, the amount of capital raised by railways, mainly through joint-stock companies, increased from £200,000 to £230 million, more than one thousand-fold.[13]

"One of the most important by-products of the introduction and extension of the railway system," observed M.C. Reed in *Railways and the Growth of the Capital Market,* was the part it played in "assisting the development of a national market for company securities."[14] Railways, in both the United States and England, demanded more capital investment than could be provided by the relatively small coterie of wealthy men who invested in corporations at the start of the nineteenth century. By the middle of the century, with railway stocks flooding markets in both countries, middle-class people began, for the first time, to invest in corporate shares. As *The Economist* pronounced at the time, "everyone was in the stocks now ... needy clerks, poor tradesman's apprentices, discarded service men and bankrupts—all have entered the ranks of the great monied interest.[15]

One barrier remained to broader public participation in stock markets, however: no matter how much, or how little, a person had invested in a company, he or she was *personally* liable, without limit, for the company's debts. Investors' homes, savings, and other personal assets would be exposed to claims by creditors if a company failed, meaning that a person risked financial ruin simply by owning shares in a company. Stockholding could not become a truly attractive option for the general public until that risk was removed, which it soon was. By the middle of the nineteenth century, business leaders and politicians broadly advocated changing the law to limit the liability of shareholders to the amounts they had invested in a company. If a person bought $100 worth of shares, they reasoned, he or she should be immune to liability for anything beyond that, regardless of what happened to the company. [...]

[...] People worried that limited liability would, as one parliamentarian speaking against its introduction in England said, attack "The first and most natural principle of commercial legislation ... that every man was bound to pay the debts he had contracted, so long as he was able to do so" and that it would "enable persons to embark in trade with a limited chance of loss, but with an unlimited chance of gain" and thus encourage "a system of vicious and improvident speculation."[16]

Despite such objections, limited liability was entrenched in corporate law, in England in 1856 and in the United States over the latter half of the nineteenth century (though at different times in different states). With the risks of investment in stocks now removed, at least in terms of how much money investors might be forced to lose, the way was cleared for broad popular participation in stock markets and for investors to diversify their holdings. Still, publicly traded corporations were relatively rare in the United States up until the end of the nineteenth century. Beyond the railway industry, leading companies tended to be family-owned, and if shares existed at all they were traded on a direct person-to-person basis, not in stock markets. By the early years of the twentieth century, however, large publicly traded corporations had become fixtures on the economic landscape.[17]

Over two short decades, beginning in the 1890s, the corporation underwent a revolutionary transformation. It all started when New Jersey and Delaware ("the first state to be known as the home of corporations," according to its current secretary of state for corporations[18]), sought to attract valuable incorporation business to their jurisdictions by jettisoning unpopular restrictions from their corporate laws. Among other things, they

- Repealed the rules that required businesses to incorporate only for narrowly defined purposes, to exist only for limited durations, and to operate only in particular locations
- Substantially loosened controls on mergers and acquisitions; and
- Abolished the rule that one company could not own stock in another

Other states, not wanting to lose out in the competition for incorporation business, soon followed with similar revisions to their laws. The changes prompted a flurry of incorporations as businesses sought the new freedoms and powers incorporation would grant them. Soon, however, with most meaningful constraints on mergers and acquisitions gone, a large number of small and medium-size corporations were quickly absorbed into a small number of very large ones—1,800 corporations were consolidated into 157 between 1898 and 1904.[19] In less than a decade the U.S. economy had been transformed from one in which individually owned enterprises competed freely among themselves into one dominated by a relatively few huge corporations, each owned by many shareholders. The era of corporate capitalism had begun. [...]

Notes

1 Tom Hadden, *Company Law and Capitalism* (London: Weidenfeld and Nicolson, 1972), 14.

2 John Carswell, *The South Sea Bubble* (London: Cresset Press, 1960), 42 ("Spaniards"), 55 ("profits").

3 Ibid., 173.

4 Ibid.

5 Hadden, *Company Law and Capitalism*, 16.

6 Carswell, *The South Sea Bubble*, 210.

7 Especially in high-technology companies, where stock options are widely used to compensate employees, failure to account for them unduly inflates reported earnings, sometimes by hundreds of millions of dollars. Yet, despite criticsm of the practice by investor groups, accounting bodies, and the likes of Alan Greenspan and Warren Buffett, the federal government seems reluctant to stop it. Why? Likely because powerful business interests unduly influence what government does. True, many large companies—Coca-Cola, General Electric, Home Depot, Dow Chemical Company, and General Motors—now voluntarily count stock options as compensation expenses, but these are not companies that make significant use of the practice. Business interests lobbied and successfully in the early 1990s to block attempts by the Financial Accounting Standards Board (the body responsible for setting accounting standards) to fix the problem and are likely to prevail over any future attempts at reform in this area.

8 The Sarbanes-Oxley Act, Pub. L. No.107–204, 116 Stat. 745, was signed into law by the president on July 30, 2002. Among other things, the act limits the extent to which an accounting firm can serve as both an auditor of and consultant to the to the same corporation. That practice, which contributed notoriously to Arthur Andersen's complicity in Enron's misdeeds, generates an obvious conflict of interest. An accounting firm that wants to protect its lucrative consulting contracts with a corporation has every incentive to cooperate with, rather than oversee, the corporation's financial reporting; obviously that compromises its abiltity to audit the corporation objectively. The Sarbanes-Oxley Act, and regulations created under it by the Securities and Exchange Commission (SEC), though imperfect and containing some

wide loopholes, do go some of the way toward remedying the problem by barring a firm from auditing aclient for which it provides certain kinds of consulting services. It also enhances the powers of corporations' audit committees, requires CEOs and CFO's to certify fiancial reports (and face up to ten years in prison for "knowing" falsification and twenty years for "willing" falsification), and strengthens disclosure requirements. Several problems are likely to limit the act's effectiveness, however. First, the SEC has discretion to allow a firm to provide consulting services to an audit client on the prohibited list, so long as "it is reasonable to conclude that the results of these services will not be subjected to audit procedures" when the client is audited. Second, certain services are not on the prohibited list, such as routine preparation of tax returns, a lucrative practice for accounting firms and one that clearly has a direct impact on audited financial statements. Third, the SEC is "ludicrously underfinanced," as Paul Krugman states in "Business as Usual," *The New York Timdes*, October 22, 2002, and thus may not be effective in ensuring firms comply with the act. Fourth, the SEC has, according to some critics, watered down the act's requirements (see, e.g., Fulcrum Financial Inquiry, "Through Rule-Making, SEC Continues to Weaken Sarbanes-Oxley," January 27, 2003, available at www.fulcruminquiry.com).

9   Hadden, *Company Law and Capitalism*, 13.

10 John   Lord,   *Capital   and   Steam   Power*,   1925,   available   at www.history.rochester.edu/steam/lord.

11 Scott Bowman, *The Modern Corporation and American Political Thought: Law, Power and Ideology (University Park, Pa.: Pennsyslvania State University Press, 1996)*, 41.

12 Bowman, *The Modern Corporation and American Political Thought*, 41–42.

13 Paddy Ireland, "Capitalism Without the Capitalist: The Joint Stock Company Share and the Emergence of the Modern Doctrine of Separate Corporate Personality," *Jornal of Legal History* 17 (1996): 63.

14 Cited in ibid., 62.

15 Cited in ibid., 65.

16 Cited in Barbara Weiss, *The Hell of the English: Bankruptcy and Victorian Novel* (Lewisburg, Pa.: Bucknell University Press, 1986), 148.

17 Morton Horwitz, "Santa Clara Revisited: The Development of Corporate Theory," in *Corporations and Society: Power and Responsibility*, ed. Warren Samuels and Arthur Miller (New York: Greenwood Press, 1987), 13.

18 Interview with Dr. Harriet Smith Windsor.

19 Roland Marchand, *Creating the Corporate Soul: The Rise of Public Relations and Corporate Imagery in American Big Business* (Berkeley: University of California Press, 1998), 7.

22

Crime and capitalist business corporations
Frank Pearce

[...] According to legal reasoning and practice a limited-liability corporation is made up of five elements: (1) the corporation itself, with its own legal personality; (2) its shareholders who can buy or sell stakes in the company and who are entitled to shares of the profits but who are not personally liable for its actions or its debts; (3) its directors, who are legally responsible for determining the corporation's policy goals, organization, and the kind of business it does; (4) its managers who are responsible for the day-to-day activities of the corporation's factories, chemical plants, and supermarket stores; and (5) the corporation's lower-level employees who cannot commit the corporation to particular lines of action but whose actions can create vicarious liability for their employer.

One implication of this corporate form is that shareholders can reap large profits at relatively low risk to themselves and given the volume of corporate crime it is clear that shareholders routinely benefit from such illegal activities (Clinard and Yeager, 1980; Snider, 1993). Directors and managers also are usually not personally liable for what the corporation does, or are insured against such liability. Routinely, when corporations are prosecuted for environmental and health and safety violations, it is only the corporation as a juristic person that is prosecuted and given the resources of most corporations, the fines result in little more than a minor tax (Etzioni, 1993). In fact, the law, in its use of the corporate personality:

> is both naive and sophisticated. It is naive because it does not, cannot, recognise the reality of corporate structure; it is sophisticated because its inclusive reasoning system enables it to do so with impunity ... The criminal law, rather than recognising the fact that decisions are the product of systemic processes, focuses instead on individual intentionality. Until conscious changes are made to the law through legislation (such changes are unlikely if not impossible within the law's own analogic reasoning system) this crass anthropomorphism will persist (Weait, 1992, pp. 59–60).

On the other hand, once the corporation is recognized as a legal personality there is a tendency to view it as being like a private individual, free to engage in lawful private transactions, with its internal life and actions equally private, privileged, and unregulated. In the United States this has even included the right of corporations to have protection under the first, fourth, fifth, sixth, seventh, and fourteen amendments, severely limiting governmental regulation, investigation, and intervention (Mayer, 1990).

Although corporations may be treated as if they are persons for legal purposes, they only share some of the attributes of human beings, and lack many others. The contradictions that derive from the differences between a naturalized person (an individual human subject) and the naturalized legal person (a legal construct) is exemplified clearly in the issue of aggregation (Moran, 1992). The focus on individual actors is entirely inappropriate for a large corporation "because the way that responsibilities are distributed through a corporate body makes it extremely unlikely that the necessary fault will ever reside entirely in a single identifiable individual. Companies gain many benefits from the principle of aggregation" (Slapper, 1993, p. 435). Thus it is notable that the two convictions for corporate manslaughter in England and Wales have both been against small companies where the identification of the controlling mind is straightforward. In this respect, as in so many others, larger, complexly organized corporations enjoy an unequal advantage (Cahill, 1997).

Both corporations and individual human beings may engage in actions that further some basic overall goal. Individuals, however, often also are concerned with such nonteleological elements as integrity, autonomy, and responsibility even when these concerns cannot be shown to further a basic goal such as happiness. We regard them as intrinsically important and valuable and not simply as means to other more basic ends. On the other hand, as formal organizations, with particular goals such as the maximization of profits, growth, and survival, other things have ethical value for business corporations only insofar as they are instrumental in furthering their ultimate goals. Honesty and keeping one's word when dealings with other members of the organization are important to the extent that these operating principles ensure overall efficiency and the realization of the organizations' goals. And in dealing with those outside the organization they are important only if they are seen to function as operating conditions that set the upper limits to an organization's operations, for example, the scarcity of resources, of equipment, and of trained personnel. In organizational decision-making and planning such conditions must be taken into account as *data*. In this respect information about them is logically consistent with other information utilized in planning and decision-making, for example, cost–benefit computations. It is therefore pointless to expect an industrial organization actively to avoid polluting the atmosphere on purely noninstrumental moral grounds. From the standpoint of the logic of organizational behavior such actions would be irrational (Benjamin and Bronstein, 1987). It is equally pointless to expect those managing such an organization for profit to be concerned with community interests out of an active communal identification with members of local communities. On the other hand, it is possible to include in the memoranda of association of organizations specific legally binding moral and political constraints—for example, that independent unions should be recognized and arms manufacture avoided.

THE CAPITALIST BUSINESS CORPORATION AND ITS
ORGANIZATIONAL FORMS

In addition to the legal definition of a corporation, it can be defined as "an organization for the accumulation of capital in order to maximize profits, in order to accumulate more capital, leading to more profits ..." (Glasbeek, 1988, p. 373). Thus its managers experience pressure to achieve high profits from the company's major shareholders and major creditors, from stock market evaluations of the corporation's performance *vis-à-vis* their competitors, and because their own interests are linked with the company's since significant components of their own remuneration is related to profit returns and/or is in shares in that company. They will therefore do everything possible to maximize output and to minimize costs and external constraints.

The relationships between corporations and profit maximization require some elaboration. First, precisely how "profitability" should be calculated has been, and remains, subject to dispute (Cutler et al., 1977; 1978). And there is little doubt that different positions on this question have real, practical consequences. What is not in doubt is that corporate management is under pressure to maximize profitability, however, the latter term is defined or calculated. Relatedly, the disciplines of business policy and business strategy reveal a range of competing arguments (in the form of techniques) as to how the aim of profit maximization might be secured (see, for example, Mintzberg and Quinn, 1996). Second, and related to the previous point, a key variable in terms of the calculation of profitability is the time span over which profitability in general, and returns on investment in particular, is calculated. The calculative attitude that is central to corporate decision-making and behavior can involve a commitment either to short-term profits or to long-term profits and to judgments regarding continuing economic viability. Thus a central element of corporate strategy may be to assume "the cloak of social responsibility" for actions that "are in the long-run interest of a corporation" (Friedman, 1970). Third, we should also be clear that while profit maximization is the key corporate goal, corporations do not necessarily make accurate calculations as to how this should be achieved, or manage to implement effective strategies and policies to reach this end. In other words, corporations do not always accurately or successfully calculate. They may be unsuccessful for a variety of reasons, and are sites of bounded, multiple, and competing rationalities. For these reasons, it is perfectly possible that corporations, operating as rational actors, might not appear as such.

It is more realistic to view the corporation not as a private person, but more as a political entity. In some senses it is a shareholder's republic in that every shareholder, usually, has the vote and the capacity to withdraw from what is, after all, a voluntary association. On the other hand, shareholders are many and relatively atomized compared to the top management who are few, unified, and in control of information. Do the latter, then, control the corporation?

If yes, are these managers socially conscious as Berle and Means (1967) believed or, as others less sanguine argue, do they use the corporation for their own advantage rather than that of anybody else, increasing the size of the organization to boost their salaries, for example (Marris, 1964). Now, there is a great deal of evidence that the management in many large corporations has significant relative autonomy from all or most shareholders but that, at the same time, top managerial groups are not simply self-selecting, but require the endorsement of key sections of capital, whether stock holders, shareholders, or large creditors, like the banks. The phenomena of corporate raiding, shareholder revolts, and massive dividend bonuses involve struggles between different groups of shareholders and between shareholders and top management. Such struggles despite "the rituals of a democratic contest" and "the deployment of the symbols of democracy" are often only "contests between adversary political machines" controlled by rival wealthy shareholders (Latham, 1961. p. 225). For example, in the United States, Zeitlin (1989, p. 89) has identified such ownership interests in 40 percent of the top 500 U.S. firms. Further, he has shown that the wealthiest one percent of American families own "a fifth of all the real estate (and over twice that much of commercial real estate), three-fifths of corporate stock, and over four-fifths of all the trust assets" (Zeitlin, 1989, p. 141). Moreover, the "major banks are major lenders of funds to the top corporations and own significant stock in them as do the major insurance companies" (Zeitlin, 1989, p. 29) and large corporations also own stock in the large banks and in each other. Zeitlin's empirical analysis provides strong arguments why, as a matter of course, "the corporate veil" should be pierced (Clark, 1986, pp. 71–74). Nevertheless, who is in control needs to be empirically established, and it is important to recognize that the exercise of control by large owners of stock is usually only partial, and won through struggle.

Thus the corporation is an aristocratic or oligopolistic republic, and one subject to bloody struggles between its elites. Like other political entities, the corporation pursues its goals through a system consisting of: "(1) an authoritative allocation of principal functions; (2) a symbolic system for the ratification of collective decisions; (3) an operating system of command; (4) a system of rewards and punishments; and (5) institutions for the enforcement of the common rules" (Latham, 1961, p. 220). The corporation's goals and its authoritative allocation of principal functions are specified, but only in part, by the "constitution" provided by the corporation's "Memorandum of Association" and its "Articles of Association." These are then interpreted in the interests of those who rule the organization, either by the rules themselves or by their representatives who govern for them. In either case, the controllers, as we have seen, are chosen politically. [...]

[...] The limited-liability corporation has a strong proclivity to engage in antisocial, illegal, and criminal conduct. As a capitalist business it is essentially dedicated to making continuous and, if possible, ever-increasing profits. It is intrinsically indifferent to what commodities it produces as long as there is a market for them; thus in the United States the carcinogen tobacco was produced mainly for domestic consumption, but as this market has become smaller, tobacco firms began targeting overseas markets. In order to maximize profits, there is always a need to cut costs. This means that efforts are made to make it difficult for workers to join effective trade unions, or to demand safe workplaces. These tendencies are exacerbated by the limited-liability corporate form. Shareholders invest in a wide range of companies, and since their only concern is with the return of their investments they are indifferent to what occurs within different production processes and rarely live in the areas where these take place. They are legally protected from most of the negative consequences of company actions. Company executes are also fundamentally concerned with profitability, and with "willful blindness" are again often distanced from (and legally protected from the consequences of) production, conceive of it abstractly and, in turn, pressure managers to produce as much and as cheaply as possible. This creates a form of structural irresponsibility where it is often difficult to identify how decisions are made and how well or poorly they relate together. [...]

23

The theory of business enterprise
Thorstein Veblen

[...] The pioneers, especially in that North-Atlantic seaboard community that has been chiefly effective in shaping American traditions, brought with them a somewhat high-wrought variant of the English preconception in favor of individual discretion, and this tradition they put in practice under circumstances peculiarly favorable to a bold development. They brought little of the remnants of that prescriptive code that once bound the handicraft system, and the conditions of life in the colonies did not foster a new growth of conventional regulations circumscribing private initiative. America is the native habitat of the self-made man, and the self-made man is a pecuniary organism.[1]

Presently, when occasion arose, the metaphysics of natural liberty, pecuniary and other, was embodied in set form in constitutional enactments. It is therefore involved in a more authentic form and with more incisive force in the legal structure of this community than in that of any other.

Freedom of contract is the fundamental tenet of the legal creed, so to speak, inviolable and inalienable; and within the province of law and equity no one has competence to penetrate behind this first premise or to question the merits of the natural-rights metaphysics on which, it rests. The only principle (attested habit of thought) which may contest its primacy in civil matters is a vague "general welfare" clause; and even this can effectively contest its claims only under exceptional circumstances. Under the application of any general welfare clause the presumption is and always must be that the principle of free contract be left intact so far as the circumstances of the case permit. The citizen may not be deprived of life, liberty, or property without due process of law, and the due process proceeds on the premise that property rights are inviolable. In its bearing upon the economic relations between individuals this comes to mean, in effect, not only that one individual or group of individuals may not legally bring any other than pecuniary pressure to bear upon another individual or group, but also that pecuniary pressure cannot be barred.

Now, through gradual change of the economic situation, this conventional principle of unmitigated and inalienable freedom of contract began to grow obsolete from about the time when it was fairly installed; obsolescent, of course, not in point of law, but in point of fact. Since about the time when this new conventional standardization of the scheme of economic life in terms of free contract reached its mature development, in the eighteenth century,[2] a new standardizing force, that of the machine process, has invaded the field.[3] The standardization and the constraint of the system of machine industry differs from what went before it in that it has had no conventional recognition, no metaphysical authentication. It has not become a legal fact. Therefore it neither need nor can be taken account of by the legal mind. It is a new fact which fits into framework neither of the ancient system of prescriptive usage nor of the later system of free personal initiative. It does not exist *de jure*, but only *de facto*. Belonging neither to the defunct system nor to the current legal system, since it neither constitutes nor traverses a "natural right," it is, as within the cognizance of the law, non-existent. It is, perhaps, actual, with a gross, material actuality; but it is not real, with a legal, metaphysically competent reality. Such coercion as it may exert, or as may be exercised through its means, therefore, is, in point of legal reality, no coercion.

Where physical impossibility to fulfill the terms of a contract arises out of the concatenation of industrial processes, this physical impossibility may be pleaded as invalidating the terms of the contract. But the pecuniary pressure of price or subsistence which the sequence and interdependence of industrial processes may bring to bear has no standing as such in law of equity; it can reach the cognizance of the law only indirectly, through gross defection of one of the contracting parties, in those cases where the pressure is severe enough to result in insolvency, sickness, or death. The material necessities of group of workmen or consumers, enforced by the specialization and concatenation of industrial processes, is, therefore, not competent to set aside, or indeed to qualify, the natural freedom of the owners of these processes to let work go on or not, as the outlook for profits may decide. Profits is a busing proposition, livelihood is not.[4]

Under the current *de facto* standardization of economic life enforced by the machine industry, it may frequently happen that an individual of a group, *e.g.*, of workmen, has not a *de facto* power of free contract. A given workman's livelihood can perhaps, practically, be found only on acceptance of one specific contract offered, perhaps no at all. But the coercion which in this way bears upon his choice through the standardization of industrial procedure is neither assault and battery nor breach of contract, and it is, therefore, not repugnant to the principles of natural liberty. [...]

[...] The discrepancy between law and fact in the matter of industrial freedom has had repeated illustration in the court decisions on disputes between bodies of workmen and their employers or owners. These decisions commonly fall out in favor of the employers or owners; that is to say, they go to uphold property rights and the rights of free contract. The courts have been somewhat broadly taken to task by a certain class of observers for alleged partiality to the owners' side in this class of litigation. It has also been pointed out by faultfinders that the higher courts decide, on the whole, more uniformly in favor of the employer-owner than the lower ones, and especially more so than the juries in those cases where juries have found occasion to pass on the law of the case. The like is true as regards suits for damages arising out of injuries sustained by workmen, and so involving the question of the employer's liability. Even a casual scrutiny of the decisions, however, will show that in most cases the decision of the court, whether on the merits of the case or on the constitutionality of the legal provisions involved,[5] is well grounded on the metaphysical basis of natural liberty. That is to say in other words, the decisions will be found on the side of the maintenance of fundamental law and order, "law and order" having, of course, reference to the inalienable rights of ownership and contract. [...]

Notes

1   Cf., *e.g.*, Ashley, "The Economic Atmosphere of America," in *Surveys, Historic and Economic*, pp. 406 et seq.
2   This date is true for England. For America the discipline favorable to the growth of the natural-liberty dogma lasted nearly a century longer. In America the new, modern, technological and business era can scarcely be said to have set in good vigor until the period of the Civil War. Hence, with a longer and later training, the preconceptions of natural liberty are fresher and more tenacious in America. For the Continental peoples the case is different again. With them the modern technological and business situation is of approximately the same date as in America, but their training up to the date of the transition to the modern situation was in a much less degree a training in individual initiative, free scattered industry, and petty trade. The Continental peoples for the most part made a somewhat abrupt transition after the middle of the nineteenth century from a stale and dilapidated system of guild and feudalistic prescriptions to the (for them) exotic system of modern technology and business principles.
3   See Chapter II. above and chapter IX. below.
4   Under the system of handicraft and petty trade the converse was true. Livelihood was the fundamental norm of business regulations; profits had but a secondary standing, if any.
5   *E.g.*, as to employer's liability for accidents or unsanitary premises, the safeguarding of machinery, age limit of laborers or hour limit of working time, etc.

24

Corporations and criminal responsibility

Celia Wells

[...] In the Roman tradition persons are creations or artefacts of the law itself. Corporations can be subject to this fiction, like any other entity.[1] In historical terms, it may have been an understandable path given the 'passive' social function of many of the 'proto-corporations' such as universities, guilds, and the Church.[2] The problem of deciding who owned the Church once the power of the local landowners had dwindled was resolved in the twelfth century by saying that church property was owned by 'the Church' meaning the congregation.[3] This was a foretaste of the use of the legal fiction of person as a device for holding property through incorporation.

All human beings have legal personality although their responsibilities and rights may vary according to their age and status.[4] A group of people—for example, a club, association, or partnership—does not generally have a legal existence separate from its individual members. Blackstone explains, in this passage, why this may cause problems and how they may be overcome:

> As all personal rights die with the person; and, as the necessary forms of investing a series of individuals, one after another, with the same identical rights, would be very inconvenient, if not impracticable; it has been found necessary, when it is for the advantage of the public to have any particular rights kept on foot and continued, to constitute artificial persons, who may maintain a perpetual succession, and enjoy a kind of legal immortality. These artificial persons are called bodies politic, bodies corporate (*corpora corporata*), or corporations: of which there is a great variety subsisting, for the advancement of religion, of learning, and of commerce; in order to preserve entire and for ever those rights and immunities, which, if they were granted only to those individuals of which the body corporate is composed, would upon their death be utterly lost and extinct.[5]

The origins of both separate personality, and the connected development of limited liability, can be found in Roman law. However, it is ironic that limited liability emerged at that stage in order to protect the public property of municipalities, whereas its clear function now is to protect private investors from the claims of third parties.

The early corporations had little, if anything, in common with business corporations. They were more like guilds, functioning as a mechanism for controlling the right to engage in specific business activities.[6] The resolution of the East India Company in 1612 that thenceforth trading should only be carried on by the corporation is cast by Stone as the turning point in the development of the modern business corporation. '[T]he company, through its officers, was no longer merely laying down by-laws under which the members would engage among themselves, directly as entrepreneurs'.[7] The diffusion between capital and management was only then properly beginning. Until then membership in the company merely gave a right to exercise the exclusive trading privileges of the company. By the nineteenth century, investors were protected through limited liability and corporations began to be sued in tort for some of the injuries they caused. [...]

[...] Although treated separately here, it is important to note that the recognition of the corporation as a legal person is not a fact whose provenance can be pin pointed, but rather it is a tidemark subject to the ebb and flow of many different factors. By the end of the nineteenth century courts were quite familiar with the idea that, for some purposes, the word 'person' in a criminal statute might include a corporation. This received endorsement in *Royal Mail Steam Packet Co* v. *Braham*[8] when the Privy Council advised that 'person' in a legal sense was an apt word to describe a corporation. [...]

[...] Under the Sale of Food and Drugs Act 1875 it was an offence under section 6 for a person to 'sell to the prejudice of the purchaser any article of food or any drug which was not of the nature, substance and quality of the articles demanded by the purchaser'. This applied to a joint stock company incorporated under the Companies Act.[9] Corporate liability under this legislation was taken further when a corporation was convicted of the section 20 offence of giving a false warranty to the purchaser of food or drugs sold.[10] Since there was a defence if the seller proved that when he gave the warranty he had reason to believe that the statements or descriptions were true, its application to a company indicates that companies could not expect easily to evade liability on the 'person' ground. [...]

[...] The industrial revolution and improved transportation resulted in changes in corporations and in the function they played in society. Many smaller enterprises came to need capital and many others became large enough to need the services of a full-time administrator. The development of corporate executive structures clearly challenged a legal response. The one-person entrepreneur was being replaced by more complex business arrangements, and in terms of activity, the development of the railways transformed the landscape, the economy, and mobility. Corporations began to cause damage and injury both to property and person. Plaintiffs discovered that the individual at fault might riot be capable of being sued or worth suing. It emerged that what was the simplest for the injured party was also the safest for management: to treat the corporation as the actor. The emergence of civil claims against corporations provides only part of the background to the development of corporate criminal liability. As the discussion below reveals the history of liability of local authorities and later railway companies for breaches of duty also played a significant role. There was also a move in the late eighteenth and early nineteenth centuries towards a broader notion of manslaughter; carelessness became less tolerated and the penalties and scope of manslaughter liability were extended.[11]

It is only later in the story that the problem of whether a corporation is capable of committing criminal offences really emerged. The first step, as Welsh pointed out, was to overcome the 'real difficulty' of how an individual could be vicariously liable to pay damages for the wrongful act or negligence of his servant.[12] When the problem of establishing liability for an injury which he had not authorized and might even have expressly forbidden was sidestepped, 'the difficulty of ascribing wrongful intention to an artificial person was in truth only a residue of anthropomorphic imagination'.[13] The emergence of the common law principle that masters had 'vicarious' liability for their servants facilitated the development both of civil and criminal liability of corporations. '[I]t was only a short step from the idea of a master as a human person to the master as a corporate person.'[14] This 'modern' vicarious liability of masters was itself a revival of an ancient principle, which had been eroded in the medieval period, of absolute liability for *all* the wrongful actions of servants.[15] By the time that the corporation began to appear as a significant social and economic force the liability of masters for their servants' criminal wrongs had almost completely vanished except where the master had given his command or consent.[16] This limitation on masters' liability of course protected corporations since it could be argued that they were incapable of giving such command or consent. But there were exceptions, such that masters *were* strictly (i.e. absent command or consent) liable for public nuisance: if any member of his household 'layeth or casteth anything out of his house into the street or common highway, to the damage of any individual or the common nuisance of his majesty's leige people'.[17]

Corporate liability was founded on a combination of this exception, extending an individual master's liability, and the parallel liability of municipalities to maintain roads and waterways running through their jurisdiction. Local authorities' liability for public nuisance provided a model for the application of the juristic person concept to the newly developing collective body, the corporation. The basis of local authority liability for nuisance was itself rooted in an analogy with the master/servant relationship. They were liable as 'masters' when their 'servants', the local officials, created a public nuisance in streets through failing to maintain them.

At the same time, many of the early large corporate bodies such as the railway companies were set up under special charters or private Acts which imposed specific duties upon them, analogous to the municipal duties of local authorities.[18] Thus, it was not a huge step to hold them liable, at first for failing in those duties, non-feasance,[19] and later for misfeasance, as in the key decision of *R* v. *Gt North of England Railway Co* in 1846.[20] The company had unlawfully destroyed a highway in the construction of its own bridge. While those who voted to erect it and those who built it might be liable, Lord Denman said:

the public knows nothing of the former; and the latter, if they can be identified, are commonly persons of the lowest rank, wholly incompetent to make any reparation for the injury. There can be no effectual means for deterring from an oppressive exercise of power for the purpose of gain, except the remedy by an indictment against those who truly commit it, that is, by the corporation, acting by its majority.[21]

As Bernard comments, 'The point is that, according to the statutory provision, the obligation to construct five bridges lay with the corporation itself, rather than with any individual officers. [...]

[...] But the real problem came with traditional offences in general and *mens rea* in particular. In the *Great North of England Rlwy Case* Lord Denman had highlighted some *dicta* from old cases:

'A corporation cannot be guilty of treason or of felony.' It might be added 'of perjury, or offences against the person'. The Court of Common Pleas lately held that a corporation might be sued in trespass; but nobody has sought to fix them with acts of immorality. These plainly derive their character from the corrupted mind of the person committing them, and are violations of the social duties that belong to men and subjects. A corporation which has no such duties, cannot be guilty in these cases: but they may be guilty as body corporate of commanding acts to be done to the nuisance of the community at large.[22]

On the one hand, a conventional view emanated which said that capacity to commit crime 'presupposes an act of understanding and ah exercise of will'[23] and that, as had been said repeatedly since the *Case of Sutton's Hospital* in 1612,[24] a corporation is incapable of an act of understanding and it has no will to exercise.[25] On the other hand, the implications of pushing the doctrine to its logical conclusion had been largely evaded in the English law of contract and tort through the use of wide principles of agency and vicarious liability. 'A corporation is not, in the eye of the law, so abstract, impalpable or metaphysical that it cannot be regarded as a principal or master.'[26] (Welsh is using the word metaphysical here in its restricted sense of intangible.) Vicarious liability was assumed to be confined to those offences which required no *mens rea*. There are numerous examples of statutory constructions of words such as 'use', 'cause', and 'permit'. In some of these, the word itself is taken to import vicarious liability whereas others ('permit', for example) are seen as 'personal' which precludes vicarious liability. (It is not proposed to deal in detail with these.)[27]

Procedural problems are often mentioned as a factor which obstructed steps towards a more general liability of corporations. Not only was it difficult to contemplate a corporation being immoral or corrupt (see Lord Denman, above) but most felonies attracted punishments such as imprisonment or death that could have no application to an inert body.[28] [...]

Notes

1   French 1984: 34.
2   Stone 1975 ch. 2; Bernard 1984: 4.
3   Bernard 1984: 4.
4   And historically according to their sex. See generally Fredman 1997 ch. 1 and on the corporation, Corcoran 1997: 222.
5   Blackstone 1765: 455.
6   Bernard 1984: 4.
7   Stone 1975: 15.
8   1877.
9   *Pearks, Dunston & Tee Ltd* v. *Ward* (1902).
10 *Chuter* v. *Freeth and Pocock Ltd* (1911).
11 Beattie 1986: 89–91; Wiener 1991:78.
12 Welsh 1946: 51; see also Hager 1989: 600 ff.
13 Pollock 1911: 235.
14 Bernard 1984: 5.
15 Holdsworth 1944: iii. 46–7.
16 Bernard 1984: 6.
17 Ibid. See also Welsh 1946.
18 Elkins 1976:76; and see French 1984: 174.
19 *R* v. *Birm. and Glos. Rlwy* 1842.
20 1846.
21 1846 at 1298.
22 1846 at 1298.
23 Archbold 1943: 11.
24 *Case of Suttons Hospital* (1612).
25 Welsh 1946: 347.
26 Ibid.
27 A full account is found in Leigh 1982a. See also the discussion of strict liability in Ch. 4.2.
28 Felonies were only finable if statute expressly provided, as with Offences Against the Person 1861, s.5 for manslaughter. This presumption against fines was removed by Criminal Justice Act 1948, s.13. This obstacle did not prevent the US federal court from upholding and indictment for an imprisonable only offence: *US* v. *Van Schaick* (1904).

25

Wealth by stealth

Harry Glasbeek

[...] Corporate misconduct is clearly treated differently than is misfeasance by the poor, the marginal, workers, and, in general, ordinary citizens. It is not that the corporate conduct unplanned; it is not that the consequences of the corporate conduct could not have been foreseen. Indeed, in some cases it was foreseen. It is not that the corporate conduct, in the cases presented here, did not clearly breach established standards of behaviour. The irony is that the liberal-democratic polity prides itself on its adherence to the rule of law and on the care it takes with the application of criminal law—to ensure evenhanded treatment and, thereby, the legitimacy of the system. But still it tolerates this apparent privileging of the corporate sectors. [...]

[...] Before the state can use its awesome coercive powers legitimately, it must establish that the offending conduct involved an *individual who intended to engage in it*. The emphasis, as we would expect in a liberal polity, is on the responsibility of individuals for their actions. This emphasis also dovetails with the basic premise of idealized market capitalism, which posits that we are all sovereign actors, capable of exercising our free will as we go about doing what nature demands, namely optimize our opportunities. Logically, therefore, we will be held responsible for how we exercise our individual choices.

This basic formulation of the constituent elements of criminal responsibility permits us to excuse those who do not have the mental capacity to make free choices and allows us to provide defences for people who acted in self-defence or under extreme provocation or, in egregious circumstances, out of undeniable necessity. In such circumstances criminal culpability does not attach because the transgressing individual did not have the freely formed intent, known as *mens rea* to lawyers, that demands criminal punishment.

It is easy to manufacture reasons that render corporations immune from the application of a branch of law that requires an individual to have committed an act with a subjectively wrongful intention. Unsurprisingly, defenders of the status quo and of the corporation's legitimacy have employed all of these many easily available arguments at various times. While most of those arguments have been rejected, over time a useful climate, from a corporate point of view, has been created. The application of criminal law to corporations continues to be seen as aberrational, as a matter requiring justification.

Initially the defenders contended that, because a crime required an intentional breach of a legal norm, a corporation could not be a criminal because it was merely an artifice created by the state. We should assume, so the defenders claimed, that the state would never empower its own creatures to act with evil intent. When this argument did not bite, the advocates offered a variant that had a somewhat longer shelf life: as a non-human, as a mere fiction, the corporation could not have a state of mind, nor could it carry out an act. This old—and now discredited—argument demonstrates, once again, that the captains of industry, finance, retail, and everything else, who use invisible friends to produce and protect their profits, are willing to resort to any argument, no matter how threadbare, how transparently insincere, to avoid responsibilities. Today, the same people, still seeking to avoid responsibility for acts committed via their invisible friends, make a diametrically opposed argument. Now they argue that if anyone is to be held responsible, it should be the corporations, rather than the human beings who act through them.

The courts began to make inroads on the "a fiction cannot commit a crime" contentions by holding that, if the offending conduct was the omission by a certain party to do something that the law required to be done by that party—for example, to build a bridge—a corporation could be held responsible for its failure to act because there was no requirement in that case to prove the intentional nature of the act. That courts even resorted to this logically feeble argument shows that they were looking for ways of pinning criminal responsibility on the creatures to which they had given legitimacy, corporations. This pressure resulted in the gradual expansion of the concept of corporate criminal responsibility. Next, courts went on to hold corporations criminally responsible if their conduct constituted a public nuisance in that it inconvenienced the public and/or breached a statutory standard; and if the statute merely stated that an offence was committed if the act was done, regardless of the actor's motive or state of mind—for example, trading on a Sunday when that act was forbidden by legislation.

What motivated the courts to extend the application of the strictures of the criminal law to corporations was their recognition, from the nineteenth century onwards, that corporations' activities had the capacity to impose a great deal of harm and costs on society if left unchecked This acknowledgement of the need to hold corporations to account permeated the whole of the regulatory field—civil, administrative, or criminal—demonstrating the interconnectedness and comple-mentary nature of the discrete spheres of regulation. Thus, in 1915, the British House of Lords held that a corporation could be held civilly liable for the damages its activities had inflicted on another person. This pronouncement came in an unusual civil case in which civil law, like criminal law, required some evidence of an intention to do an act by the defendant. The defendant corporation had taken the still fashionable point that it was incapable of forming an intention. The House of Lords held that it was sufficient to demonstrate that those who made the corporate decisions had the necessary intent. This intent would then be taken to be the intent of the corporation. The intention of the people who were characterized as the guiding mind and will of the corporation was to be attributed to the corporation. The corporation could now form an intention and do an act This doctrine of attribution, which became known as the identification doctrine, was to become the way in which courts could determine whether corporations had formed the necessary intent to be held criminally responsible. But it would take a while before this radical civil ruling crystallized as the rule in criminal law.

After the House of Lords decision in the civil law case, corporations continued to make arguments as to why the criminal law proper should not be applied to them. Most of these arguments were technical and procedural and were relatively easy to overcome when the political will was mustered to do so. These arguments included the self-serving one that, as corporations had no body and no soul, punishment meant nothing to them. Flogging and incarceration, or deportation, made no sense; the stigmatization of a non-human was a nonsense. Accordingly, the argument went, other regulatory regimes, those that did not require the infliction of physical and psychic pain, should be deployed to control corporate behaviour. To counter these lines of defences to the application of criminal law to corporations, all the courts needed were amendments that gave them an arsenal of different sanctions, such as the right to fine instead of jailing, the right to make restitution orders, or the power to supervise reformed structures and future behaviour or to order the making of public apologies. Some of these measures were duly established; others are still being urged. In any case the arguments against applying criminal punishment to corporations were not ones based on principle. Their rebuttal required no rethinking of the fundamentals of criminal law.

Another argument maintained that to charge corporations criminally would deny them due process and, therefore, be unfair. The point made was that corporations, unlike human defendants, could not appear physically and could not confront their accusers directly—that is, corporations, because of their nature, could not be extended the safeguards that the criminal processes offered flesh and blood accused persons to help offset the might of the coercive state. This was an argument being put forth by the same group that contended that, because a corporation is not a human being, criminal law should not be applicable to it. Here, showing a certain unmitigated gall, the same sector was now claiming that the corporation should be granted the safeguards bestowed on human beings because of their very, well, human nature. Inevitably, this fanciful argument was trumped. The courts held that a corporation could indeed appear in court through its guiding mind and will and/or lawyers.

These and other similar made-up difficulties disappeared when the courts finally determined that they could no longer justify not applying criminal law to corporations. Evenhandedness in the justice system and the concrete impact of corporate harm mandated this change in approach. By 1941 a Canadian court had used the identification doctrine developed by the House of Lords in the 1915 English civil case to hold a corporation criminally responsible for a fraud committed through its leading director and executive. Since then neither legal principles nor technical difficulties have inhibited the uses of criminal law vis-à-vis the corporate vehicle, although the political will to do so remains a long way from being cemented in place. What is obvious, though, is that there was a pressing need to vanquish the long-standing corporate opposition to the potential employment of the state's most repressive weapon of regulation. The relative immunity of corporations from the criminal process tended to bring into view some delegitimating features of the corporate vehicle. [...]

[...] The neglect and/or wilful disregard to well-known standards to behaviour1 attributed to countless other large corporations has caused grievous harm: Shell (allegedly associated with brutal repression in Nigeria), Union Carbide (of Bhopal fame), Dow (which had earned a nasty reputation for its production of Agent Orange before it cranked out malfunctioning breast implants), Ford Motor Company (manufacturer of the Pinto, which proved to be explosive rather than reliable), General Electric (leading light in the still notorious heavy electrical equipment conspiracy), and Johns-Manville (a leader amongst the asbestos killers). The shareholders in these and other corporations have little financial incentive to ensure that the managers involved behave legally, ethically, or decently. As investors who do not legally own the property used to do the harm, they have no personal responsibility for its deployment by the corporation's managers. Further, the privilege of limited liability means that they are unlikely to be seriously hurt by the losses incurred by the corporation should it be held responsible for the management's failure to make a profit as a consequence of the harm-doing or for the corporation's losses should it be made to pay damages to third parties or a fine to the government. In law, the shareholders are personally untouchable, which includes their private wealth. In law, then, the shareholders of wrong-doing corporations are irresponsible.

The position is little better when it comes to the managers who make the corporate decisions to carry out acts that we now want to characterize as criminal. Precisely because we identify these senior managers as the guiding minds and will of the corporation—that is, because we identify them as *the* corporation when they are thinking and acting on its behalf—they are not seen by law to be thinking and acting in their own right, as you and I would be, as ordinary, not incorporated human beings. Unless they expressly make the impugned conduct their own, it will be attributed to the corporation, not to them. In law, the senior managers who constitute the guiding mind and will of the invisible friends of the rich are, like the rich themselves, irresponsible. [...]

[...] Just like some substances or chemicals that, by their very nature, without any malice, induce cancers and are, therefore, labelled carcinogenic, corporations, by their very nature, without any malice towards any particular victim, will engage in criminal behaviour. They will do so because there are no strong internal disincentives for them to do otherwise; while, at the same time, their single-minded goal—profit-maximization—which is also the driving motivation of the irresponsible shareholders, makes it rational for them to do so.

The early failure to hold corporations responsible for criminal activities, then, drew attention to the understanding that no one (not shareholders, not managers) was being held responsible for the evils inflicted on consumers, the environment, workers, and the markets. That is why the identification doctrines evolved and why the laying of criminal charges against corporations was eased. [...]

[...] Gradually, courts and legislators are distorting the legal construction of the corporation to make it amenable to the criminal process. But, precisely because the judicial and legislative responses have distorted, rather than changed, the legal structure of the corporation, the defenders of the status quo have not solved their problems. Corporations continue both to be anti-social and to evade legal responsibility for many acts. The corporate hand may have been twisted into shape to fit inside the criminal glove, but it still seeks to revert to its original, ill-fitting, shape. [...]

SECTION 5:
Explanations

The organisation of domination

The readings in this section reflect a range of perspectives that have been developed to explain the causation of state crime and corporate crime. And there are themes that run across the readings in this section that allow us to explore some core commonalities and contradictions in those explanations. What connects these readings together is their attempt to explain how the crimes of states and corporations arise from the particular way that relations of power and domination are structured in, and by, those institutions.

In the previous sections we saw how the physical distance created between the victims and perpetrators of crimes of the powerful was a key feature of capitalist development. For Zygmunt Bauman, crimes of the powerful – specifically the crime of genocide – are made possible by modernity itself. In other words, organisational violence is not simply a product of the *capitalist* organisation of society, but a product of the bureaucratisation of modern relations of power that enable violence to be centralised and dehumanised. Just as we saw in the context of corporations in Sections 3 and 4, modern state bureaucracies are characterised by the capacity to render violence invisible, to remove it from scrutiny. For Bauman, that space, or distance, in both a practical and mental sense that is created by highly complex and organised structures of modernity, is what makes modern bureaucratised societies capable of genocide. Bauman locates this aspect of 'modern genocide' in the cold, calculating desire to perfect the order of things, to meet no other purpose than a more ordered and pure world. Genocide in the context of Hitler's Germany was a product of a quest for 'civilisation', a quest that legitimised the most barbaric means.

Again, as we saw in the introductions to Sections 3 and 4, the notion of distance and space is important here, in the sense that the bureaucratic structure of states that produces a physical and moral distance. Those structures physically and ontologically remove the perpetrators from even the most extreme acts of violence. Although this is not always made explicit in the text, *Modernity and the Holocaust* can be understood as developing classic perspectives on bureaucratisation (Weber), the division of labour (Durkheim) and the normalisation of violence (Arendt). Where Bauman departs from those authors is that he views morality not in relativist or social constructionist terms, but argues that all humans have an innate moral capacity. He therefore argues (principally in Chapter 7 of *Modernity and the Holocaust)* that, as human beings, we all share the ability to tell right from wrong. It is the inhumanity of bureaucracy that shatters our ability to find a common morality.

The extract by Stanley Cohen is also concerned with the moral universe of the perpetrators of state crimes. His starting point is to seek a way of explaining the 'motivational vocabularies' available to actors and observers and to understand how they are consistent with legality and morality. As a starting point for answering this question, he uses Sykes and Matza's earlier (1957) sociological theory that explored how shared subcultural values were derived from a legal-moral architecture. Their primary task was to explain youth deviance. But, as Sykes and Matza had themselves noted, the moral flexibility of the law is best illustrated by the example of war, where a universal moral injunction against killing ceases to apply when the person to be killed is an 'enemy'. Yet, the contradictory aspect of wartime violence is revealed when the moral injunction not to kill is reasserted after an enemy is captured and held as a prisoner of war. Cohen brings Sykes and Matza's theoretical insights squarely back into the arena of militarised violence by describing the 'techniques of neutralisation' that enable human rights abusers and torturers to commit extreme acts of violence. For Cohen, the key to explaining state crimes is an understanding of how the state provides the moral context for 'denial' by state servants. First, authorisation replaces existing moral principles with the duty to obey. Second, once the moral barrier is passed initially, then the ongoing pressure to commit those acts becomes normalised or routinised. And third, the process of dehumanising the victim allows the normal rules of moral conduct to be suspended. Note that Cohen refers to the suspension of the normal moral code, rather than suspension of the rule of law or a conventionally understood 'state of exception' discussed in Section 1 of this book. Yet the self-suspension of a set of values subjectively held by an individual, as opposed to a set of norms established in a body of rules or law, is clearly a different process. Cohen's work therefore probes the interrelation-ship between state deviance and the deviant acts or behaviour of state servants.

The extract by Edwin Sutherland, the first of two in this book, is also concerned with how normative rules of behaviour are reconstructed in an organisational context. In the extract reproduced here, his focus is on the dynamics of economic competition and co-operation between business. Suther-land argues that the standards of behaviour that develop in corporations can be understood as arising from a process of 'differential association' through which criminality is learned by association with those who already practise criminal activities. Criminal practice occurs as a result of both a general ideology that becomes accepted by individuals within corporations and the diffusion of illegal practices between competitors. Sutherland had already developed this theory to apply to other forms of criminal subculture, and, therefore, like Cohen, was concerned with applying 'mainstream' criminological theory to crimes of the powerful. He proposed that in order to understand the prospects for the control of illegal corporate activity, it was necessary to assess levels of organisation and disorganisation in social groups. His conclusion was that business criminality depends, on the one hand, upon highly co-ordinated forms of social organisation and, on the other, upon the disorganisation of the means to regulate or control organisational offending.

Nikos Passas's work is heavily influenced by 'strain' theory[1] and as such seeks to locate offending or 'deviance' from moral or legal norms in the broader context of their macro-social causes. Strain theory was developed by the sociologist Robert Merton (1949) to explain how 'crime' or 'deviance' arises from a strain between the attainment of the goals set by cultural expectations and the limited opportunities to achieve those goals. For Merton, the almost universal cultural expectation was the post-war American dream of material wealth and success. If this goal could not be achieved legitimately, then people turned to illegitimate – or criminal – means. Passas proposes that strain theory accurately allows us to explain the motivational structure for corporate crime. Just as businesses depend upon executives for their success, so do executives depend on meeting organisational goals for their success. This is where individual and organisational cultural values coincide to cause a phenomenon that Matza (1969) had called an 'episodic release from moral constraint'. In the context of business executives (rather than young offenders, for example) this means acting upon the assumption that illegal practices may be necessary to remain competitive, profitable and so on. Indeed, it means acting on the assumption that law violation is part of the general culture of business – 'everybody breaks the law' (Passas, 1990: 167).

Whereas Passas understands corporate crime as a form of release from moral constraint, Frank Pearce and Steve Tombs start from an entirely different position. They reject any presumption that corporations are capable of acting morally and argue that corporate decision-making operates within an environment that is intrinsically *amoral*: even if a corporation – or its senior officers – wanted to act 'morally', then this would mean that they would have to ignore the rationale for their existence. For corporations, when they do act rationally, act only to maximise profits in the long term, and, as we saw in the previous section, senior officers are bound by law to put this goal above all others. But Pearce and Tombs also note that corporate rationality is bounded by other, contingent, features of their operating environment – their own incompetence, their political citizenship, and the wider pressures imposed upon them by their operating environments, by economic pressures and so on. Thus, corporations are always amoral actors, even if this means that they are rarely, if ever, guided by a pure rationality.

Pearce and Tombs's argument therefore counters the assumption that is prevalent in the mainstream literature on corporate social responsibility whereby corporations project themselves as *moral* citizens – as capable of making moral decisions. This argument is often made in business interventions in debates about regulation as a means of countering punitive or strict enforcement strategies (see the introduction to Section 6). The argument that corporations can act as moral citizens is closely linked to the claim that the deterrent sanction of the criminal law is less applicable in cases of corporate crime than it is in individual crime. We will discuss the implications of this for criminalising corporations in the introduction to Section 7. In the meantime, it is enough to note that the argument that corporate crime is best dealt with as a process of negotiation and bargaining between regulatory agencies and offenders is one that is never applied in cases of interpersonal killing or other forms of serious crime.

The use of the full force of the law against individual criminals who commit serious crimes is supported by a range of theoretical propositions. But always foremost amongst them is the principle of deterrence, usually based upon the following logic: if the punishment is severe enough and the chances of being caught are severe enough, then a rational thinking individual will calculate that the losses are more than the benefits of financial gain or 'gratification' of offending. But where individuals are not particularly capable of taking rational decisions on this basis, corporations and corporate officials are. If corporations do not act with a pure rationality, Pearce and Tombs's argument, following Edwin Sutherland (1949), is that corporations are much *more likely* than individuals to make decisions after a reasoned assessment and calculated understanding of the costs and benefits of those decisions.

This argument can be supported in three ways. First, corporate decision-makers have resources and forms of awareness that are not available to individual 'criminals' acting alone or in small groups. Although most individuals do not possess the information necessary to calculate rationally the probability of detection and punishment, large bureaucratic organisations *do* have the re-sources to deploy sophisticated information-gathering systems and to call upon lawyers and accountants. Both companies and their directors do make calculated decisions, based not upon perfect knowledge, but upon a range of knowledge resources available to them which allow them to make calculated decisions. They draw upon information from company accountants and balance sheets; they are generally aware of how often an environmental or health and safety inspector is likely to call, what the likely punishment is for non-compliance and so on. Much more than other types of ('street' or 'mainstream') criminals, they act within the constraints of a bounded rationality. Whilst clearly much of this information is not precise, the point is that corporate decision-makers (individually and collectively) have resources available to them that individuals simply do not possess.

Second, companies and their senior officers do have some motivation to consider the long-term future consequences of their decisions, and the costs of punishment to their business and their social position. Corporations are 'future oriented' (Braithwaite, 1989). Organisations and their senior officers use cost-–benefit analysis to assess the future implications of strategic decisions as a routine procedure. Often they are involved in speculative activities precisely because of their future projections. Investments in temporary 'loss leaders' are commonplace across industrial sectors; and many oligopolistic industries have the ability to ride out temporary falls in the price of commodities to protect the longer-term interests of the corporation.

Third, as Chambliss (1969) argued, deterrence can appropriately be used against white-collar offenders because they satisfy two conditions: first, they do not have a commitment to crime as a way of life; and second, their offences are instrumental rather than expressive. In other words, the crimes they commit are less likely to be spontaneous or emotional crimes than calculated risks that are taken as part of the long-term strategy of meeting organisational goals. The complex construction of morality that this brief discussion highlights, then, is that the fictional notion of the amoral, rational choice calculator is difficult to sustain where it is most applied: to the individual. And yet it is much more plausible where it is least applied: to the corporation.

The contributions by W.G. Carson and by Sally Simpson and Lori Ellis explore the connection between corporate crime and the social conditions that shape corporate action. These contributions focus on how capitalism and patriarchy respectively act as structures of domination. In the context of the UK oil industry, Carson describes the process of encouraging rapid development to the point that the social harms caused by rampant profiteering are left largely unchecked. Carson very clearly located dangerous working conditions in unequal power relations that are given force by particular regimes of production. His emphasis – significant in the context of the preceding section in this book – was upon the way that government policy developed a regime of speedy production through the structuring of the licensing and regulatory systems. What he called a political economy of speed (Carson, 1982) allowed the development of an 'extraordinary situation with regard to the law governing offshore safety' (Carson, 1980: 249–50) whereby the North Sea remained exempt from the regulations that applied to onshore industries, and responsibility for regulating safety remained outside the remit of the Health and Safety Executive. Instead, the Department of Energy (the 'sponsoring department' responsible for encouraging production) retained responsibility for safety regulation and allowed it to be left to a tiny, over-stretched and woefully underresourced inspectorate (Carson, 1980). Now what is important about this argument is that it locates deaths and injuries in the sector not in any features of the industry that made it inherently unsafe (as both the oil companies and the government claimed) but in the political economy of speed. As the extract by Carson points out, the chances of being killed in the 1970s UK oil industry were six times higher than in quarrying, nine times higher than in mining, and 11 times higher than in construction. Understood within the context of a very particular political economy, those remarkably high rates of death and injury were aided and abetted by the UK-government; they were, to use the concept introduced in the previous section, state-facilitated crimes.

The extract by Simpson and Elis provides a brief account of liberal and radical Marxist feminist approaches to explaining corporate crime. According to the latter perspective, the corporate victimisation of women results from the patriarchal structure of managements in corporations and a lack of formal equality in the workplace and the marketplace. And according to the former perspective, the corporate victimisation of women can be explained by the structural subordination of women in a labour market where men hold a privileged position. The patriarchal organisation of the labour process allows this structure of domination to persist because it perpetuates a higher valuation of the male contribution to production. Capital also benefits economically from this structure of patriarchal domination through its ability to divide workers along gendered lines and sustain a relatively unprotected, cheap female labour force. Simpson and Elis also begin to incorporate a class dimension to explanations of how victimisation is structured, pointing out, particularly in relation to birth-control technologies, that female victimisation is aggravated in different ways according to race and class. The following two examples show clearly how corporations act as structures of class/race/gender domination in the ways outlined by Simpson and Elis.

In the 1970s and 1980s the pharmaceutical company A.H. Robbins produced the Dalkon Shield contraceptive intra-uterine device. The company marketed and advertised the Dalkon Shield using falsified claims about its safety, despite senior management being made aware of serious health risks at an early stage of its distribution. In the US alone, it was reported that the Dalkon Shield injured 235,000 and killed 33 women, and caused 200 cases of spontaneous septic abortion. Soon after it began to discover problems in the US, A.H. Robbins began an aggressive export policy to 'dump' the devices on Third World economies. Subsidised by the government agency USAID, as part of its policy of promoting birth control in the developing world, the company sold 4.5 million unsterilised Dalkon Shields in relatively poor countries, eventually distributing a total of 4.5 million in 80 countries. They did so in the knowledge that less developed countries would have even lower standards of regulation, and even less access to product information than the US (Mintz, 1985).

The case of Norplant, a contraceptive implant sold in the US, is in many ways comparable with the more widely known case of the Dalkon Shield. Norplant is a plastic tube that is implanted into the arms of women to slowly release an artificial hormone to prevent pregnancy for up to 5 years. The product was aggressively marketed in the 1990s, mainly at women in low-income groups. Particular incentives were offered, through schemes administered by USAID, to users in developing countries and several states offered financial payments to women who agreed to use Norplant. Very soon after Norplant had been distributed, users reported experiencing a range of side-effects, including head-aches, heavy and continuous menstrual bleeding, blood clots, nausea, excessive weight gain, abdominal pain, depression and visual impairment. Yet, despite a growing body of evidence and mounting complaints, the company Wyeth Pharma-ceuticals continued to distribute the implant. Those side-effects gave rise to 400 class actions involving 50,000 women. Because Norplant was targeted at low-income groups and in states where there was a relatively large black population, the victims of its side-effects were disproportionately black women. Indeed, Roberts (1997) views the Norplant saga as another episode in the long history of state control over African-American women's reproductive freedom. Norplant was launched in the UK in 1993 and then withdrawn in 1999 not, according to the company, because it was unsafe, but because of adverse publicity and because of the US legal actions (*BBC News*, 30 April 1999). Neither Wyeth nor A.H. Robbins – nor for that matter their directors or chief executives – were prosecuted for any criminal offence in either of those cases. The legal actions against them were all civil cases taken by private citizens.

Beyond the clear resonance with the Simpson and Elis extract, those cases illustrate usefully the relevance of each of the perspectives developed in this section. First of all, they raise questions about whether cases like this could have occurred without the existence of a bureaucratised moral distance between corporate managements and the consequences of their decisions. Could they have occurred without the use of techniques of neutralisation by management hierarchies? In the pharmaceutical industry, a 'higher loyalty' to the pursuit of a healthy society is often used to legitimise the distribution of untested products (Braithwaite, 1984). Is the marketing of unsafe products made easier by the process of differential association? How far can the cases be understood as the result of the bounded rationality and amorality of corporate decision-making? And to what extent can they be explained by a political economy that encourages speedy profits at all costs? Finally, to what extent were each of the cases a result of the features of consumer market structures that thrive on, and reproduce, gendered and racialised inequalities? To recognise that each of the perspectives in this section might offer relevant and powerful explanations for the crimes of the powerful is not to say that they offer equally applicable explanations but it is to say that because the phenomena that we study have complex origins they also require complex explanations.

There have, over the years, been a number of attempts to build an integrated theory of corporate and white-collar crime that captures the multi-level complexity of institutionally produced crime (for example, Coleman 1987; Punch 2000; Vaughan 1992). However, such a search for an integrated theory may be pointless, given the shifting social formations and hugely different institutional contexts that give rise to crimes of the powerful. It is doubtful that Bauman's theory of the Holocaust could easily be applied to the case of the Rwandan genocide, just as it is doubtful that Sutherland's theory of differential association is as relevant to understanding the organisational deviance of the transnational corporations of today, as it was to understanding the crimes of General Motors in 1930s America. This is not to devalue those approaches. But it is to say that the quest for a universal theory of crimes of the powerful is ultimately prevented by the complexity and ever-changing forms through which power is realised in contemporary societies. Moreover, no matter how sophisticated, it may be that an integrated theory of crimes of the powerful is not achievable because what is at issue when we seek to explain their origins and incidence is not simply 'crime' but, more fundamentally, 'the manner in which that power is exercised in our society' (Geis and Meier, 1977: 19). As we will see in the next section, what needs explaining is how crimes of the powerful occur in ways that are sympto-matic of, and at the same time organise the ongoing, and ever-shifting, domination of, powerful groups and institutions. In other words, what is at stake in understandings of crimes of the powerful is not merely how a particular criminal event occurs, but how the organisation of domination is achieved and reproduced.

Note

1 Merton's strain theory was a development of French sociologist Emile Durkheim's concept of anomie. The basic idea in anomie is that deviance from dominant social values is encouraged by the instability (or state of anomie) of a given society, since rapid social change undermines the moral regulation that binds the society around a particular set of values.

References

Bauman, Z. (1989) *Modernity and the Holocaust*. Cambridge: Polity Press.

Braithwaite, J. (1984) *Corporate Crime in the Pharmaceutical Industry*. London: Routledge, Kegan & Paul.

Braithwaite, J. (1989) *Crime, Shame and Reintegration*. Cambridge: Cambridge University Press.

Carson, W.G. (1980) 'The Other Price of Britain's Oil: Regulating safety on offshore oil installations in the British sector of the North Sea', *Contemporary Crises*, 4: 239–66.

Carson, W.G. (1982) *The Other Price of Britain's Oil*. Oxford: Martin Robertson.

Chambliss, W. (1969) *Crime and the Legal Process*. New York: McGraw-Hill.

Coleman, J. (1987) 'Toward an Integrated Theory of White-collar Crime', *American Journal of Sociology*, 93(2): 406–39.

Geis, G. and Meier, R. (1977) 'Introduction' in G. Geis and R. Meier (eds) *White-Collar Crime: Offences in business, politics and the professions*. New York: Free Press.

Matza, D. (1969) *Becoming Deviant*. Englewood Cliffs, NJ: Prentice Hall.

Merton, R. (1949) *Social Theory and Social Structure*. New York: Free Press.

Mintz, M. (1985) *At Any Cost: Corporate greed, women and the Dalkon Shield*. New York: Pantheon.

Passas, N. (1990) 'Anomie and Corporate Crime', *Contemporary Crises*, 14.

Passas, N. (2000) 'Global Anomie, Dysnomie, and Economic Crime: Hidden consequences of neoliberalism and globalization in Russia and around the world', *Social Justice*, 27(2).

Punch, M. (2000) 'Suite Violence: Why managers murder and corporations kill', *Crime, Law and Social Change*, 33: 243–80.

Roberts, D. (1997) *Killing the Black Body: Race, reproduction and the meaning of liberty*. New York: Vintage.

Sutherland, E. (1949) *White-Collar Crime*. New York: Holt, Reinhart and Winston.

Sykes, G. and Matza, D. (1957) 'Techniques of neutralisation: A theory of delinquency', *American Sociological Review*, 22: 664–70.

Vaughan, D. (1992) 'The Macro-Micro Connection in White-collar Crime Theory' in K. Schlegel and D. Weisburd (eds) *White-Collar Crime Reconsidered*. Boston: Northeastern University Press. pp. 124–45.

Wells, C. (2001) *Corporations and Criminal Responsibility*, 2nd edition. Oxford: Oxford University Press.

26

Modernity and the Holocaust
Zygmunt Bauman

[...] Murderous motives in general, and motives for mass murder in particular, have been many and varied. They range from pure, cold-blooded calculation of competitive gain, to equally pure, disinterested hatred or heterophobia. Most communal strifes and genocidal campaigns against aborigines lie comfortably within this range. If accompanied by an ideology, the latter does not go much further than a simple 'us or them' vision of the world, and a precept 'There is no room for both of us', or 'The only good injun is a dead injun'. The adversary is expected to follow mirror-image principles only if allowed to. Most genocidal ideologies rest on a devious symmetry of assumed intentions and actions.

Truly modern genocide is different. *Modern genocide is genocide with a purpose.* Getting rid of the adversary is not an end in itself. It is a means to an end: a necessity that stems from the ultimate objective, a step that one has to take if one wants ever to reach the end of the road. *The end itself is a grand vision of a better, and radically different, society.* Modern genocide is an element of social engineering, meant to bring about a social order conforming to the design of the perfect society.

To the initiators and the managers of modern genocide, society is a subject of planning and conscious design. One can and should do more about the society than change one or several of its many details, improve it here or there, cure some of its troublesome ailments. One can and should set oneself goals more ambitious and radical: one can and should remake the society, force it to conform to an overall, scientifically conceived plan. One can create a society that is objectively better than the one 'merely existing' – that is, existing without conscious intervention. Invariably, there is an aesthetic dimension to the design: the ideal world about to be built conforms to the standards of superior beauty. Once built, it will be richly satisfying, like a perfect work of art; it will be a world which, in Alberti's immortal words, no adding, diminishing or altering could improve. [...]

[...] Stalin's and Hitler's victims were not killed in order to capture and colonize the territory they occupied. Often they were killed in a dull, mechanical fashion with no human emotions – hatred included – to enliven it. They were killed because they did not fit, for one reason or another, the scheme of a perfect society. Their killing was not the work of destruction, but creation. They were eliminated, so that an objectively better human world – more efficient, more moral, more beautiful – could be established. A Communist world. Or a racially pure, Aryan world. In both cases, a harmonious world, conflict-free, docile in the hands of their rulers, orderly, controlled. People tainted with ineradicable blight of their past or origin could not be fitted into such unblemished, healthy and shining world. Like weeds, their nature could not be changed. They could not be improved or re-educated. They had to be eliminated for reasons of genetic or ideational heredity – of a natural mechanism, resilient and immune to cultural processing.

The two most notorious and extreme cases of modern genocide did not betray the spirit of modernity. They did not deviously depart from the main track of the civilizing process. They were the most consistent, uninhibited expressions of that spirit. They attempted to reach the most ambitious aims of the civilizing process most other processes stop short of, not necessarily for the lack of good will. They showed what the rationalizing, designing, controlling dreams and efforts of modern civilization are able to accomplish if not mitigated, curbed or counter-acted.

These dreams and efforts have been with us for a long time. They spawned the vast and powerful arsenal of technology and managerial skills. They gave birth to institutions which serve the sole purpose of instrumentalizing human behaviour to such an extent that any aim may be pursued with efficiency and vigour, with or without ideological dedication or moral approval on the part of the pursuers. They legitimize the rulers' monopoly on ends and the confinement of the ruled to the role of means. They define most actions as means, and means as subordination – to the ultimate end, to those who set it, to supreme will, to supra-individual knowledge. [...]

[...] There are two antithetical ways in which one can approach the explana-tion of the Holocaust. One can consider the horrors of mass murder as evidence of the fragility of civilization, or one can see them as evidence of its awesome potential. One can argue that, with criminals in control, civilized rules of behaviour may be suspended, and thus the eternal beast always hiding just beneath the skin of the socially drilled being may break free. Alternatively, one can argue that, once armed with the sophisticated technical and conceptual products of modern civilization, men can do things their nature would otherwise prevent them from doing. To put it differently; one can, following the Hobbesian tradition, conclude that the inhuman pre-social state has not yet been fully eradicated, all civilizing efforts notwithstanding. Or one can, on the contrary, insist that the civilizing process has succeeded in substituting artificial and flexible patterns of human conduct for natural drives, and hence made possible a scale of inhumanity and destruction which had remained inconceivable as long as natural predispositions guided human action. I propose to opt for the second approach, and substantiate it in the following discussion.

The fact that most people (including many a social theorist) instinctively choose the first, rather than the second, approach, is a testimony to the remarkable success of the etiological myth which, in one variant or another, Western civilization has deployed over the years to legitimize its spatial hegemony by projecting it as temporal superiority. Western civilization has articulated its struggle for domination in terms of the holy battle of humanity against barbarism, reason against ignorance, objectivity against prejudice, progress against degeneration, truth against superstition, science against magic, rationality against passion. It has interpreted the history of its ascendance as the gradual yet relentless substitution of human mastery over nature for the mastery of nature over man. It has presented its own accomplishment as, first and foremost, a decisive advance in human freedom of action, creative potential and security. It has identified freedom and security with its own type of social order: Western, modern society is defined as *civilized* society, and a civilized society in turn is understood as a state from which most of the natural ugliness and morbidity, as well as most of the immanent human propensity to cruelty and violence, have been eliminated or at least suppressed. The popular image of civilized society is, more than anything else, that of the absence of violence; of a gentle, polite, soft society. [...]

[...] What in fact has happened in the course of the civilizing process, is the redeployment of violence, and the re-distribution of access to violence. Like so many other things which we have been trained to abhor and detest, violence has been taken out of sight, rather than forced out of existence. It has become invisible, that is, from the vantage point of narrowly circumscribed and privatized personal experience. It has been enclosed instead in segregated and isolated territories, on the whole inaccessible to ordinary members of society; or evicted to the 'twilight areas', off-limits for a large majority (and the majority which counts) of society's members; or exported to distant places which on the whole are irrelevant for the life-business of civilized humans (one can always cancel holiday bookings).

The ultimate consequence of all this is the concentration of violence. Once centralized and free from competition, means of coercion would be capable of reaching unheard of results even if not technically perfected. Their concentration, however, triggers and boosts the escalation of technical improvements, and thus the effects of concentration are further magnified. As Anthony Giddens repeatedly emphasized (see, above all, his *Contemporary Critique of Historical Materialism* (1981), and *The Constitution of Society* (1984), the removal of violence from the daily life of civilized societies has always been intimately associated with a thoroughgoing militarization of inter-societal exchange and inner-societal production of order; standing armies and police forces brought together technically superior weapons and superior technology of bureaucratic management. For the last two centuries, the number of people who have suffered violent death as the result of such militarization has been steadily growing to reach a volume unheard of before. [...]

[...] All division of labour (also such division as results from the mere hierarchy of command) creates a distance between most of the contributors to the final outcome of collective activity, and the outcome itself. Before the last links in the bureaucratic chain of power (the direct executors) confront their task, most of the preparatory operations which brought about that confrontation have been already performed by persons who had no personal experience, and sometimes not the knowledge either, of the task in question. Unlike in a pre-modern unit of work, in which all steps of the hierarchy share in the same occupational skills, and the practical knowledge of working operations actually grows towards the top of the ladder (the master knows the same as his journeyman or apprentice, only more and better), persons occupying successive rungs of modern bureaucracy differ sharply in the kind of expertise and professional training their jobs require. They may be able to put themselves imaginatively into their subordinates' position; this may even help in maintaining 'good human relations' inside the office – but it is not the condition of proper performance of the task, not of the effectiveness of the bureaucracy as a whole. In fact, most bureaucracies do not treat seriously the romantic recipe that requires every bureaucrat, and particularly those who occupy the top, to 'start from the bottom' so that on the way to the summit they should acquire, and memorize, the experience of the entire slope. Mindful of the multiplicity of skills which the managerial jobs of various magnitudes demand, most bureaucracies practise instead separate avenues of recruitment for different levels of the hierarchy. Perhaps it is true that each soldier carries a marshal's baton in his knapsack, but few marshals, and few colonels or captains for that matter, keep soldiers' bayonets in their briefcases.

What such practical and mental distance from the final product means is that most functionaries of the bureaucratic hierarchy may give commands without full knowledge of their effects. In many cases they would find it difficult to visualize those effects. Usually, they only have an abstract, detached awareness of them; the kind of knowledge which is best expressed in statistics, which measure the results without passing any judgement, and certainly not moral ones. In their files and their minds the results are at best diagramatically represented as curves or sectors of a circle; ideally, they would appear as a column of numbers. Graphically or numerically represented, the final outcomes of their commands are devoid of substance. The graphs measure the *progress* of work, they say nothing about the nature of the operation or its objects. The graphs make tasks of widely different character mutually exchangeable; only the quantifiable success or failure matter, and seen from that point of view, the tasks do not differ. [...]

[...] Another, equally important effect of bureaucratic context of action is *dehumanization of the objects of bureaucratic operation*; the possibility to express these objects in purely technical, ethically neutral terms. [...]

[...] Dehumanization starts at the point when, thanks to the distantiation, the objects at which the bureaucratic operation is aimed can, and are, reduced to a set of quantitative measures. For railway managers, the only meaningful articulation of their object is in terms of tonnes per kilometre. They do not deal with humans, sheep, or barbed wire; they only deal with the cargo, and this means an entity consisting entirely of measurements and devoid of quality. For most bureaucrats, even such a category as cargo would mean too strict a quality-bound restriction. They deal only with the financial effects of their actions. Their object is money. Money is the sole object that appears on both input and output ends, and *pecunia*, as the ancients shrewdly observed, definitely *non olet*. As they grow, bureaucratic companies seldom allow themselves to be confined to one qualitatively distinct area of activity. They spread sideways, guided in their movements by a sort of *lucrotropism* – a sort of gravitational pulling force of the highest returns on their capital. As we remember, the whole operation of the Holocaust was managed by the Economic Administration Section of the *Reichsicherheithauptamt*. We know that this one assignment, exceptionally, was not intended as a strategem or a camouflage.

Reduced, like all other objects of bureaucratic management, to pure, quality-free measurements, human objects lose their distinctiveness. They are already dehumanized – in the sense that the language in which things that happen to them (or are done to them) are narrated, safeguards its referents from ethical evaluation. In fact, this language is unfit for normative-moral statements. It is only humans that may be objects of ethical propositions. (True, moral statements do extend sometimes to other, non-human living beings; but they may do so only by expanding from their original anthropomorphic foothold.) Humans lose this capacity once they are reduced to ciphers.

Dehumanization is inextricably related to the most essential, rationalizing tendency of modern bureaucracy. As all bureaucracies affect in some measure some human objects, the adverse impact of dehumanization is much more common than the habit to identify it almost totally with its genocidal effects would suggest. Soldiers are told to shoot *targets*, which *fall* when they are *hit*. Employees of big companies are encouraged to destroy *competition*. Officers of welfare agencies operate *discretionary awards* at one time, *personal credits* at another. Their objects are *supplementary benefit recipients*. It is difficult to perceive and remember the humans behind all such technical terms. The point is that as far as the bureaucratic goals go, they are better not perceived and not remembered.

Once effectively dehumanized, and hence cancelled as potential subjects of moral demands, human objects of bureaucratic task-performance are viewed with ethical indifference, which soon turns into disapprobation and censure when their resistance, or lack of co-operation, slows down the smooth flow of bureaucratic routine. [...]

[...] Bureaucracy contributed to the perpetuation of the Holocaust not only through its inherent capacities and skills, but also through its immanent ailments. The tendency of all bureaucracies to lose sight of the original goal and to concentrate on the means instead – the means which turn into the ends – has been widely noted, analysed and described. The Nazi bureaucracy did not escape its impact. Once set in motion, the machinery of murder developed its own impetus: the more it excelled in cleansing the territories it controlled of the Jews, the more actively it sought new lands where it could exercise its newly acquired skills. With the approaching military defeat of Germany, the original purpose of the *Endlösung* was becoming increasingly unreal. What kept the murdering machine going then was solely its own routine and impetus. The skills of mass murder had to be used simply because they were there. The experts created the objects for their own expertise. We remember the experts of Jewish Desks in Berlin introducing every new petty restriction on German Jews who had long before all but disappeared from German soil; we remember the SS commanders who forbade the *Wehrmacht* generals from keeping alive the Jewish craftsmen they badly needed for military operations. But nowhere was the morbid tendency of substituting the means for the ends more visible than in the uncanny and macabre episode of the murder of Romanian and Hungarian Jews, perpetrated with the Eastern Front just a few miles away, and at an enormous cost to the war effort: priceless rail carriages and engines, troops and administrative resources were diverted from military tasks in order to cleanse distant parts of Europe for the German habitat which was never to be.

Bureaucracy is intrinsically *capable* of genocidal action. To *engage* in such an action, it needs an encounter with another invention of modernity: a bold design of a better, more reasonable and rational social order – say a racially uniform, or a classless society – and above all the capacity of drawing such designs and determination to make them efficacious. Genocide follows when two common and abundant inventions of modern times meet. It is only their meeting which has been, thus far, uncommon and rare. [...]

27

Human rights and crimes of the state: the culture of denial
Stanley Cohen

[...] More familiar ground to criminologists, is the body of literature known as "motivational accounts" or "vocabulary of motives" theory. The application of this theory in Sykes and Matza's (1957) "techniques of neutralisation" paper is a criminological classic; there is no need to explain the idea to this audience.

The theory assumes that motivational accounts which actors (offenders) give of their (deviant) behaviour must be acceptable to their audience (or audiences). Moreover, accounts are not just *post facto* improvisations, but are drawn upon in advance from the cultural pool of motivational vocabularies available to actors and observers (and honoured by systems of legality and morality). Remember Sykes and Matza's original list; each technique of neutralisation is a way of denying the moral bind of the law and the blame attached to the offence: denial of injury ("no one got hurt"); denial of victim ("they started it"; "it's all their fault"); denial of responsibility ("I didn't mean to do it", "they made me do it"); condemnation of the condemners ("they are just as bad") and appeal to higher loyalties (friends, gang, family, neighbourhood).

Something very strange happens if we apply this list not to the techniques for denying or neutralising conventional delinquency but to human rights violations and state crimes. For Sykes and Matza's point was precisely that delinquents are *not* "political" in the sense implied by subcultural theory; that is, they are not committed to an alternative value system nor do they withdraw legitimacy from conventional values. The necessity for verbal neutralisation shows precisely the continuing bind of conventional values.

But exactly the same techniques appear in the manifestly political discourse of human rights violations – whether in collective political trials (note, for example, the Nuremberg trials or the Argentinian junta trial) or official government responses to human rights reports (a genre which I am studying) or media debates about war crimes and human rights abuses. I will return soon to "literal denial", that first twist of the denial spiral which I identified earlier (it didn't happen, it can't happen here, they are all liars). Neutralisation comes into play when you acknowledge (admit) that something happened – but either refuse to accept the category of acts to which it is assigned ("crime" or "massacre") or present it as morally justified. Here are the original neutralisation techniques, with corresponding examples from the realm of human rights violations:

- *denial of injury* – they exaggerate, they don't feel it, they are used to violence, see what they do to each other.
- *denial of victim* – they started it, look what they've done to us; they are the terrorists, we are just defending ourselves, we are the real victims.
- *denial of responsibility* – here, instead of the criminal versions of psychological incapacity or diminished responsibility (I didn't know what I was doing, I blacked out, etc) we find a denial of individual moral responsiblity on the grounds of obedience: I was following orders, only doing my duty, just a cog in the machine. (For individual offenders like the ordinary soldier, this is the most pervasive and powerful of all denial systems).
- *condemnation of the condemners* – here, the politics are obviously more explicit than in the original delinquency context. Instead of condemning the police for being corrupt and biased or teachers for being hypocrites, we have the vast discourse of official denial used by the modern state to protect its public image: the whole world is picking on us; they are using double standards to judge us; it's worse elsewhere (Syria, Iraq, Guatamala or wherever is convenient to name); they are condemning us only because of their anti-semitism (the Israeli version), their hostility to Islam (the Arab version), their racism and cultural imperialism in imposing Western values (all Third World tyrannies).
- *appeal to higher loyalty* – the original subdued "ideology" is now total and self-righteous justification. The appeal to the army, the nation, the *volk*, the sacred mission, the higher cause – whether the revolution, "history", the purity of Islam, Zionism, the defence of the free world or state security. As the tragic events of the last few years show, despite the end of the cold war, the end of history and the decline of meta narratives, there is no shortage of "higher loyalties", old and new.

Let us remember the implications of accounts theory for our subject. Built into the offender's action, is the knowledge that certain accounts will be accepted. Soldiers on trial for, say, killing a peaceful demonstrator, can offer the account of "obeying orders" because this will be honoured by the legal system and the wider public. This honouring is, of course, not a simple matter: Were the orders clear? Did the soldier suspect that the order was illegal? Where in the chain of command did the order originate from? These, and other ambiguities, make up the stuff of legal, moral and political discourses of denial.

I have no time here to apply each of these theoretical frameworks – psychoanalysis, cognitive psychology, bystander theory, motivational accounts etc – to my case study of reactions to knowledge of human rights violations and state crimes. (There are obviously also many other relevant fields: political socialisation and mobilisation, mass media analysis, collective memory). For illustration only, let me list some elementary forms of denial which these theories might illuminate.

I will distinguish three forms of denial, each of which operates at (i) the individual or psychic level and (ii) at the organised, political, collective or official level.

(1) Denial of the Past

At the individual level, there are the complex psychic mechanisms which allow us to "forget" unpleasant, threatening or terrible information. Memories of what we have done or seen or known are selected out and filtered.

At the collective level, there are the organised attempts to cover up the record of past atrocities. The most dramatic and successful example in the modern era is the eighty years of organised denial by successive Turkish governments of the 1915–17 genocide against the Armenians – in which some one and a half million people lost their lives (Hovanissian, 1986). This denial has been sustained by deliberate propaganda, lying and cover-ups, forging of documents, suppression of archives and bribing of scholars. The West, especially the USA, has colluded by not referring to the massacres in the UN, ignoring memorial ceremonies and by surrendering to Turkish pressure in NATO and other arenas of strategic cooperation.

The less successful example, of course, is the so called "revisionist" history of holocaust of European Jews, dismissed as a "hoax" or a "myth".

At both levels, we can approach the process of denial through its opposite: the attempt to recover or uncover the past. At the individual level, the entire psychoanalytic procedure itself is a massive onslaught on individual denial and self-deception. At the political level, there is the opening of collective memory, the painful coming to terms with the past, the literal and metaphorical digging up on graves when regimes change and try to exorcise their history.

(2) Literal Denial

Here we enter the grey area sketched out by psychoanalysis and cognitive theory. In what senses can we be said to "know" about something we profess not to know about? If we do shut something out of knowledge, is this unconscious or conscious? Under what conditions (for example, information overload or desensitisation) is such denial likely to take place?

There are many different versions of literal denial, some of which appear to be wholly individual, others which are clearly structured by the massive resources of the state. We didn't know, we didn't see anything, it couldn't have happened without us knowing (or it could have happened without us knowing). Or: things like this can't happen here, people like us don't do things like this. Or: you can't believe the source of your knowledge: – victims, sympathisers, human rights monitors, journalists are biased, partial or ignorant.

The psychological ambiguities of "literal denial" and their political implications are nicely illustrated by the psychoanalyst John Steiner's re-interpretation of the Oedipus drama (Steiner, 1985 and 1990).

The standard version of the legend is a tragedy in which Oedipus is a victim of fate who bravely pursues the truth. At the beginning he does not know the truth (that he has killed his father, that he had sexual relations with his mother); at the end he does. This is taken as a paradigm for the therapeutic process itself: the patient in analysis to whom, gradually and painfully, the secrets of the unconscious art revealed. But alongside this version, Steiner shows, Sophocles also conveys a quite different message in the original drama: the message is that the main characters in the play must have been aware of the identity of Oedipus and realised that he had committed patricide and incest. There is a deliberate ambiguity throughout the text about the nature of this awareness – just how much did each character know? Each of the participants (including Oedipus himself) and especially the various court officials, had (good) different reasons for denying their knowledge, for staging a cover up. The Oedipus story is not at all about the discovery of truth, but the denial of truth – a cover up like Watergate, Iran, Contra. Thus the question: how much did Nixon or Bush "know"?

The ambiguity about how conscious or unconscious our knowledge is, how much we are aware of what we say we are unaware, is nicely captured in Steiner's title "Turning a Blind Eye". This suggests the possibility of *simultaneously* knowing and not knowing. We are not talking about the simple lie or fraud where facts are accessible but lead to a conclusion which is knowingly evaded. This, of course is standard in the organised government cover up: bodies are burnt, evidence is concealed, officials are given detailed instructions on how to lie. Rather, we are talking about the more common situation where "we are vaguely aware that we choose not to look at the facts without being conscious of what it is we are evading' (Steiner, 1985, p 61)

(3) Implicatory Denial

The forms of denial that we conceptualise as excuses, justifications, rationalisations or neutralisations, do not assert that the event did not happen. They seek to negotiate or impose a different construction of the event from what might appear the case. At the individual level, you know and admit to what you have done, seen or heard about. At the organised level, the event is also registered but is subjected to cultural reconstruction (for example, through euphemistic, technical or legalistic terminology). The point is to deny the implications – psychological and moral – of what is known. The common linguistic structure is "yes, but". Yes, detainees are being tortured but there is no other way to obtain information. Yes, Bosnian women are being raped, but what can a mere individual thousands of miles away do about it?

"Denial of Responsiblity", as I noted earlier, is one of the most common forms of implicatory denial. The sociology of "crimes of obedience" has received sustained attention, notably by Kelman and Hamilton (1989). The anatomy of obedience and conformity – the frightening degree to which ordinary people are willing to inflict great psychological and physical harm to others – was originally revealed by Milgram's famous experiment. Kelman and Hamilton begin from history rather than a university laboratory: the famous case of Lieutenant Calley and the My Lai massacre during the Vietnam War in May 1968 when a platoon of American soldiers massacred some 400 civilians. From this case and other "guilt free" or "sanctioned" massacres, they extract a rather stable set of conditions under which crimes of obedience will occur:

(i) *Authorisation*: when acts are ordered, encouraged, or tacitly approved by those in authority, then normal moral principles are replaced by the duty to obey;

(ii) *Routinisation*: the first step is often difficult, but when you pass the initial moral and psychological barrier, then the pressure to continue is powerful. You become involved without considering the implications; it's all in a day's work. This tendency is re-inforced by special vocabularies and euphemisms ("surgical strike") or a simple sense of routine. (Asked about what he thought he was doing, Calley replied in one of the most chilling sentences of all times: "It was no big deal");

(iii) *Dehumanisation*: when the qualities of being human are deprived from the other, then the usual principles of morality do not apply. The enemy is described as animals, monsters, gooks, sub-humans. A whole language excludes them from your shared moral universe.

The conditions under which perpetrators behave can be translated into the very bystander rationalisations which allow the action in the first place and then deny its implications afterwards. As Kelman and Hamilton show in their analysis of successive public opinion surveys (in which people were asked both to imagine how they would react to a My Lai situation themselves and to judge the actual perpetrators), obedience and authorisation are powerful justifications. And observers as well as offenders are subject to desensitisation (the bombardment by horror stories from the media to a point that you cannot absorb them any more and they are no longer "news") and dehumanisation. [...]

28

White collar crime: the uncut version
Edwin Sutherland

[...] As a part of the process of learning practical business, a young man with idealism and thoughtfulness for others is inducted into white collar crime. In many cases he is ordered by managers to do things which he regards as unethical or illegal, while in other cases he learns from those who have the same rank as his own how they make a success. He learns specific techniques of violating the law, together with definitions of situations in which those techniques may be used. Also he develops a general ideology. This ideology grows in part out of the specific practices and is in the nature of generalization from concrete experiences, but in part it is transmitted as a generalization by phrases such as "We are not in business for our health," "Business is business," and "No business was ever built on the beatitudes." These generalizations, whether transmitted as such or constructed from concrete practices, assist the neophyte in business to accept the illegal practices and provide rationalizations for them.

All the preceding documents came from young men in subordinate positions and are in no sense a random sample of persons in such positions. Unfortunately, similar documents even of a scattered nature are not available for the managers of large industries. No firsthand research study from this point of view has ever been reported. Gustavus Meyer in his *History of American Fortunes,* and Lundberg in his *America's Sixty Families* have demonstrated that many of the large American fortunes originated in illegal practices. On the other hand, they pay little attention to the process by which illegal behavior develops in the person. [...]

[...] Business firms have the objective of maximum profits. When one firm devises a method for increasing profits, other firms become aware of the method and adopt it, perhaps a little more quickly and a little more generally if the firms are competitors in the same market than if they are not competitors. The diffusion of illegal practices which increase profits is facilitated by the trend toward centralization of the control of industry by investment banks and by the conferences of business concerns in trade associations. The process of diffusion will be considered first in relation to competition, and subsequently with reference to other relations.

The diffusion of illegal practices among competitors is illustrated in the following incident in a food manufacturing concern. A chemist who had been employed to advise this firm as to the scientific basis for claims in advertising made the following statement regarding his experiences with the firm.

When I got members of the firm off in a corner and we were talking confidentially, they frankly deplored the misrepresentations in their advertisements. At the same time they said it was necessary to advertise in this manner in order to attract the attention of customers and sell their products. Since other firms were making extravagant statements regarding their products, we must make extravagant statements regarding our products. A mere statement of fact regarding our products would make no impression on customers in the face of the ads of other firms. [...]

[...] General Motors devised the fraudulent advertisement of its interest rate on installment purchases at 6 percent, when in fact the rate was more than 11 percent. The other automobile companies also had interest rates of about 11 percent, but they advertised their interest rate as 6 percent as soon as General Motors began to do so. Again, when one automobile company published an advertisement of the price and specifications of a certain model, together with a picture of a more expensive model, thus misrepresenting their products, the other companies in the automobile industry generally published similar advertisements with similar misrepresentations. Within a few months after the tire dealers had solemnly adopted a code of ethics in advertising, including a pledge not to use misrepresentations, one tire manufacturer announced a special cut-rate price for tires on the Fourth of July and Labor Day, in which the savings were grossly and fraudulently misrepresented; the other tire manufacturers promptly made similar announcements of cut-rate sales with similar misrepresentations.

Thus competition in advertising drives the participants to the extremes and when one corporation violates the law in this respect other corporations do likewise.

Practices in restraint of trade are similarly diffused. [...] More frequently practices in restraint of trade are diffused by conferences and agreements among competitors. Sometimes definite coercion is employed in forcing competitors into illegal practices in restraint of trade. This is illustrated by the case in which the Aluminum Company of America, after failing to persuade the Dow Chemical Company to enter into an illegal agreement regarding magnesium, initiated an infringement suit against the latter company; this suit was withdrawn as soon as Dow Chemical Company agreed to enter into the illegal conspiracy. [...]

[...] Differential association is a hypothetical explanation of crime from the point of view of the process by which a person is initiated into crime. Social disorganization is a hypothetical explanation of crime from the point of view of the society. These two hypotheses are consistent with each other and one is the counterpart of the other. Both apply to ordinary crime as well as to white collar crime.

Social disorganization may be either of two types: anomie, or the lack of standards which direct the behavior of members of a society in general or in specific areas of behavior; or the organization within a society of groups which are

in conflict with reference to specified practices. Briefly stated, social disorganization may appear in the form of lack of standards or conflict of standards.

Two conditions are favorable to disorganization of our society in the control of
business behavior: first, the fact that the behavior is complex, technical, and not
readily observable by inexperienced citizens; second, the fact that the society is
changing rapidly in its business relations. In any period of rapid change, old
standards tend to break down and a period of time is required for the development
of new standards.

The anomie form of social disorganization is related to the change from the
earlier system of free competition and free enterprise to the developing system of
private collectivism and governmental regulation of business. The tradition has
been that a government should not intervene in the regulation of business but that
free competition and supply and demand should regulate economic processes.
This tradition was generally held by the people of the United States in the earlier
period. While that tradition has been largely abandoned in practice, it retains great
force as an ideology, which has been designated "the folklore of capitalism." In
practice businessmen are more devoted than any other part of current society to
the policy of social planning. This is social planning in the interest of businessmen.
Social planning for the more inclusive society is criticized by businessmen as
"regimentation," "bureaucracy," "visionary," and "communistic." In this transition
from one social system toward a different social system, anomie has existed in two
forms. First, the businessmen passed through a period of uncertainty [...] They
were dissatisfied with the system of free competition and free enterprise and had
no substitute on which they could reach consensus. This period cannot be sharply
limited but is located within the three to six decades after the Civil War. Second,
the general public has passed or is passing through the same uncertainty and
conflict of standards, starting at a later period than the businessmen did and
continuing after businessmen had reached a new general consensus.

Conflict of standards is the second form of social disorganization. This is
similar to differential association in that it involves a ratio between organization
favorable to violations of law and organization rather than social disorganization.
Business has a rather tight organization for the violation of business regulations
while the political society is not similarly organized against violations of business
regulations.

Evidence has been presented in previous chapters that crimes of business are
organized crimes. This evidence includes references not only to gentlemen's
agreements, pools, trade associations, patent agreements, cartels, conferences, and
other informal understandings, but also to the tentacles which business throws out
into the government and the public for the control of those portions of the society.
The definition of specified acts as illegal is a prerequisite to white collar crime, and
to that extent the political society is necessarily organized against white collar
crime. The statutes, however, have little importance in the control of business
behavior unless they are supported by an administration which is intent on
stopping the illegal behavior. In turn the political administration has little force in
stopping such behavior unless it is supported by a public which is intent on the
enforcement of the law. This calls for a clear-cut opposition between the public

and the government, on the one side, and the businessmen who violate the law, on the other. This clear-cut opposition does not exist and the absence of this opposition is evidence of the lack of organization against white collar crime. What is, in theory, a war loses much of its conflict because of the fraternization between the two forces. White collar crimes continue because of this lack of organization on the part of the public. [...]

29

Anomie and corporate deviance
Nikos Passas

[...] A central proposition of anomie theory is that discrepancies between cultural goals and institutional means available to people for the achievement of these goals make for a weaker commitment to prevailing standards (i.e., anomie or anomie trends) and deviant behaviour. It stresses the point that the over-emphasis on success goals and the striving for the realisation of continuously higher targets are culturally induced. Because of limited access to opportunities, the lower classes have been seen by Merton as more vulnerable to pressures conducive to anomie and deviance than the upper classes. By consolidating anomie theory with reference group and relative deprivation analysis, however, it can be shown that, as the meaning and content of success goals vary from one part of the social structure to another, similar difficulties in attaining diversely defined goals may be faced by people in the upper social reaches too; they are, therefore, far from immune to pressures towards deviance (cf. Passas 1987; Passas 1988: chapters 4 and 5).

Further, it is essential to note that the maxime of ceaseless striving for success – especially monetary success – is not simply a cultural message, which just happens to obtain in contemporary societies. It is also reinforced by the capitalist mode of production in Western countries. It is inherent to this mode of production and, one might argue, it corresponds to a "condition of its existence". This is not to say that the one exists because of the other, but rather that they are mutually supportive. In this context, some of the prominent goals set for business and organisations in general are profit, growth and efficiency. Although large corporations "may have other goals, such as the increase or maintenance of corporate power and prestige, along with corporate growth and stability, their paramount objectives are the *maximisation of profits* and the general financial success of the corporation ..." (Clinard 1983: 18, emphasis added). So, it is not only that profits have to be made; the target is maximum possible profits (obviously, this is a simplification, for analytical purposes, and it should not be taken as an empirical assertion that this is always so; but, one may plausibly assume that this is frequently the case). There is no defined and definite stopping point, the target is a moving one; the game chased by capitalists and capitalist corporations is typically Hydra-headed. The capitalist "race" is never-ending as competitors keep joining in. So, "even as some firms fall behind or drop out of the race, new firms enter afresh, and even the leaders must worry about this potential competition" (Bowles and Edwards 1985: 88).

Thus, cultural prescriptions correspond, in a sense, to necessities in the realm of business and corporations. Never-ending achievement, mostly measured or measurable in terms of money, is "required" for the participation in this race. These aims which shape and determine to a great extent the functioning of organisations can be best achieved when they are passed on to those working in and for them, especially to those who occupy the higher ranks. A certain degree of harmony between organisational values and goals and those of the organisation's members can be, thus, secured. Training classes and socialisation processes are promoted to attune members to the organisational goals, because, as "business firms depend on their members' skills to attain goals, they must ensure that members' motivations and values are consistent with the organisation's needs" (Vaughan [1983], 1985: 69; cf. also Peters and Waterman 1982; Ermann and Lundman 1982: 7–8).

The members' commitment to their firm's goals is further enhanced by the realisation that the attainment of their own ends depends largely on the prosperity of the firm. People's involvement in high positions in organisations, corporations, industry etc. not only facilitates and "requires" such a commitment, but may also be seen as instrumental to their personal success. It is not only in the scientific community that "the institutional goal and the personal reward are tied together" (Merton 1957: 659). In a similar manner, the personal interests of highly placed individuals are connected with those of the corporation – although they need not always coincide (comp. Vaughan [1983] 1985: 70). Thus, a combined effect of culturally propagated themes of success and continuous striving, the peculiar "business ethic", and organisational demands may be, as Gross has found upon a survey of various data, that people at the top of organisations tend to be "ambitious, shrewd and possessed of a nondemanding moral code". [...]

[...] Matza introduced the concept of "drift" to describe the "episodic release from moral constraint", a crucial part of the process leading to delinquency (Matza 1964: 69). He has avoided the related term "anomie", partly because of its polysemy and partly to "suggest the episodic rather than constant character of moral release" (Matza 1964: 69). Given that "anomie", as employed here, is a matter of degree and refers to tendencies towards the weakening of people's allegiance to prevailing social standards, Matza's contribution is relevant and can be regarded, to a certain extent, as complementary. It may be proposed that cultural messages of success, structural strains, neutralisations converting "infraction into mere action" and enabling "drift" (Matza 1964: 176), and anomie may be part of a complex circle conducive to deviant behaviour.

It must be stressed, however, that we are not dealing here with juvenile "drifters", but with respected adults in powerful and influential positions. Similarities in the mechanisms leading to deviance, in general, ought not to cloud the differences in the extent, content and consequences of techniques of neutralisation and rule-breaking behaviour in diverse structural locations. Slogans, such as "I didn't do it for myself", which prepare the ground for law violations (cf. Sykes and

Matza 1957), are not only available to young delinquents, but also to company executives. However, the demands of the larger society are not sacrificed for those of a gang or friendship clique, but in the interest of small and large corporations and their shareholders. Furthermore, unlawful practices are known and common enough for corporate officials to resort to them as the only way of coping with competition. The wider environment and economic necessities may jointly make for deviance and anomie, since highly placed managers sometimes operate on the assumption (if not certainty) that other companies do break the law. As a study of top executives among the Fortune 500 corporations has revealed, they feel that, when the interests of their shareholders are concerned, they have no right to wrap themselves "in the mantle of moral philosophers and judges". More interestingly, some argued that the economic survival of the corporation "sometimes dictated that they violate the law; if they did not, *their stockholders would suffer, and other firms 'with less scrupulous management' would win out*" (Silk and Vogel 1976: 228, emphasis added). [...]

[...] In an environment dominated by concerns of costs and benefits, a lack of effective social control is likely to promote processes resulting in deviance and anomie. It seems that deterrence of corporate deviance is not among the priority targets of societies pursuing "law and order". This is small wonder, given that implicated in such activities are people of great social significance, economic and political power. The relative immunity and impunity of executives (especially those at the top), which has been found to be a factor contributing to corporate deviance (cf. Clinard and Yeager 1980), and the complicated issues involved in the legislation and implementation of laws regulating corporations are reiterated in the literature (cf. Carson [1971], 1975; Pearce 1976; Conklin 1977; Tiedemann 1977; Carson 1982; Box 1983; Braithwaite [1984], 1986), and we need not go into detail.

It is essential, however, to note that the laxity of authorities, which fails to deter corporate deviance, is a consequence of structural contradictions. It is certainly true that corporations maintain good relations with controlling agencies, and actively participate in the drafting of government regulations. With rapid social changes, aided by technological advancements, some patterns of corporate deviance seem inevitable. This, as well as the "non-conformity" of corporate officials, can be analysed in terms of what Merton has called "institutionalised evasions of institutional norms". These develop "when practical exigencies confronting the group or collectivity (or significantly large parts of them) require adaptive behaviour which is at odds with long-standing norms, sentiments, and practices" (Merton 1968: 372). Merton has also outlined processes of interaction between controllers and controlled, whereby the extent of unavoidable deviations from rules and their degree of visibility are continuously re-arranged, so that the maximum objectives of both groups can be attained. The unrestricted observability of role-performance is resisted because strict conformity is often made difficult by situational demands, and because the interests involved are often divergent. Illustrating this, Merton has remarked that, "The strong hostility toward 'close supervision' in business and industry evidently expresses this doubly reinforced objection to the surveillance of role-performance" (Merton 1968: 397). [...]

[...] [A]nother (perhaps, parallel) effect may be the creation of a wider anomic context. In many cases the gap between principles and practices cannot be closed effectively without disrupting economic life. There are also social and technical-legal difficulties, when it comes to sanctions against law violations of large corporations. When the company itself is sentenced, its members and the public at large may be affected. Fines, for instance, may be included in the cost of production and result in increased prices of final products or services. To cite a concrete example, top executives of the companies involved in the electrical conspiracy and fined a total of $1.8 million, "persuaded the Internal Revenue Service that all legal expenses, fines, and damages could be written off as 'ordinary and necessary' expenses of doing business" (McCaghy 1985: 226). Further, it may not be possible to identify guilty individuals. Inaction, on the other hand, or perceived undue lenience can bring about anomic attitudes: disrespect for criminal law or withdrawal of allegiance to the values underpinning it. [...]

30

Ideology, hegemony and empiricism
Frank Pearce and Steve Tombs

[...] The assumption that most corporations are not in fact amoral calculators—in other words, that their adherence to regulations is not conditional upon their interpretation of their own (short-term or longer-term) self-interest—is common in the work of all those associated with the compliance theories of regulation (Hutter, Kagan and Scholz, Jamieson, Richardson *et al.*). Perhaps its clearest and most explicit expression is to be found in Bardach and Kagan's *Going by the Book* (1982), described by Keith Hawkins as 'the most important publication which argues that in some circumstances regulatory enforcement can be too stringent'.[1] In this text, these authors actually attempt to quantify the proportion of all corporations which are amoral calculators, or 'bad apples'. In fact, they assume, 'for analytical purposes', that 'bad apples'

> make up about 20 per cent of the average population of regulated enterprises in most regulatory programs ... This distribution almost certainly overesti-mates the proportion of bad apples in most regulatory programs, but it does square roughly with what commentators have said and with much regulatory practice ... (Bardach and Kagan 1982: 65)

Despite the empirical arbitrariness of such a figure—we are given no indication of the basis upon which it was arrived at—the claim that certain corporations can do anything other than attempt to maximize long-term profitability is theoretically untenable. Even if a corporation wished to act with a primary commitment to social responsibility, this would entail ignoring the very rationale of the corporation and the nature of the existing economic system. This is *not* to argue that such rational calculation necessarily means that all regulations are ignored by corpora-tions, nor that any particular corporation will in practice necessarily succeed either in forming a correct interpretation of what is rational, or in acting in accordance with that interpretation—we accept that, at times, corporations will act 'irration-ally'; what the 'compliance school' call incompetence and political citizenship are both perfectly compatible with a concept of corporations as amoral calculators. Nor is it to imply that business firms or the individuals who hold positions of power and take decisions within them will all act criminally. It is simply to recognize that, as Box has argued, the nature of the capitalist mode of production forces corporations to attempt to exert as much control as possible over their operating environments, and that this pushes them into violating those regulations which seek to prevent individual corporations from using their corporate power to exert certain forms of control over consumers, workers, governments, other corporations, and so on (Box 1983). Indeed, although recent theorists differ somewhat about the appropriate models for describing business organizations, few, if any, give any credibility to the notion of the 'soulful corporation'.[2] Thus, theoretically, we are largely in agreement with Edwin Sutherland, when he argued that

> the corporation probably comes closer to the 'economic man' and to 'pure reason' than any person or any other organization. The executives and directors not only have explicit and consistent objectives of maximum pecuniary gain but also have research and accountancy departments by which precise determination of results is facilitated ...

> The rationalistic, amoral, and nonsentimental behavior of the corporation was aimed in earlier days at technological efficiency; in later days more than previously it has been aimed at the manipulation of people by advertising, salesmanship, propaganda and lobbies.

> ... the corporation selects crimes which involve the smallest danger of detection and identification and against which victims are least likely to fight. ... The corporations attempt to prevent the implementation of the law and to create general goodwill ... (Sutherland 1983: 236–8)

It is further the case that the empirical evidence as to the spread of illegalities among all types of corporations seems, *contra* Bardach and Kagan, to support a view which sees the commitment of corporations to regulations as essentially contingent. [...]

[...] [E]xisting empirical evidence suggests that regulatory deviance is not confined to a tiny proportion of all firms. Carson found that every one of the 200 firms visited in the course of his research on the Factory Inspectorate violated health and safety laws at least twice, and the average number of violations per firm was nineteen (Carson 1970a). More recent HSE industry 'blitzes' have also revealed widespread regulatory violations. While enforcement notices are normally issued at an average rate of 0.03 per cent a visit, a recent Factory Inspectorate proactive initiative on small textile firms issued such notices at a rate of 7 per cent; prosecutions were taken out as a result of 0.7 per cent of visits as opposed to 0.005 per cent normally; *191 of the 300 premises inspected were not even registered with local regulatory agencies, as required by law* (HSE 1985d). Similarly, in summer 1987, the Inspectorate concentrated on construction sites. As a result of inspecting the work of about 4,500 contractors, 868 prohibition notices were issued requiring firms to stop work immediately because of dangerous conditions—that is, work on approximately one in five building sites visited had to be stopped (HSE 1987*b*).

It is not only small firms that engage in such violations. Elsewhere, Pearce has presented evidence that violations and prosecutions relating to regulatory law in general and health and safety laws in particular undermine the claims by many larger companies that problems of regulatory deviance within their industries are confined to 'fly-by-night' operators (Pearce 1989). Violations are widespread among companies of all sizes and in all sectors of the economy (see also Clinard and Yeager 1980: 130; Carson 1982). Even if these data are not held to be conclusive as to the commonplace and routine nature of regulatory deviance with respect to health and safety law, they surely call into question empirically that which we earlier questioned theoretically—namely, the claim that only a minority of corporations should be treated as if they are amoral calculators. [...]

Notes

1 This remark was made in a personal communication from Keith Hawkins to Steve Tombs, 13 April 1989, as part of a critical commentary upon an earlier version of this paper.
2 Braithwaite (1984) and Pearce and Tombs (1989) provide critical discussions of this literature and Glasbeek (1988*b*) makes excellent use of Friedman (1962), among others, in a devastating critique of the 'social responsibility' movement.

31

The other price of Britain's oil: regulating safety on offshore oil installations in the British sector of the North Sea

W.G. Carson

[...] Whatever the priority allocated to safety in the planning and execution of offshore operations, the frontier image is one that readily reconciles readers to the inevitability of accidents. People are killed at inhospitable frontiers. Thus, a further image which is often projected in discussions of offshore safety is that of necessary sacrifice for the common weal. While we may dismiss as mere, if possibly inappropriate humour the view of one Treasury man who explained to an early collaborator on this project that, "with the economy in the state that it was, the people who were dying there were dying for the greater good", the suggestion of necessary sacrifice is often quite explicit and quite serious. Thus, for example, in 1977 Anthony Wedgwood Benn, the then Secretary of State for Energy, wrote about the reduction of offshore risks and, having outlined the vital contribution which oil and gas could make to Britian's future, turned his attention to "the penalties" which "as with all things ... are to be paid". In terms possibly more redolent of the Cenotaph than of the North Sea he went on: "too many have already paid the ultimate penalty with their lives, which is tragically the price so often extracted of pioneers". More recently, *The Guardian* deployed the metaphor of cost-benefit analysis to provide a stark caption for a discussion of "The human price of Britain's oil billions". This and several of the other images already mentioned were cogently combined in one editorial in the *Aberdeen Press and Journal*:

> North Sea oil and gas will be worth a staggering £7,200 million this year – and we owe an enormous debt to all who have helped to bring this about. The costs have been high and grievously so in regard to the loss of life which has been incurred. Only yesterday we had another grim reminder of the human toll involved in this vast and crucial operation, in often severely testing conditions which demand taking technology to its outer limits.

Not all of the images associated with offshore employment can be dismissed as false. More specifically, there is little doubt that, at least until very recently, the North Sea has been a very dangerous place indeed to work. While the "human toll" of around 100 killed and 400 seriously injured may not seem particularly appalling in absolute terms, the incidence rates lying behind these stark statistics compare very unfavourably with other reputedly dangerous occupations. Thus, for example, between 1974 and 1976 the overall risk of being killed on or around an oil installation in the British sector (excluding accidents on vessels, for which no employment figures are available) was around six times that for the quarrying industry, nine times that for the mining industry and eleven times as great as the risk of death in the course of construction work. When diving, probably the most hazardous civilian occupation in contemporary Britain, is left out of the account, the gap narrows (to four times, six times and eight times, respectively) but by no means disappears; when the figures relating to diving, itself, are calculated over the same period, the resulting incidence rate for fatalities is in the region of eight per thousand or twenty-six times the death rate in quarrying, thirty-eight times that in mining and fifty times that in the construction industry. While the record for diving, as for the industry as a whole, has shown very substantial improvement in 1977 and 1978, there is no doubt that the North Sea thoroughly deserved its dangerous reputation during the most crucial phase of its development in the mid-1970s.

If such is the case, it becomes germane to ask why offshore employment has been so hazardous? This is a question to which some of the other images already mentioned have considerable relevance since they suggest, at least by implication, that the casualty rate has been an inevitable consequence of working at technological frontiers and in consistently adverse climatic conditions. No less important, they imply that there is relatively little that law could have done, or can do to minimize a human cost exacted by the unique exigencies of the offshore situation rather than by anything else. The other price of Britain's oil, they suggest, is not negotiable.

In the course of this research it has been possible to examine fatal accident files compiled by the Scottish legal authorities in connection with something approaching two-thirds of all oil-related fatalities which occurred in the British sector of the North Sea between 1971 and 1978. Additionally, quarterly summaries of fatal and serious accident reports produced by the British Department of Energy have been scrutinized for the period from 1974 onwards. What emerges from these two sources is that although there is no denying the industry's technological sophistication or the harshness of the setting in which it has to conduct operations, neither of these factors, so salient in the imagery woven around the North Sea oil industry, can be held primarily accountable for the rate of death and injury which has taken place. On the contrary, the evidence overwhelmingly supports the view that offshore accidents largely emanate from the same set of relatively mundane factors that cause the majority of accidents in any industrial context. While space precludes the protracted elaboration of what would necessarily be detailed evidence in this respect, the following example makes the point fairly forcefully – not least because it concerns a double fatality which has become probably the most technologically 'celebrated' accident to have occurred thus far in the British North Sea:

In early 1977, two divers carried out an operational dive to a depth of around 380′ for the purpose of clearing rope and wire cable that had fouled a blowout preventor stack. To accomplish this, they descended in a bell which was pressurized to the appropriate depth with the necessary mix of around 5 percent oxygen and 95 percent helium. Because of the well-known problems of hypothermia (cold) associated with North Sea diving, steam-heating in the deck compression chamber to which they would return was turned on. After the dive was completed, the bell returned to the surface and some difficulty was encountered in establishing a good seal between it and the "transfer under pressure chamber" through which the two men would pass on their way to the main chamber. At a second attempt, a satisfactory connection was made but, as the divers were in the process of changing the bell controls, a slight loss of pressure was noted. Although this was corrected by two short bursts of 100 percent helium, a further slight loss of pressure suggested to the diving supervisor that the original problem with the connection was recurring. Accordingly, the divers were ordered into the transfer chamber and told to seal off the bell. The latter they were unable to do and, since a small pressure loss was still registering, they were instructed to proceed to the main complex and shut the door. On entering the main decompression chamber, the two men complained of the heat, and the heating, which had earlier been registered at a high but not unacceptable level of around 110° fahrenheit, was switched off. But a loss in pressure was still being recorded on the master gauge, and more helium was therefore introduced to the main chamber. This still did not improve the reading, so the supervisor now concluded that he was facing a major emergency. At this point also, he suddenly realized that he was not, in fact, monitoring the decompression chamber but the bell, and when the necessary gauge alterations were carried out, it became evident that the series of helium injections into the former had re-pressurized it to a depth of 650′. This in itself was not particularly dangerous, but pressurization increases temperature, while the high temperature-conductivity of helium feeds heat to the human body at a high rate. Both divers showed increasing signs of acute distress, possibly to the point of panic, but there was no means of accelerating the pace of temperature reduction, even though the real nature of the emergency was now clear. Shortly afterwards, the victims were seen to collapse on the chamber floor, and subsequent investigation showed them to be dead. In a profession well-known for its high risk of hypothermia, they had died of *hyper*thermia (heatstroke).

This accident has been described at some length because, more than any other single incident, it has been picked up by the media and by others as epitomizing the way in which diving takes its practitioners close to and sometimes across the threshold of the known and the familiar. Indeed, one legal text on offshore law cites it as "a good example" of the fact that fatalities occur in situations, "where very little can be done in any event, or in a totally unforeseen manner" and as an illustration of how, "divers are operating at the limits of modern underwater and medical technology". Such a conclusion might indeed seem to be justified by the bare facts recounted above, as by a point made by the Sheriff at the fatal accident inquiry which ensued:

> Although all the components in this tragedy were known to science – particularly to heat physiologists – their possible conjunction in a compression chamber had never previously been recorded or, so far as the evidence showed, foreseen by those engaged in practice and research throughout the long history of deep diving.

The affair assumes a rather different complexion, however, when some of the other findings reached by the inquiry are taken into account. The pressure gauge in question was fitted to the main deck decompression control panel but could be made to monitor pressure in any other part of the complex by the opening and closing of valves. Its use was preferred to that of the available, fixed gauges for each individual part of the complex because of its finer calibration. Thus, it was possible for the supervisor to think he was monitoring one unit while actually monitoring another, an error which the fatal accident inquiry found to be substantially responsible for the accident. Moreover, and quite apart from the inherent deficiencies of a system that has a gauge "capable of being used to indicate pressure in a compartment other than that for which it was clearly labelled", it was held that this particular layout was especially dangerous since there was a prominent notice saying *MAIN LOCK* (i.e. main compression chamber) prominently displayed over the gauge in question. High technology, perhaps, but a comparatively straightforward design issue coupled with operational error which, it should be remembered, is amenable to proper operational rules.

The broad import of this story could be replicated many times over both in relation to diving accidents and to the other categories of offshore activity reputedly involving 'special' hazards because of their very nature and setting. As with diving, so too with cranes which have collapsed and all too often fallen overboard under the strain of 'snatch-loading' from heaving decks; so too with drilling and its notoriety so taken for granted that some installation managers will even justify a higher than usual accident rate on the grounds that this operation is taking place; so too with construction accidents which are often accepted as the inevitable consequence of the engineering impertinence involved in erecting massive structures in such a location; so too with casualties on vessels which are frequently attributed to the "freak waves" that, as one sceptical Health and Safety official observed, "seem to happen every five minutes in the North Sea". In all these cases, the evidence suggests that we should be wary of the superficially attractive explanation of high accident rates in terms of technological frontiers or adverse operating conditions. Rather, it supports the view that the offshore record is traceable to a catalogue of causative factors which are not only well-known to anyone concerned with general industrial safety, but also, and more important in the context of this paper, are potentially amenable to regulation through law. Unsafe working practices, poor design and maintenance, inadequate communications and supervision, short-cuts taken under pressure, and lack of elementary safety precautions play an all too familiar role in the genesis of accidents in the North Sea; but they are also the kinds of issue upon which properly constructed and systematically enforced law can purportedly intervene to create a safer working environment. [...]

[...] To understand the chequered history of how British law has dealt with the issue of safety in the North Sea, it is necessary to go back to the specific nexus of structural relationships which dominated offshore developments in their earliest stages during the 1960s. Throughout that decade, as writers like Longstreth have argued, finance capital (banking and the City) maintained a position of institutionalized dominance within the British state, a dominance that was exercised through the Bank of England and its connections with the Treasury, and that found its expression in recurrent policy preoccupations with the value of the Pound and with the balance of payments. [...]

[...] This nexus between finance capital and strategically located agencies within the state apparatus was to prove crucial in shaping British policy with regard to North Sea oil. As Adrian Hamilton has pointed out, the inter-departmental committee (Ministry of Power, Treasury and Cabinet Office) which preceded the first North Sea licensing round in 1964 opted firmly for as rapid exploration and exploitation as possible in order to meet the "overriding need" for a balance of payments. Indeed, so pressing was the Treasury's preoccupation with this aspect of the matter that it even positively favoured foreign investment in the early years "because of the immediate benefits to the capital account". [...]

[...] At the heart of the regulatory relationship with regard to offshore developments, then, there lies not only a set of policies emanating from the institutionalized domination of strategic parts of the British State by finance capital, but also a related pattern of give and take between the State and the oil majors. Just as the policy of rapid development required the assistance of the latter, so they, too, required the services of the State in creating the preconditions under which large amounts of capital could be safely raised and deployed. [...]

32

Theoretical perspectives on the corporate victimization of women
Sally Simpson and Lori Elis

[...] The development of feminist criminology parallels the development of feminist thinking in other disciplines. It began with criticism of female exclusion from the research and theoretical domain and/or the often blatant sexism in how females were portrayed when they were discussed. This early critique led to more investigations that put women and women's experiences at the center of the research endeavor. More recently, however, feminist criminologists have shifted away from an exclusive focus on females. At the heart of this shift is the recognition that social organization is *gendered*, that male and female lives are interconnected materially, culturally, and structurally.

There is no single feminist theory or perspective. Rather, feminist criminology draws from several theoretical frameworks—including liberal feminism, marxist feminism, socialist feminism, radical feminism, and women-of-color feminism.[1] Each of these perspectives has something useful to say about the nature of gendered corporate crime victimization, but like Gerber and Weeks,[2] we believe that socialist feminism (with modifications from women of color) offers the keenest and broadest interpretations.

Briefly, each orientation differs as to (1) the historical development and source of gendered social organization, (2) who benefits from such social organization and how, and (3) tactics for change.[3] Liberals tend to view gender inequality as stemming from the separation of public and private spheres after industrialization. This separation, they claim, caused the development of distinct gender roles and attitudes that justified and reinforced differential treatment of males and females; men worked outside the home while women cared for the house and family. As society has modernized, however, this organization is outdated and exclusionary for both sexes—males who would like to develop a more nurturing side as well as females who want equal access to societal opportunities. Changes in attitudes and opportunities, liberals argue, can be achieved through legal interventions combined with basic changes in institutional socialization, such as the use of gender-neutral language in educational learning materials. Although liberal feminists (primarily those in the humanitarian camp) acknowledge that this type of gendered social organization has negative consequences for males, the focal concern of liberals is to gain equality for women, that is, they assume that women want what men have.

A liberal feminist approach to corporate victimization of women would analyze the problem in several ways. First, to the extent that males and females are treated differently as victims or plaintiffs, liberals advocate adopting gender-neutral legislation for equal protection under the law. For instance, they believe that reproductive harms should be studied and calculated for both males and females. If one or both sexes are affected by workplace exposure, instead of excluding women from employment in those positions, companies have an obligation to abate the hazard.[4] If abatement is not possible, job relocation at similar wages should occur—a policy of rate retention.[5] Second, because few women are in positions of power and decision making within corporations, regulatory agencies, and court systems, female voices and concerns are not heard. Thus, liberals assert that better integration of women into these positions will offer more protection and support for female victims of corporate crime.[6]

Marxist, socialist, and radical feminist approaches offer more of a systemic critique of capitalist, patriarchal social organization that gives rise to gender oppression and subordination. Their perspectives differ as to whether the basis of gender conflict lies in relations of production, relations of reproduction and consumption, or a combination of the two. Marxist feminists cite the first, radical feminists emphasize the second, and socialist feminists combine both elements.[7] Recognizing the class basis of material relations in a capitalist society, marxist feminists would examine the ways in which women's victimization by corporations, general lack of protection, and limited access to redress serve the interests of capital. A shift from capitalism to socialist or communist social organization will eliminate class divisions (other types of stratification will necessarily follow), and the basis for corporate crime will be eradicated. Radical feminists, on the other hand, look to male subordination of women and control of women's sexuality to understand the ways in which women are victimized by corporations (for example, prescription drugs to prevent miscarriage that harm both the mother and fetus; birth control devices aimed at controlling female, not male, fecundity; protective legislation that excludes females, not males, from hazardous workplaces due to reproductive threats; and so forth).

A socialist-feminist perspective analyzes both social class and patriarchy as intersecting systems of dominance that allow males to appropriate the labor power of females (paid and unpaid labor) and to control their sexuality. Patriarchal gender relations structure criminality—both in terms of who does what kind of offending and the kind of victimization likely to occur. For instance, Messerschmidt hypothesizes that patriarchal capitalist societies produce two types of people: the powerless (women and the working classes) and the powerful (a group composed of men and the capitalist class). While both groups commit crimes, Messerschmidt argues that the greatest amount and most serious of these (corporate crime, sexual violence) are committed by the powerful against the powerless (working classes and women).[8]

From this viewpoint, corporate victimization of women represents the power of capitalist males to expropriate women's labor and reproductive power for the males' benefit. Thus, the fact that women's occupations have fewer health and safety standards and that some are not covered by workers' compensation demonstrates working women's relatively powerless status vis-à-vis working men. Women's occupations are seen primarily as an outgrowth of their roles in the home, namely, nurturing and providing service. Consequently, they tend not to be as well compensated, are assumed not to carry the same industrial risks as "real" jobs (read men's work), and therefore are not considered to be in need of special avenues for redress—in sum, all conditions that benefit capital. Men's work, in contrast, is more highly valued; is assumed (based on empirical studies of occupational hazards) to be riskier; and contains provisions that allow compensation, although limiting the amount injured workers may seek. Men benefit from this situation in that their contributions to production are acknowledged and given limited protection within the capitalist system. Capital benefits economically because workers' compensation places limitations on the amount of the award (thus, there is little substantial threat to capitalist profits). Capital benefits ideologically by demonstrating its concern for labor issues.

Because the domestic realm of housework, child care, and consumption (women's unpaid labor) does not directly contribute to production in capitalist societies, it is devalued. Moreover, because legally the home is viewed as a distinct and separate sphere, what happens in the home is often viewed as a private matter, beyond regulation and legal intervention. This view of the home benefits both capital and men. Capital benefits because reproduction, child care, homemaking, and consumption all reproduce the labor force with little cost to capital. Additionally, unemployed women make up a large portion of the reserve labor force that can be called into service as a means to increase competition among workers and depress wages. Finally, the isolation of women in the home (a private domain) reinforces the notion of *caveat emptor* (buyer beware). If a woman, as household consumer or domestic laborer, is injured by a household chemical (say, a cleaning product that is toxic, carcinogenic, or flammable), her home labor is not protected by a special body of law (such as labor law); nor does she have the kind of institutional supports, such as labor unions, offered to other types of workers. The home is not a regulated environment, and manufacturers are therefore less accountable to these kinds of victims.

Males, primarily husbands, benefit from these domestic arrangements. Studies demonstrate that the bulk of home labor is conducted by women even if they are employed full-time outside the home.[9] Thus, males expropriate the productive labor power of women. While men do not directly benefit from the corporate victimization of women in the domestic realm, they do benefit from the lack of regulation and intervention into the private sector, where patriarchal power and privilege are normative.

So, too, do males benefit from modern birth control developments. While males benefit from the sexual freedom women gain as the threat of unwanted pregnancies is removed, women's actual freedom is curtailed and mediated through the medical community—typically, upper-class white males.[10] Medical controls over female reproduction reinforce the dominant gender stereotypes about sex and responsibility, namely, that women are responsible for male sexuality. The most direct benefit that males reap from the technological control of women's reproduction is that they themselves are spared similar experimentation and corporate victimization.

Socialist-feminist perspectives, while offering important insights into the problem of corporate victimization of women, are problematic for a number of reasons: First, they fail to incorporate race and racial oppression systematically as a distinct and intersecting system of dominance into the analytic framework.[11] All males and all females, with a salute to class differences, are viewed as essentially the same. Second, socialist-feminist perspectives are too macro in orientation and do not "account for the intentions of actors and for how action, including crime, is a meaningful construct in itself."[12] In other words, theory should provide insight into how individuals experience gender, race, and class relations and, in turn, how experiences shape social actions and social structures. Finally, socialist feminism does not reject marxist analytical categories but instead attempts to accommodate gender within them. Thus, production and reproduction are viewed as separate systems, one being the site of class relations and the other the site of patriarchy. Critics argue that these systems are reciprocal and complementary. "Reproductive labor is simultaneously productive labor and vice versa."[13]

A modified version of socialist-feminist criminology, one that is sensitive to micro processes and intragender diversity,[14] would better account for the ways in which all women, including minorities, are victimized by corporations and the extent to which access to redress is structured not just by gender but also by race. Further, differing conceptions of masculinity and femininity by race influence how females interpret their own victimization and how they are likely to respond to it. An example is helpful here.

The history of the birth control movement in the United States reflects two primary concerns: the individual freedom of women and population control.[15] These concerns were structured by race and social class in that it was primarily white, middle-class freedoms that were sought and the fertility of working-class and minority women that was controlled. "What was demanded as a 'right' for the privileged came to be interpreted as a 'duty' for the poor."[16] After decades of involuntary sterilizations, women of color came increasingly to view birth control as "genocide" and to reject its use. These different experiences, according to our modified theory, should influence both social action (that is, who is apt to use birth control) and aggregate patterns of victimization. [...]

Notes

1   K. Daly and M. Chesney-Lind, "Feminism and Criminology," *Justice Quarterly* 5 [1988]: 497–538; Simpson, "Feminist Theory."

2   Gerber and Weeks, "Women as Victims."

3   See Simpson, "Feminist Theory," for a summary of this literature.

4   Katz. "Hazardous Working Conditions."

5   U.S. Department of Labour, *Lost in the Workplace*.
6   See, e.g., Steinman, "Women, Medical Care."
7   Daly and Chesney-Lind, "Feminism and Criminology"; Simpson, "Feminist Theory."
8   Messerschmidt, *Capitalism, Patriarchy, and Crime, 156*.
9   A Hochschild. *The Second Shift* (New York: Viking, 1989).
10 L. Gordon. "The Politics of Birth Control, 1920–1940: The Impact of Professionals," in *Women and Health: The Politics of Sex in Medicine*, ed. E. Fee (Farmingdale, NY: Baywood, 1982), 151–75, 157–59.
11 S. S. Simpson, "Caste, Class, and Violent Crime," *Criminology* 29 (1991): 115–35.
12 Messerschmidt, *Masculinities and Crime*, 57.
13 Ibid., 59.
14 S. S. Simpson and L. Elis, "Sorting Out the Castle and Crime Conundrum," *Criminology* 33 (1995): 47–81.
15 Gordon, "The Politics of Birth Control," 151
16 A. Y. Davis, *Women, Race and Class* (New York: vintage, 1983), 210.

SECTION 6:

Definitions

In the eye of the beholder: between crime and harm

The reading by Ed Herman that starts off this section is part of a much larger body of work that had consistently analysed contradictions in state definitions of terrorism (Chomsky and Herman, 1979; Herman and O'Sullivan, 1990). In this work he has shown clearly how the political violence used by the state very often falls squarely into dictionary and indeed 'official' definitions of terrorism. The United Nations, for example, defines terrorism as 'criminal acts intended or calculated to provoke a state of terror in the general public, a group of persons or particular persons for political purposes'. All of the acts of violence committed by states that are described by Herman here would fall easily into this definition, as would the Anglo-American coalition attacks on civilian populations during and following the invasion of Iraq in 2003. The assaults upon Fallujah in 2004, for example, can be very clearly defined as terrorist acts (on Fallujah as a war crime, see Boyle, 2004).

The US diplomat, Edward Peck, has concisely summed up the definitional problem that confronts the state:

> In 1985, when I was the Deputy Director of the Reagan White House Task Force on Terrorism ... they asked us to come up with a definition of terrorism that could be used throughout the government. We produced about six, and each and every case, they were rejected, because careful reading would indicate that our own country had been involved in some of those activities.

Of the current definition of terrorist activities in US law, Peck has noted:

> Yes, well, certainly, you can think of a number of countries that have been involved in such activities. Ours is one of them. Israel is another. And so, the terrorist, of course, is in the eye of the beholder.[1]

Work by Herman and his colleagues has consistently shown how states continually change definitions of political violence and terrorism in ways that are politically convenient. For example, as he shows in the extract reproduced here, there has been tendency to define terrorism as 'international' acts of political violence. This is done in order to neatly sidestep the violence used by governments to terrorise and intimidate their own populations.

Historically states have dealt with the problem of definition by supplementing the common feature on all definitions of terrorism (the provocation of a state of terror in the general public) with an act of political violence *against* the state Thus, the League of Nations definition, adopted in 1937, is: 'All criminal acts directed against a State and intended or calculated to create a state of terror in the minds of particular persons or a group of persons or the general public'. More recent developments in the definition have consolidated the definition of terrorism as counter-state violence. Article 1 of the European Union Framework Decision on Combating Terrorism sets out a list of offences against property and against the person that

> may be seriously damaging to a country or an international organisation … where committed with the aim of: (i) seriously intimidating a population; or (ii) unduly compelling a Government or international organisation to perform or abstain from performing any act; or (iii) destabilising or destroying the fundamental political, constitutional, economic or social structures of a country or an international organisation.

As the UK campaign group Statewatch has noted, this definition, focusing as it does upon the destabilising of political, economic and constitutional structures is broad enough to include protests against governments and international institutions such as the G8 (Bunyan, 2002). Thus this definition succeeds in shifting the definitional terrain away from the violence of the state to activities directed against the state.

Those shifting features of definitional terrain are made in order to allow the terms of the debate to be framed by those who have the power to label particular groups or individuals as 'terrorists'. The power of definition has therefore been guided by a rudimentary and partisan political reasoning that, as Herman points out, shifts the focus to 'sub-state' terrorism, a form of political violence that is dwarfed, in terms of the relative numbers of its victims, by state terrorism and state political violence. And this is where the process of definition takes on an important function: it enables the reconstruction of a generally held idea of what terrorism is and what states can legitimately do about it. As we saw in the introduction to Section 1 of this book, the definition of terrorism itself plays an important role in constructing the state's *raison d'état*.

A similar observation in the context of business crime was used as a starting point for Edwin Sutherland's research in the 1940s. Sutherland (1945, 1949) established that powerful and respectable business and professional men routinely committed crimes and that these crimes were much more frequent and everyday than other forms of crime committed by relatively lower-class individuals. Yet, this offender type hardly featured in public discussion of the crime problem and attracted very little in the way of state censure. For Sutherland, this gaping hole in our knowledge about crime led to gross distortion of our understanding of the 'crime problem' and the state response to crime. The lack of attention upon relatively high-status offenders led us to associate crime with poverty and to assume that criminals tended to be from relatively poor social groups (he noted, for example, that only 2% of those given custodial sentences were members of the upper classes).

Sutherland did not reject a value-based or purely relativistic reasoning out of hand, but embraced a new definition of 'crime' that was carefully grounded in concepts of law and criminal justice. His definition of 'white-collar crime' was developed with two aspects of criminal process in mind. First, he used a range of sources of (administrative, regulatory and civil) law to show how crimes of the powerful were often separated from the normal criminal legal process. Second, he identified a fundamental difference between offences that are *punishable* and those that are *punished*. Sutherland argued that although the criminal justice system went to great lengths to organise separate categories for business offending, this institutional segregation was compounded by the fact that a large number of offences that *were* punishable were never investigated as legal breaches, or, if they were, never reached the courts. Thus numerous acts and failures on the part of white-collar offenders and corporations were simply not treated as crimes by investigation and prosecution authorities. Therefore the definition of crime for Sutherland was not merely contingent upon the legal status of an act or failure, but was also contingent upon the decisions made by state authorities.

Moreover, the decision-making process was shaped, according to Sutherland, from a position of class bias. This manifests itself in the mutual ideological perspectives of regulated and regulator that prevent business offenders being viewed as real criminals (and this point will be developed in the following section). And because legislators, policy-makers and regulators generally regard those offenders as 'respectable' members of society, they are not treated as criminals at all.

Paul Tappan argued that Sutherland used the term 'crime' too loosely. For Tappan, 'crime' as a label needs to be reserved for clear violations of criminal law that are successfully prosecuted in the courts (see also Tappan, 1960). So, Tappan articulates a 'black letter' approach to law, but this is not all he articulates. The debate between Tappan and Sutherland is too easily reduced to a stand-off between law and sociology, or between a narrow legal positivism and an open textured social science. His critique of Sutherland's definition of 'white-collar crime' made three broad points that are relevant to sociological approaches to crime.

First, he argued, business offences have qualities that make them character-istically different from mainstream crimes. They are offences that very often arise from normal business activities. Thus, the merchant who 'puffs' or overprices his wares to mislead customers, or breaches labour law in order to extract more profits from his workforce is, in Tappan's terms, merely breaching the *trust* of his customers or workers and not clearly in breach of the criminal law. It is because they are generally breaches of trust or breaches of administrative regulations that they are not normally dealt with by the criminal law. Those phenomena Sutherland described as crimes are more accurately described as the 'norms of ordinary business practice'. What is interesting here is that Tappan locates the framework of norms not in social expectations of the general populace, or in the administrative standards set by regulations, but in the standards set by business itself. In this sense, the argument is a circular one: the normative standards of business crime cannot be regarded as criminal because they do not breach the normative standards of business.

Second, and following the previous point, he argued that 'crime' should not be reduced to a moralising label and its use should not be reduced to propaganda. For Tappan there are clear dangers with using the term 'crime' too loosely. The term 'criminal' cannot reasonably be applied to a relatively lower-status individual who has not been tried in a court of law. Therefore, he questions why this label should apply to white-collar offenders who have not been prosecuted under the normal rules of due process.

Third, the consequence of a lack of precision in definitions of the 'criminal' and 'crime' is that the distinction between harm and crime becomes blurred. This is significant for Tappan because the institutional response to 'crime' we expect from the state is different from responses to more generalised issues that are defined as 'harm' or 'social injury'. As Tappan notes in a section of the article not included in the extract, 'law has defined with greater clarity and precision the conduct which is criminal than our anti-legalistic criminologists promise to do' (Tappan, 1947: 100). Devoid of this clarity and precision, notions of crime are far removed from the just or consistent outcomes that we should expect from the criminal justice system.

It is in this argument that we begin to see the essential difference between the authors. Whereas Tappan retains a notion of law and criminal justice as a set of institutions that seek to achieve justice and consistency, Sutherland dissents from such a view. As we have seen in the previous section, it is possible to understand law and criminal justice as a set of institutions that provide the conditions to reproduce *in*justice and *in*equality. For Sutherland, the law and its institutions support a fundamentally unjust and unequal order.

There is a further, perhaps irresolvable, issue that is brought to the surface in the debate between Sutherland and Tappan. In Tappan's terms, the harms produced by corporations must be regarded as little more than normal business practice if they are not clearly criminalised. The problem with this position is that it is assumed that the law is a rational and efficient means of dealing with harm. The assumption here is that the law prohibits the most socially harmful business activities. But this assumption is difficult to sustain.

Take the example of air and water pollution. In this case, the law intervenes to limit pollution below a specified threshold. Most harmful pollution is licensed or permitted by regulatory agencies. Only when those conditions of licensing are breached do they become punishable. Thus, the subset of environmental harms that are sanctionable by law constitute only a small subset of corporate activities that harm the environment. 'Crime' can never be a concept that entirely captures the most harmful corporate activities. To focus upon 'crime' is to focus upon a relatively small state-defined subcategory of a much broader set of social injuries.

In other words, why study 'crime', when the key problems produced in capitalist societies remain uncriminalised? Laureen Snider places this question in the context of the recent trends in 'deregulation'. As Snider argues, '[b]ecause its survival is contingent on the passage and enforcement of "command and control" legislation, corporate crime can "disappear"' (extract: 172) as a result of decriminalisation, deregulation and the downsizing of the state's enforcement capacity. Here we are confronted with the logical conclusion of Tappan's argument: when corporate crimes are decriminalised and become part of accepted business practice, they cease to be 'crimes'.

A similar problem is raised by state violence. For it is possible to argue that many of the most damaging acts of violence committed by states are entirely lawful: violence as a result of 'legal' wars, the creation of economic inequalities that kill thousands every day through starvation, lack of water, lack of basic health provision and vaccinations that are readily available in other, relatively wealthy parts of the world and so on. All of this raises the important question of whether it is helpful to use a concept of state and corporate *crime* as a starting point for understanding state and corporate harm.

Julia and Herman Schwendinger's work seeks to break this impasse between 'crime' and 'harm'. They argue against adopting a positivist framework that is derived from legal definitions of crime, or, like Sutherland's definition, remains 'in accord with established legal precedents' (Schwendinger and Schwendinger, 1970: 137). There are two important points in this extract that are worth drawing out. First, Schwendinger and Schwendinger argue that no criminologist can escape the use of subjectivist or normative standards. In other words, Sutherland, in arguing that the definition of crime should also reflect what states ought to do rather than simply what they do, is basing his argument to some extent on normative assumptions. The question this raises for Schwendinger and Schwendinger, then, is why criminologists like Sutherland remain constrained by a definition of 'crime' in the first place. If they are engaging in a normative or value-based form of reasoning, why not take this reasoning to its logical conclusion; why not focus upon the much broader terrain of 'social injury' or 'public wrongs'? Second, by relying upon some form of *legal* reasoning, criminologists remain within a framework of thinking that acts, as we saw in Section 4, to reproduce capitalist social relations. Legal frameworks operate segregated and insulated from the conditions of social inequality that law reproduces. For Schwendinger and Schwendinger, the consequence of remaining locked into a legalistic framework is that it provides an organising category that allows criminologists to analyse something called 'law' whilst ignoring the social inequalities that law reproduces. Thus, their call is for criminologists to reject the legalistic framework and instead work towards building a society based upon equality. Their solution is to adopt a human rights framework with minimum standards of basic material requirements of human beings, a framework that would allow imperialism, racism, sexism and poverty to be described appropriately as crimes.

Following the arguments developed by Schwendinger and Schwendinger, Penny Green and Tony Ward attempt to address the contradictions of applying a state-defined notion of crime identified by those authors and at the same time retain crime as a meaningful concept. Their solution is to use human rights standards to invoke a notion of state deviance. They argue that human rights standards have the status of an internationally recognised set of norms. Elsewhere they note that no government has openly repudiated the United Nations Universal Declaration of Human Rights (Green and Ward, 2004). Thus it is possible to measure deviation from human rights standards – even in the absence of institutions to enforce and punish their transgressions – as a method of deriving a more precise and workable definition of state crime. The concept of deviance is key to understanding Green and Ward's approach, since their definition of state crime is based upon the 'deviant' avoidance of or violation of human rights norms, as opposed to policies that are not egalitarian or policies that lead to poverty. The point at which we can invoke the label 'crime' is the point at which states deviate from a generally accepted set of norms. By embracing human rights standards, Green and Ward thus attempt to broaden out the notion of crime beyond a narrow legalism and at the same time avoid a subjective or moralising form of analysis.

David and Jessica Friedrichs extend the type of analysis offered by Green and Ward into relatively uncharted territory by applying human rights norms and other international legal norms to a supra-state institution, the World Bank. This extract argues that the World Bank is complicit in a range of crimes and yet is less bound to legal standards of conduct than nation states. After all, the World Bank breaches human rights norms in the knowledge that it is not a signatory to international treaties and therefore cannot be held liable for human rights violations. Yet, the violations that Friedrichs and Friedrichs point to indicate a high degree of complicity in the denial of basic rights and in environmental degradation (see also Mackenzie, 2006). The case referred to elsewhere in the article is the construction of the World Bank-funded Pak Mun Dam in Thailand. As a result of the construction project, the dam flooded a significant area of community forest, contravening the World Bank's own policies on the destruction of cultural property. Stagnant water and changes to the flow of the river system created by the dam have created serious health problems for local people; and a decline in the fish supply destroyed the local economy and forced people to seek work in the cities or to eek out a living scavanging landfill sites for recyclable materials. In addition, 1700 households lost their home, land or both. There was also evidence that the government was hiring thugs to physically attack protestors. The claims disseminated by the World Bank failed to warn of any of those problems and indeed only reported potential benefits to local people, none of which have materialised. Neither has World Bank addressed any of the villagers' concerns. In so far as the World Bank can be held ultimately responsible for forced resettlement, the denial of basic material needs and the fraudulent claims made about the impact of the dam, it is characterised here as a fundamentally criminal institution.

The question that the readings in this section raise, albeit in different ways, is whether a notion of 'crime' (or, in the case of the Herman extract, 'terrorism') can be usefully applied to crimes of the powerful. How can we label states as criminal if, as we saw in Section 1, states claim the exclusive right to invoke a state of exception that allows them to act outside the rule of law? And how can we label corporations as criminal if, as we saw in Section 4, their status allows them to escape criminal liability? A notion of 'social harm' (or what Schwendinger and Schwendinger call 'social injury') can therefore have two functions. First, it can release us from a state-defined conceptual framework of 'crime' and open up new possibilities for censuring harmful behaviour. Second, it can allow us to look at crimes of the powerful more objectively, without having to constantly redefine the conceptual terrain on which we operate (for a broader discussion of the crime/harm debate, see Stitt and Giacopassi, 1993; Muncie, 2000; Hillyard et al., 2004; Friedrichs and Schwartz, 2007).

But, as we have seen, adopting a notion of harm also has its pitfalls. 'Harm' does not carry the weight of social censure or the moral bind that 'crime' does. The importance of a robust and actionable notion of 'crime' is illustrated by recent debates on 'corporate social responsibility' (CSR). CSR is used by companies strategically to support arguments against the use of legally binding standards (see Glasbeek, 1988; Fauset, 2006; Christian Aid, n.d.). As we saw in the introduction to the previous section, the basic premise of CSR is that companies can self-regulate in a way that negates the need for legal regulation. Whilst, as we have seen in relation to the data discussed earlier in the chapter, 'crime' can never be a concept that entirely captures even the most harmful corporate or state activities, the criminalisation of harm remains an important means of developing accountability and attributing responsibility for states and corporate crime. Having made this point, we are still left with a problem that underpins the readings throughout this book (and in particular in Sections 1 and 4): the problem of criminalisation. Indeed, the insufficiency of conventional definitions of crime identified in this section – as the extracts by Sutherland and Tappan perhaps indicate most clearly – arise directly from the failure to criminalise crimes of the powerful. And it is to various aspects of the 'problem of criminalisation' that the next section will turn its attention.

Note

1   Radio interview with Amy Goodman, *Democracy Now*, 28 July 2006.

References

Boyle, F. (2004) 'A War Crime in Real Time: Obliterating Fallujah', *Counterpunch*, 15 November.
Bunyan, T. (2002) *The War on Freedom and Democracy: An analysis of the effects on civil liberties and democratic culture in the EU*, Statewatch Analysis no. 13. London: Statewatch.
Chomsky, N. and Herman, E. (1979) *The Washington Connection and Third World Fascism*. Cambridge, MA: South End Press.

Christian Aid (n.d.) *Behind the Mask: The real face of corporate social responsibility.* London: Christian Aid.

Fauset, C. (2006) *What's Wrong with Corporate Responsibility.* Oxford: Corporate Watch.

Friedrichs, D. and Schwartz, M. (eds) (2007) Special issue of *Crime, Law and Social Change*, 48 (1–2).

Glasbeek, H. (1988) 'The Corporate Responsibility Movement – the latest in Maginot Lines to save capitalism', *Dalhousie Law Journal*, 11.

Green, P. and Ward, T. (2004) *State Crime: Governments, violence and corruption.* London: Pluto.

Herman, E. and O'Sullivan, G. (1990) *The Terrorism Industry.* New York: Pantheon Books.

Hillyard, P., Pantazis, C., Tombs, S. and Gordon, D. (eds) (2004) *Beyond Criminology: Taking harm seriously.* London: Pluto.

Mackenzie, S. (2006) 'Systematic Crimes of the Powerful', *Social Justice*, 33(1).

Muncie, J. (2000) 'Decriminalising Criminology' in G. Lewis, S. Gerwitz and J. Clarke (eds) *Rethinking Social Policy.* London: Sage.

Schwendinger, H. and Schwendinger, J. (1970) 'Defenders of Order or Guardians of Human Rights?', *Issues in Criminology*, 5(2).

Stitt, B. and Giacopassi, D. (1993) 'Assessing Victimisation from Corporate Harms', in M. Blankenship (ed.) *Understanding Corporate Criminality.* New York: Garland.

Sutherland, E. (1945) 'Is "white-collar crime" crime?', *American Sociological Review*, 5: 1–12.

Sutherland, E. (1949) *White-Collar Crime.* New York: Holt, Reinhart and Winston.

Tappan, Paul (1947) 'Who is the White Collar Criminal?' *American Sociological Review*, 12(1).

Tappan, P. (1960) *Crime, Justice and Correction.* New York: McGraw-Hill.

33

The real terror network

Ed Herman

[...] In country after country in the U.S. sphere of influence "dominoes" have been falling, with military regimes and other dependent tyrannies coming into power in virtually all of Central and South America, and in Thailand, Indonesia, the Philippines, Zaire and elsewhere. These regimes have almost uniformly displayed the following characteristics: (1) they represent a small elite interest, including the multinational corporation, which they treat kindly; (2) they all use terror, including modern forms of torture, to keep the majority unorganized, powerless, and as means to local elite and multinational corporate ends; (3) the leaderships of these states are almost invariably venal; (4) they have allowed already highly skewed income distributions to become still more unequal, and have caused a large fraction of their populations to be kept in a state of extreme deprivation.

There is, in short, a huge tacit conspiracy between the U.S. government, its agencies and its multinational corporations, on the one hand, and local business and military cliques in the Third World, on the other, to assume complete control of these countries and "develop" them on a joint venture basis. The military leaders of the Third World were carefully nurtured by the U.S. security establishment to serve as the "enforcers" of this joint venture partnership,[1] and they have been duly supplied with machine guns and the latest data on methods of interrogation of subversives. The impoverished and long abused masses of Latin America, as Penny Lernoux observes, "will not stay quietly on the farms or in the slums unless they are terribly afraid. As in Stroessner's Paraguay, the rich get richer only because they have the guns."[2] The "rich" include a great many U.S. companies and individuals, which is why the United States has provided the guns, and much more. Labor costs have been kept low under this system. The "side effects" in the form of widespread hunger, malnutrition, diseases of poverty and social neglect, millions of stunted children, and a huge reserve army of structurally unemployed and uncared for people are the regrettable but necessary costs of "growth" and "development." These side effects have not been heavily featured in the western mass media.

The terror employed by the enforcers, which helps produce these side effects, has been of fearful quality and frightening scope. In its 1974 *Report on Torture*,

Amnesty International (AI), pointed out that human torture, for several centuries largely a historical curiosity, "has suddenly developed a life of its own and become a social cancer."[3] It became a major phenomenon during the reigns of Hitler and Stalin, but in Germany it disappeared with the collapse of Nazism; and, following the death of Stalin, torture sharply declined and in many forms disappeared altogether in the Soviet Union and in the Soviet sphere of influence.[4] But it has grown by leaps and bounds in the Third World client states of the west, most notably in the U.S. sphere of influence. More than ten of the U.S. clients in Latin America are National Security States (hereafter NSSs), Third World fascist clones, directly controlled by military elites whose ideology combines elements of Nazism with pre-Enlightenment notions of hierarchy and "natural inequality."[5] These military elites and their cadres have been trained to find "subversion" in any effort or idea that would challenge the status quo in any way—Bible classes, organizing peasants, unions, proposals for land reform or tax increase on property, and the like. They have also learned that subversion, which is the same thing as Communism, is an evil that must be rooted out and destroyed in a permanent holy war. The result has been a system of self-sustaining and ruthless violence, with behavior patterns strongly reminiscent of those of the Nazi secret police. [...]

[...] The documentation on the extensiveness and innovative cruelty of torture in these client states is immense, although as I shall discuss later the U.S. public is largely spared the pain of having to confront this horror either in its gruesome details or in meaningful context. Meaningful context would, of course, involve disclosure of the enormous degree of U.S. complicity in the origination and servicing of this form of Third World fascism, a fact I will document throughout this book. Instead of facts, people in the United States are assured by their leaders that those countries are in basically good hands—as General Haig has pointed out, the rulers of these "moderately authoritarian" states believe in God, as he does. There is some confirmation of Haig's faith in the Christian qualities of the Argentinian leaders—the exclusive reading matter provided in many of that country's torture centers is *The New Testament*.[6]

Another extremely important reflection of a resurgence of terrorism has been the growth of "disappearances," a phenomenon mentioned by Hannah Arendt as one of the last and most terrible phases in the evolution and degeneration of totalitarian states.[7] The term refers to cases where individuals are seized by military, paramilitary or police agents of the state, who secretly murder and dispose of the bodies of their victims, often after torture, always without legal process, and without acknowledgement and admitted responsibility of the state. Disappearances, as described by a recent report on this subject by AI, is "a particular government practice applied on a massive scale in Guatemala after 1966, in Chile since later 1973, and in Argentina after March 1976."[8] It was a tactic used by the Nazis in the occupied territories in the 1940s under the Nacht und Nebel (Night and Fog) Decree to dispose of those resisters "endangering German security" by means of what Field Marshall Wilhelm Keitel described as "effective intimidation." The victims, in Germany as in Chile, were subject to an often violent arrest, torture, secret imprisonment and usually death. As noted by AI,

The discovery of mass graves of peoples previously believed to have "disappeared" and the testimony of survivors of secret detention camps have helped not only to fill in the factual vacuum left by each individual "disappearance" but also to refute denials of accountability on the part of government authorities in countries where the practice has become widespread.[9]

Clearly in this new proliferation of the "disappeared" in Latin America we are confronted with something monstrous: AI notes that "making people 'disappear' is an especially abhorrent method of government repression, one which violates a broad range of human rights, and inflicts widespread and continuing physical and/or psychological suffering. A government seeks thereby to ignore its responsibility to its citizens and the international community."[10] This is an understatement, given the fact of severe torture and mutilation as a commonplace in Latin American disappearances, as well as death and offical silence. We are also dealing here with a phenomenon that is quantitatively significant, the number of disappeared in Latin America in recent decades numbering several score thousands. At the First Latin American Congress of Relatives of the Disappeared, held in San José, Costa Rica, January 20–24, 1981, the estimate given for disappeared men, women and children in Latin America over the past two decades was 90,000.[11] By contrast, the CIA's most recent (newly inflated) estimate of the total number of deaths resulting from "international terrorist" violence for the period 1968–1980, numbers 3,668,[12] or about 4 percent of the number of "disappearances" for Latin America alone. [...]

[...] "Terror," according to the dictionary definition, is "*a mode of governing*, or of opposing government, by intimidation."[13] The "problem" for western propaganda arises from the fact that the dictionary definition inconsiderately encompasses in the word "terrorist" Guatemala's Garcia or Chile's Pinochet, who clearly govern by the use of intimidation, but whose kindly ministrations in the interest of "stability" and "security" are best kept in the background. This calls for word adaptations that will exclude state terrorists and capture only the petty terror of small dissident groups and individuals. All the establishment specialists and propagandists do in fact ignore Garcia, Pinochet and the South African government and concentrate on the lesser terror, by explicit or implied redefinition of "terrorist."

Walter Laqueur, who has academic ties and must therefore confront this problem directly, admits that terror has a wider meaning, and he titles his book *Terrorism*, not just the terrorism of dissidents, or the terrorism of the left. But he says: "My concern in the present study of terrorism is with *movements* that have used systematic terrorism as their main weapon; others will be mentioned only in passing."[14] The state he excludes from the class of objects called "a movement," so that state terror is thereby defined away. He doesn't try to justify this in terms of importance in the whole spectrum of terror – he just happens to be interested in studying the same thing that the *Reader's Digest, Time*, David Rockefeller, and Generals Haig and Pinochet think is an appropriate subject. One might argue on purely technical grounds, however, that on Laqueur's definition, the National Security States (NSSs) represent the triumph of a "movement" or "movements," given the extensive interconnections between them, their linkages to the U.S. military-intelligence apparatus, their common ideology, and the frequency with which they have been products of rightwing conspiracies within national military establishments. The idea that all the lesser terrorists are properly designated "movements" whose "main weapon" is terror is also absurd, but Laqueur has his political purposes and the examination of small bits of illogic in his propaganda exercise need not detain us.[15]

The CIA is also obliged to define terrorism in ita annual enumeration of "Patterns of International Terrorism." How does it cope with the need to exclude Garcia and Pinochet? It does this by concentrating on "international terrorism," not just plain terrorism. The CIA concept of terrorism itself is close to the dictionary definition cited above, and would include the state-organized violence of Guatemala and Chile. "International terrorism," however, is defined as follows: "Terrorism conducted with the support of a foreign government or organization and/or directed against foreign nationals, institutions, or governments."[16] In short, if you use "death squads" to kill 7,000 of your own citizens, this is "terrorism" but not "international terrorism." Unless, of course, you do this with "the support of a foreign government." [...]

[...] Another analyst of terrorism, J. Bowyer Bell, also concentrates on the lesser terror, although in contrast with the purer extreme right propaganda of Moss and Sterling, Bell calls attention to the great diversity of motivation of the retail terrorists, distinguishing between psychotic and self-dramatizing individuals and those who are desperate because of social oppression, with legitimate grievances unfulfilled and possibly beyond fulfillment under unjust systems. Bell has the integrity to note in a book published in 1975 that "Others asked if the more recent use of American B-52s over Hanoi was an appropriate military exercise, while the Palestinian use of incendiary grenades in Rome was not."[17] Why then *are* B-52 raids and state terror in the end excluded from Bell's analysis? He is never very clear. In part, it is a matter of definition; as with the CIA, Bell is interested in "transnational terror" and is therefore prepared to ignore internal state assaults on their own people. B-52 raids are transnational, but Bell also arbitrarily excludes warfare between states, even when based on aggression, and he shows a strange myopia in failing to see the extensive sub rosa transnational terror long perpetrated by strong states (e.g. South Africa) against weaker neighbors. [...]

Notes

1   See chapter 3 below. For a fuller discussion see Miles D. Wolpin. *Military Aid and Counterrevolution in the Third World*, Lexington, 1972.
2   Penny Lernoux, *Cry of the People*, Doubleday, 1980, p. 36.
3   Farrer, Straus, and Giroux, 1975, p. 7.
4   *Ibid.*, p. 184.
5   See Lernoux, *Cry of the People*, pp. 47–50
6   AI, *Amnesty International Report 1979*, p. 48.
7   Hannah Arendt, *The Origins of Totalitarianism*, New York, Meridian, 1958, pp. 432–3

8   AI, "'*Disappearances,' A Workbook,* New York, 1981, p. 1.
9   *Ibid.,* p. 2.
10 *Ibid.,* p. 77.
11 Acta Final Y Resoluciones, ler Congreso Latinoamericano De Familiares De Desaparecido, San Jose, Costa Rica, 20–24 Enero 1981, p. 5.
12 CIA, *Patterns of International Terrorism: 1980, June 1981, p. vi.*
13 *Webster Collegiate Dictionary,* Fifth Edition, 1945, p. 1031.
14 Walter Laqueur, *Terrorism,* Little Brown, 1977, p 7. Emphasis added.
15 For a further examination of Laqueur's work, see Chomsky and Herman, *The Washington Connection,* pp. 87–91.
16 CIA, *Patterns of International Terrorism, 1980,* June 1981, p. ii.
17 *Transnational Terror,* American Enterprise Institute and Hoover Institution, 1975, p. 3.

34

White-collar criminality
Edwin Sutherland

[...] White-collar crime is real crime. It is not ordinarily called crime, and calling it by this name does not make it worse, just as refraining from calling it crime does not make it better than it otherwise would be. It is called crime here in order to bring it within the scope of criminology, which is justified because it is in violation of the criminal law. The crucial question in this analysis is the criterion of violation of the criminal law. Conviction in the criminal court, which is sometimes suggested as the criterion, is not adequate because a large proportion of those who commit crimes are not convicted in criminal courts. This criterion, therefore, needs to be supplemented. When it is supplemented, the criterion of the crimes of one class must be kept consistent in general terms with the criterion of the crimes of the other class. The definition should not be the spirit of the law for white-collar crimes and the letter of the law for other crimes, or in other respects be more liberal for one class than for the other. Since this discussion is concerned with the conventional theories of the criminologists, the criterion of white-collar crime must be justified in terms of the procedures of those criminologists in cealing with other crimes. The criterion of white-collar crimes, as here proposed, supplements convictions in the criminal courts in four respects, in each of which the extension is justified because the criminologists who present the conventional theories of criminal behavior make the same extension in principle.

First, other agencies than the criminal court must be included, for the criminal court is not the agency which makes official decisions regarding violations of the criminal law. The juvenile court, dealing largely with offenses of the children of the poor, in many states is not under the criminal jurisdiction. The criminologists have made much use of case histories and statistics of juvenile delinquents in constructing their theories of criminal behavior. This justifies the inclusion of agencies other than the criminal court which deal with white-collar offenses. The most important of these agencies are the administrative boards, bureaus, or commissions, and much of their work, although certainly not all, consists of cases which are in violation of the criminal law. The Federal Trade Commission recently ordered several automobile companies to stop advertising their interest rate on installment purchases as 6 percent, since it was actually 11 1/2 percent. Also it filed complaint against *Good Housekeeping*, one of the Hearst publications, charging that its seals led the public to believe that all products bearing those seals had been tested in their laboratories, which was contrary to fact. Each of these involves a charge of dishonesty, which might have been tried in a criminal court as fraud. A large proportion of the cases before these boards should be included in the data of the criminologists. Failure to do so is a principal reason for the bias in their samples and the errors in their generalizations.

Second, for both classes, behavior which would have a reasonable expectancy of conviction if tried in a criminal court or substitute agency should be defined as criminal. In this respect, convictability rather than actual conviction should be the criterion of criminality. The criminologists would not hesitate to accept as data a verified case history of a person who was a criminal but had never been convicted. Similarly, it is justifiable to include white-collar criminals who have not been convicted, provided reliable evidence is available. Evidence regarding such cases appears in many civil suits, such as stockholders' suits and patent-infringement suits. These cases might have been referred to the criminal court but they were referred to the civil court because the injured party was more interested in securing damages than in seeing punishment inflicted. This also happens in embezzlement cases, regarding which surety companies have much evidence. In a short consecutive series of embezzlements known to a surety company, 90 percent were not prosecuted because prosecution would interfere with restitution or salvage. The evidence in cases of embezzlement is generally conclusive, and would probably have been sufficient to justify conviction in all of the cases in this series.

Third, behavior should be defined as criminal if conviction is avoided merely because of pressure which is brought to bear on the court or substitute agency. Gangsters and racketeers have been relatively immune in many cities because of their pressure on prospective witnesses and public officials, and professional thieves, such as pickpockets and confidence men who do not use strong-arm methods, are even more frequently immune. The conventional criminologists do not hesitate to include the life histories of such criminals as data, because they understand the generic relation of the pressures to the failure to convict. Similarly, white-collar criminals are relatively immune because of the class bias of the courts and the power of their class to influence the implementation and administration of the law. This class bias affects not merely present-day courts but to a much greater degree affected the earlier courts which established the precedents and rules of procedure of the present-day courts. Consequently, it is justifiable to interpret the actual or potential failures of conviction in the light of known facts regarding the pressures brought to bear on the agencies which deal with offenders.

Fourth, persons who are accessory to a crime should be included among white-collar criminals as they are among other criminals. When the Federal Bureau of Investigation deals with a case of kidnapping, it is not content with catching the offenders who carried away the victim; they may catch and the court may convict twenty-five other persons who assisted by secreting the victim, negotiating the ransom, or putting the ransom money into circulation. On the other hand, the prosecution of white-collar criminals frequently stops with one offender. Political graft almost always involves collusion between politicians and business men but prosecutions are generally limited to the politicians. Judge Manton was found guilty of accepting $664,000 in bribes, but the six or eight important commercial concerns that paid the bribes have not been prosecuted. Pendergast, the late boss of Kansas City, was convicted for failure to report as a part of his income $315,000 received in bribes from insurance companies but the insurance companies which paid the bribes have not been prosecuted. In an investigation of an embezzlement by the president of a bank, at least a dozen other violations of law which were related to this embezzlement and involved most of the other officers of the bank and the officers of the clearing house, were discovered but none of the others was prosecuted. [...]

[...] This difference in the implementation of the criminal law is due principally to the difference in the social position of the two types of offenders. Judge Woodward, when imposing sentence upon the officials of the H. O. Stone and Company, bankrupt real estate firm in Chicago, who had been convicted in 1933 of the use of the mails to defraud, said to them, "You are men of affairs, of experience, of refinement and culture, of excellent reputation and standing in the business and social world." That statement might be used as a general characterization of white-collar criminals for they are oriented basically to legitimate and respectable careers. Because of their social status they have a loud voice in determining what goes into the statutes and how the criminal law as it affects themselves is implemented and administered. [...]

[...] The theory that criminal behavior in general is due either to poverty or to the psychopathic and sociopathic conditions associated with poverty can now be shown to be invalid for three reasons. First, the generalization is based on a biased sample which omits almost entirely the behavior of white-collar criminals. The criminologists have restricted their data, for reasons of convenience and ignorance rather than of principle, largely to cases dealt with in criminal courts and juvenile courts, and these agencies are used principally for criminals from the lower economic strata. Consequently, their data are grossly biased from the point of view of the economic status of criminals and their generalization that criminality is closely associated with poverty is not justified.

Second, the generalization that criminality is closely associated with poverty obviously does not apply to white-collar criminals. With a small number of exceptions, they are not in poverty, were not reared in slums or badly deteriorated families, and are not feebleminded or psychopathic. They were seldom problem children in their earlier years and did not appear in juvenile courts or child guidance clinics. The proposition, derived from the data used by the conventional criminologists, that "the criminal of today was the problem child of yesterday" is seldom true of white-collar criminals. The idea that the causes of criminality are to be found almost exclusively in childhood similarly is fallacious. Even if poverty is extended to include the economic stresses which afflict business in a period of depression, it is not closely correlated with white-collar criminality. Probably at no time within fifty years have white-collar crimes in the field of investments and of corporate management been so extensive as during the boom period of the twenties.

Third, the conventional theories do not even explain lower class criminality. The sociopathic and psychopathic factors which have been emphasized doubtless have something to do with crime causation, but these factors have not been related to a general process which is found both in white-collar criminality and lower class criminality and therefore they do not explain the criminality of either class. They may explain the manner or method of crime—why lower class criminals commit burglary or robbery rather than false pretenses. [...]

35

Who is the criminal?
Paul W. Tappan

[...] A number of criminologists today maintain that mere violation of the criminal law is an artificial criterion of criminality, that categories set up by the law do not meet the demands of scientists because they are of a "fortuitous nature" and do not "arise intrinsically from the nature of the subject matter."[1] The validity of this contention must depend, of course, upon what the nature of the subject matter is. These scholars suggest that, as a part of the general study of human behavior criminology should concern itself broadly with all anti-social conduct, behavior injurious to society. [...]

[...] Another increasingly widespread and seductive movement to revolutionize the concepts of crime and criminal has developed around the currently fashionable dogma of "white collar crime." This is actually a particular school among those who contend that the criminologist should study anti-social behavior rather than law violation. The dominant contention of the group appears to be that the convict classes are merely our "petty" criminals, the few whose depredations against society have been on a small scale, who have blundered into difficulties with the police and courts through their ignorance and stupidity. The important criminals, those who do irreparable damage with impunity, deftly evade the machinery of justice, either by remaining "technically" within the law or by exercising their intelligence, financial prowess, or political connections in its violation. We seek a definition of the white collar criminal and find an amazing diversity, even among those flowing from the same pen, and observe that characteristically they are loose, doctrinaire, and invective. When Professor Sutherland launched the term, it was applied to those individuals of upper socio-economic class who violate the criminal law, usually by breach of trust, in the ordinary course of their business activities.[2] This original usage accords with legal ideas of crime and points moreover to the significant and difficult problems of enforcement in the areas of business crimes, particularly where those violations are made criminal by recent statutory enactment. From this fruitful beginning the term has spread into vacuity, wide and handsome. We learn that the white collar criminal may be the suave and deceptive merchant prince or "robber baron," that the existence of such crime may be determined readily "in casual conversation with a representative of an occupation by asking him, 'What crooked practices are found in your occupation?'"[3]

Confusion grows as we learn from another proponent of this concept that, "There are various phases of white-collar criminality that touch the lives of the common man almost daily. The large majority of them are operating within the letter and spirit of the law. ..." and that "In short, greed, not need, lies at the basis of white-collar crime."[4] Apparently the criminal may be law obedient but greedy; the specific quality of his crimes is far from clear.

Another avenue is taken in Professor Sutherland's more recent definition of crime as a "legal description of an act as socially injurious and legal provision of penalty for the act."[5] Here he has deemed the connotation of his term too narrow if confined to violations of the criminal code; he includes by a slight modification conduct violative of any law, civil or criminal, when it is "socially injurious."

In light of these definitions, the normative issue is pointed. Who should be considered the white collar criminal? Is it the merchant who, out of greed, business acumen, or competitive motivations, breaches a trust with his consumer by "puffing his wares" beyond their merits, by pricing them beyond their value, or by ordinary advertising? Is it he who breaks trust with his employees in order to keep wages down, refusing to permit labor organization or to bargain collectively, and who is found guilty by a labor relations board of an unfair labor practice? May it be the white collar worker who breaches trust with his employers by inefficient performance at work, by sympathetic strike or secondary boycott? Or is it the merchandiser who violates ethics by under-cutting the prices of his fellow merchants? In general these acts do not violate the criminal law. All in some manner breach a trust for motives which a criminologist may (or may not) disapprove for one reason or another. All are within the framework of the norms of ordinary business practice. One seeks in vain for criteria to determine this white collar criminality. It is the conduct of one who wears a white collar and who indulges in occupational behavior to which some particular criminologist takes exception. It may easily be a term of propaganda. For purposes of empirical research or objective description, what is it?

Whether criminology aspires one day to become a science or a repository of reasonably accurate descriptive information, it cannot tolerate a nomenclature of such loose and variable usage. [...]

[...] It is not criminology. It is not social science. The terms "unfair," "infringement," "discrimination," "injury to society," and so on, employed by the white collar criminologists cannot, taken alone, differentiate criminal and non-criminal. Until refined to mean certain specific actions, they are merely epithets.

Vague, omnibus concepts defining crime are a blight upon either a legal system or a system of sociology that strives to be objective. They allow judge, administrator, or—conceivably—sociologist, in an undirected, freely operating discretion, to attribute the status "criminal" to any individual or class which he conceives nefarious. This can accomplish no desirable objective, either politically or sociologically.[6]

Worse than futile, it is courting disaster, political, economic, and social, to promulgate a system of justice in which the individual may be held criminal without having committed a crime, defined with some precision by statute and case law. [...]

[...] Having considered the conceptions of an innovating sociology in ascribing the terms "crime" and "criminal," let us state here the juristic view: Only those are criminals who have been adjudicated as such by the courts. Crime is an intentional act in violation of the criminal law (statutory and case law), committed without defense or excuse, and penalized by the state as a felony or misdemeanor. In studying the offender there can be no presumption that arrested, arraigned, indicted, or prosecuted persons are criminals unless they also be held guilty beyond a reasonable doubt of a particular offense.[7]

Even less than the unconvicted suspect can those individuals be considered criminal who have violated no law. Only those are criminals who have been selected by a clear substantive and a careful adjective law, such as obtains in our courts. The unconvicted offenders of whom the criminologist may wish to take cognizance are an important but unselected group; it has no specific membership presently ascertainable. Sociologists may strive, as does the legal profession, to perfect measures for more complete and accurate ascertainment of offenders, but it is futile simply to rail against a machinery of justice which is, and to a large extent must inevitably remain, something less than entirely accurate or efficient. [...]

[...] We consider that the "white collar criminal," the violator of conduct norms, and the anti-social personality are not criminal in any sense meaningful to the social scientist unless he has violated a criminal statute. We cannot know him as such unless he has been properly convicted. He may be a boor, a sinner, a moral leper, or the devil incarnate, but he does not become a criminal through sociological name-calling unless politically constituted authority says he is. [...]

Notes

1   See, for example, Thorsten Sellin, *Culture Conflict and Crime*, pp. 20–21, (1938).

2   E. H. Sutherland, "Crime and Business," 217 *The Annals of the American Academy of Political and Social Science* 112, (1941).

3   Sutherland, "White-Collar Criminality," 5 *American Sociological Review* 1, (1940).

4   Harry Elmer Barnes and Negley K. Teeters, *New Horizons in Criminology*, pp. 42–43, (1943).

5   Sutherland, "Is 'White-Collar Crime' Crime?" Ic *American Sociological Review* 132, (1945).

6   In the province of juvenile delinquency we may observe already the evil that flows from this sort of loose definition in applied sociology. In many jurisdictions, under broad statutory definition of delinquency, it has become common practice to adjudicate as delinquent any child deemed to be anti-social or a

behavior problem. Instead of requiring sound systematic proof of specific reprehensible conduct, the courts can attach to children the odious label of delinquent through the evaluations and recommendations of over-worked, under-trained case investigators who convey to the judge their hearsay testimony of neighborhood gossip and personal predilection. Thus these vaunted "socialized tribunals" sometimes become themselves a source of delinquent and criminal careers as they adjudge individuals who are innocent of proven wrong to a depraved offender's status through an administrative determination of something they know vaguely as anti-social conduct. See Introduction by Roscoe Pound of Pauline V. Young, *Social Treatment in Probation and Delinquency*, (1937). See also Paul W. Tappan, *Delinquent Girls in Court*, (1947) and "Treatment Without Trial," 24 *Social Forces*, 306, (1946).

7   The unconvicted suspect cannot be known as a violator of the law: to assume him so would be in derogation of our most basic political and ethical philosophies. In empirical research it would be quite inaccurate, obviously, to studay all suspects or defendants as criminals.

36

The sociology of corporate crime: an obituary (or: whose knowledge claims have legs?)
Laureen Snider

[...] In the most basic sense, corporate crime has disappeared by definition: when first isolated as an object of sociological and criminological knowledge its primary characteristic was deemed to be its illegal status, corporate crimes were acts proscribed by governments.[1] This is rooted in Sutherland's definition of 'white-collar crime' as an *offence* 'committed by a person of respectability and high social status in the course of his [sic] occupation' (Sutherland, 1940: 1). Corporate crime became a variant of white-collar crime, specifically acts 'of omission or commission by an individual or group of individuals in a legitimate formal organization—which have a serious physical or economic impact on employees, consumers or the general public' (Box, 1983: 20), everything from false advertising to marketing unsafe products or falsifying the results of scientific research.[2] Because its survival as an object of study is contingent on the passage and enforcement of 'command and control' legislation, corporate crime can 'disappear' through decriminalization (the repeal of criminal law), through deregulation (the repeal of all state law, criminal, civil and administrative) and through downsizing (the destruction of the state's enforcement capability). All three have been used. And because state policy is only revolutionized by changing the minds of elite players in key institutions in particular nation-states, and each institution and nation has its own distinct histories, politics and struggles, the way and degree to which it disappeared varies by nation-state, by type of crime and by regulatory institution. [...]

[...] *Competition and combines, deceptive trade practices* Competition/combines offences are (or were) anti-competitive practices designed to inflate profits by restraining trade, through conspiracies to restrict trade, mergers and monopolies, predatory pricing, price discrimination, resale price maintenance or refusal to supply retailers deemed to be selling too cheaply. The Combines Investigation Act in Canada, passed in 1889, and the 1890 Sherman Act in the US represent early attempts to proscribe profitable economic practices in the name of citizen protection. The 96-year history of Canada's Combines Investigation Act is typical: the enabling legislation was weak (no successful prosecutions under the monopoly provisions were ever registered), it never had adequate funding or enforcement, and each attempt to strengthen it was vigorously opposed by business (Snider, 1978). [...]

[...] In 1984 a Conservative government was elected [in Canada] and the new Prime Minister, Brian Mulroney, denounced the 'anti-American', 'anti-business' stance of the preceding (Liberal) government. A blue-ribbon committee to revise the Combines Investigation Act was appointed, with representatives from the Canadian Manufacturers Association, Chambers of Commerce, Grocery Products Manufacturers of Canada and similar groups. Notably absent were labour and consumers' representatives (the Deputy Minister insisted the Consumers Association of Canada and 'interested academics' were 'also consulted'). The committee recommended abolishing the Combines Investigation Act. The resulting legislation experienced none of the delays or resistance which had characterized attempts to strengthen the Act. Its replacement, the Competition Act passed in 1986, had very different goals: it was to provide a stable and predictable climate for business, to promote competitiveness, and to enhance business prosperity (Canada, Bureau of Competition Policy, 1989). To do this it removed criminal sanctions from the merger/monopoly sector, deleted 'public interest' as a criterion for evaluating a proposed merger/monopoly, offered business advance approval for proposed mergers or monopolies, and embraced a 'compliance-centred' approach. This major policy reverse passed largely unnoticed and unremarked (Stanbury, 1986–7; Canada, Bureau of Competition Policy, 1989; Snider, 1993).

As expected, enforcement levels dropped. From 1986–9, a total of 402 merger files were opened, most were unilaterally approved. Twenty-six proposed mergers were 'monitored', seven abandoned, nine restructured, five sent to the Competition Tribunal and two appealed. Merger files declined until, in 1995–6, only 228 files were opened. In 1996–7, 319 mergers were reviewed with 23 deemed problematic enough to require follow-up. In 1997–8 369 were slated for review (Canada, Industry Canada, 1998). (This modest increase—in reviews, not charges—is described as 'a crack down by the competition cops') (*Globe & Mail*, 30 March 1998: B4).[3]

Even where law remained unchanged, as in false advertising, prosecution levels dropped. Charges for conspiracy, discriminatory and predatory pricing, misleading or deceptive practices and price maintenance declined from 37 in 1982–4 and 36 in 1984–6 to 23 in 1986–8. This was not due to lack of public interest: only in 1995–6, when all the regional offices of the Competition Bureau were closed due to budget cuts, did the number of public complaints fall. Thus the 15,130 false advertising complaints in 1991–2 decreased to 6751 in 1995–6, and the 82 follow-up inquiries commenced in 1991–2 fell to eight in 1995–6. Similarly, cases referred to the Attorney General for charges dropped from 55 to seven, prosecutions from 44 to seven and convictions from 43 to 14 (Canada, Industry Canada, 1997: 36). In the spring of 1998 the Liberal government (the party which had opposed deregulation a scant decade earlier) introduced a Bill completing the process of decriminalization and deregulation initiated in 1986 (Canada, Industry Canada, 1998: 3; *Globe & Mail*, 5 May 1998: B3). [...]

[...] *Occupational health and safety* The knowledge claims that legitimated the disappearance of social crimes were often different, but the policy outcome was identical: less state regulation, fewer and weaker laws, less state-sponsored censure. Occupational health and safety offences, illegal acts which threaten the health and safety of employees and consumers, typically include regulations covering ventilation, light and temperature in workplaces (be they mines, factories or off-shore rigs), minimum wage, maximum hours, work-breaks, overtime pay, safety equipment, guards on machines and air quality monitors. Such regulations were argued into consciousness, language and law through decades of struggle, using religious and humanitarian discourses ('it isn't right to put profit over people's lives') as well as utilitarian ones ('preventing accidents is cheaper in the long run'). But such laws have always been heavily resisted. Business resistance has three sources: first, occupational health and safety laws challenge ownership rights, the rights of employers to do what they like with 'their' employees in 'their' workplace; second, they challenge contract rights, imposing what employers consider an 'artificial' barrier between owners and employees; third, they add direct costs to production while providing no corresponding benefit (to capital) (Carson, 1980; Ursel, 1986).

In the US the election of Reagan in 1979 triggered immediate attacks on OSHA, the federal agency reponsible for occupational health and safety. Regulations requiring specific labelling of hazardous chemicals were repealed, 'walk around' pay (allowing workers to accompany inspectors on tours of workplaces) was ended, exposure standards for cotton dust (cause of 'brown lung' disease) increased (Calavita, 1983). By 1992 OSHA was reduced to 2150 inspectors to cover 5.9 million employers, meaning it could at best inspect 3 percent of workplaces, and less than one-quarter of the 526 'known carcinogens' to which 25 million workers are regularly exposed had designated exposure limits (Noble, 1995). OSHA was attacked with particular fervour because it had adopted a philosophy of strict enforcement rather than a conciliatory, 'educational' approach (Green, 1994). Public 'book burnings' (of materials informing workers of their rights to refuse unsafe work) and the appointment of OSHA's worst enemies to key executive positions as regulators attacked both effectiveness and morale (Clarke, 1990: 207).

Outright attacks on regulatory officials and agencies characterized the US under Reagan and Britain under Thatcher.[4] Elsewhere the rhetoric was softer and 'self-regulation' was touted as a cheaper means to accomplish the same end, safer workplaces. Under self-regulation teams of employees with different ranks, specializations and expertise are allowed to set their own working conditions and production goals. Teams are typically rewarded for high levels of productivity and penalized for low ones. By the early 1990s self-regulation had replaced state regulation in many industries, agencies and nations.[5] In the United Kingdom a series of disasters in the late 1980s (the Piper Alpha explosions in the North Sea in 1988 which killed 167, the sinking of the Herald of Free Enterprise at Zeebrugge, killing 188) were successfully linked to regulatory cutbacks and public pressure generated considerable re-regulation. And in the 1990s pressure from progressive trading partners in the European Union plus the return of a Labour government reinforced this trend, particularly in the chemical and nuclear industries (Pearce and Tombs, 1998). Nevertheless the Robins' system of self-regulation dominates most workplaces, safety laws are still underenforced and an anti-regulatory philosophy still dominates higher echelons of the civil service (Hutter and Lloyd-Bostock, 1992; Tombs, 1996).

The safety of employees in the re-worked, 'loosely coupled' transnational corporation or in the newly privatized workplace of the 1990s has not been improved by self-regulation—injury rates appear to be rising (Viscusi, 1986; Nichols, 1990; Beckwith, 1992; Pearce and Tombs, 1992; Tucker, 1995a).[6] With self-regulation 'the limits of acceptable discourse regarding safety regulation' (Tombs, 1996: 325) have been altered, management's traditional responsibility for ensuring worker safety has vanished, 'hazard' itself has been re-defined. When workplace 'teams' set production quotas, more 'reasonable' (employer-friendly) definitions of risk result (Walters et al., 1995). Conditions which require costly time and equipment to ameliorate are less likely to be seen as hazardous. Workers who 'collaborate' in setting safety standards are poorly positioned to complain to a state watchdog if they get injured.[7] Indeed, with state standards and watchdogs both endangered species, the problematic nature of worker 'consent' to dangerous working conditions easily escapes interrogation.

An illustrative case: at the Westray Mine in Nova Scotia, 1992, methane gas exploded, killing 26 miners underground. Subsequent investigations showed that the owners had routinely failed to take precautions or make (expensive) repairs. Coal dust, inadequate ventilation and methane gas buildup were all known hazards. Government philosophies privileged the employers' right to make money over employees' rights to a safe workplace: when inspectors did visit, they gave advance notice. Workers reporting unsafe conditions were vilified and ignored (Glasbeek and Tucker, 1992; Tucker, 1995b). Fifty-two non-criminal charges were eventually laid, all were dropped. On 1 July 1998 the three remaining criminal charges were dropped (*Globe & Mail*, 1 July 1998: A1).[8]

Crimes against the environment Laws protecting the environment are new, most originating after 1970 out of environmental movements. They too have been fiercely resisted by industry. The philosophical premises of deep (radical) ecology threaten the ideological basis of capitalism, particularly its assumption that every river, tree, idea and genome exists only to be marketed for private profit, that buying and using (up) commodities is always desirable, and that there are no natural limits to capitalism (or at least none that modern science cannot over-come). Protecting the environment, which has historically been treated as a 'free good', adds to the costs of production, especially in primary and secondary industries. However, unlike most corporate crime, environmental regulation has a constituency: there are media-savvy middle class groups lobbying for its retention and enforcement in every developed country. While this has not prevented the disappearance of environmental crime, it has produced public struggles over its wisdom, feasibility and pace.

In 1995 a mandatory review of the 1988 Environmental Protection Act, Canada's primary federal legislation, revealed that a total of 28 investigators and 31 inspectors were responsible for enforcing environmental law throughout a territory bigger than the US or continental Europe. Despite policy directives specifying 'strict compliance', a permissive philosophy of 'compliance promotion' reigned (Canada, Environment Canada, 1995). From 1988–95, 66 prosecutions were launched, with a total of 51 convictions registered, an average of 7.2 actions per year. The most common 'sanctions' assessed under the Act were warnings—in 1993–4, for example, 120 warnings and three prosecutions resulted from 1548 inspections. The Environmental Assessment process is 'a disaster', lacking standards, penalties and basic rules specifying when public reviews must be held (Nikiforuk, 1997: 17). Cabinet can overrule their recommendations if reviews are held. With no definition of 'expert', companies can shop for industry-friendly 'scientists' to support their claims; there are cases of experts selling their services to the highest bidder or re-doing reports to make them 'more benign' (Nikiforuk, 1997: 17). Canada, like most industrial countries, has more than 60,000 industrial chemicals in use, with 1000 new ones introduced annually. Yet Environment Canada's 'Domestic Substances List' designated only 44 of 28,000 substances as regulatory priorities and assessed only five in 10 years, a rate which translates into '38 bureaucrat years per chemical' (Leiss, 1996: 132).

Dominant anti-regulatory philosophies in Environment Canada, relentless lobbying by industry, and massive and continuous downsizing have produced this situation (Doern and Conway, 1994; Doern, 1995; Leiss et al., 1996). Under the Regulatory Efficiency Act in 1992–3, Environment Canada lost 30 percent of its budget. In 1994–5 the budget was cut again, from $705 million to $507 million. Personnel have been reduced from 10,000 in 1992–3 to under 4000 in 1994–5. As well, the Department of Environment lost its designation as a senior Ministry, giving it less clout inside Cabinet, less voice in government priorities and decisions, and (even) fewer resources (*Globe & Mail*, 30 July 1997: A3; 19 August 1997: A1; 27 May 1998: A3). Federal environmental charges have dropped 78 percent since 1992 (*Globe & Mail*, 23 March 1999: A7).

In the province of Ontario environmental protection has been targeted ideologically since 1995, when a neo-liberal government took over from the left-leaning NDP (in office from 1991–5). From 1987–8 to 1993–4 Ontario's Ministry of the Environment was one of the best in the country, with high conviction rates and 200–300 annual prosecutions (Gallon, 1996). But in 1995–6 725 enforcement and investigation officials were let go, charges dropped from 1640 in 1994 to 724 in 1996. Prosecutions in some regions dropped 74 percent, fines declined 57 percent from 1995 to 1996. The average pollution fine dropped from a high of $3,633,095 in 1992 to $1,204,034 in 1997.[9] In 1997 several hundred officials monitoring and researching air and water quality were dismissed, the number of pollution inspectors fell 28 percent between 1995 and 1998 (*Globe & Mail*, 22 June 1998: A1). The annual operating budget, $390 million in 1993–4, stood at $150 million in 1995–6, and was cut by another third in 1997. Overall, charges have dropped by 50 percent from 1992 to 1997.[10] [...]

[...] What, then, were the knowledge claims that legitimized the disappearance of corporate crime, and how are they related to hegemonic interests? The corporate counter-revolution overall is grounded in arguments associated with monetarism and the neo-liberal economics of the 'Chicago School'. These ideas are not based in natural science but they do speak the language of statistics:

seminal articles all grounded their claims in complex mathematical models and formulae. These claims, which have restructured western capitalism over the last two decades, present an ontology of property and markets and a theory of action that explains production. Adherents argue that the unimpeded operation of market forces is the primary imperative driving capitalist economies. Market forces create wealth, which drives progress, modernity and creates all the benefits of industrialized societies (Friedman, 1962). The initial goal of neo-liberal[11] economists was the intellectual displacement of Keynesian economics, blamed for legitimating government intervention in the economy and inventing the welfare state. Keynesians departed from laissez-faire schools by arguing that state programmes which stimulated demand to create full employment made capitalist systems more, not less, efficient (Marchak, 1991). This is heresy to neo-liberalism which argues that market systems can only operate at maximum efficiency when there are no artificial barriers such as government regulations, tariffs or subsidies, to impede them. Markets must be 'set free' to follow their internal logic, which is profit maximization. The state has no role except to get out of the way. Governments must therefore repeal all policies aimed at regulating, humanizing or disciplining market forces (Posner, 1976, 1977). The idea that underlaid the welfare state, that government had a duty to protect citizens from the excesses of capitalist systems, is dismissed. Regulation is conceptualized as misguided interference in citizens' financial affairs at best, gross and unforgiveable theft at worst. When popularized by the business press, regulation becomes a 'cowardly' way for government to raise levels of taxation (editorial in *The Economist*, reprinted in *Globe & Mail*, 29 July 1996: A15). [...]

[...] These arguments were supplemented by traditional philosophical and legal objections to corporate crime and business regulation, such as claims that criminal law should never be applied to business executives because they are not 'real criminals'. ('Real' criminals are poor people, outsiders—the young, black/native male.) Business offences are *mala prohibita* offences, not *mala in se* (that is, wrong because prohibited by government, not intrinsically evil). Unlike 'normal' theft and assault, they do not hurt anybody. Or business transgressions were portrayed as rare, accidental events caused by technology or organizational complexity. Finally, ironically, sociological arguments from corporate crime literatures showing that criminal law has been very ineffective in dealing with business crime were cited. As these literatures show, enforcing criminal law is expensive, laws are badly written and full of loopholes, regulators have to let offences continue to get evidence that will stand up in court, thereby multiplying the damage done, and judicial reluctance to assess serious penalties had made business crime a high-profit, low-risk investment (Clinard and Yeager, 1980; Bardach and Kagan, 1982; Hawkins, 1984; Levi, 1984, 1993; Shapiro, 1984, 1985; Braithwaite, 1985b; Grabosky and Braithwaite, 1986, 1993; Gunningham, 1987; Coleman, 1989; Tucker, 1990; Yeager, 1991; Ayres and Braithwaite, 1992).

Why, then, were anti-regulatory arguments heard in the 1980s and 1990s, but not in the 1960s and 1970s, when policy makers were more attuned to the discourse of corporate crime with its claims that criminal law should be strengthened to deal with corporate criminals, regulation of all kinds should be increased, and rich and poor offenders, corporate and individual, should be treated the same? Certainly no new evidence proving that monopolies and oligopolies were a good thing was produced. And some of the claims employed to support deregulation are blatantly ideological, such as suggestions that anti-social acts committed by corporate executives are *mala prohibita* while those of unemployed street kids are *mala in se*. Deconstructed, this means that upstanding corporate executives (that is, 'people like me') do not intentionally do harmful things. But every ghetto kid who sells crack to his buddies 'really intends' to addict the entire neighbourhood. And every drunk driver whose reckless act leads to the deaths of innocent people, who ends up serving many years in prison, is somehow more culpable than the mining executive who kills dozens by repeatedly failing to fix dangerous conditions underground. (This argument is advanced despite the fact that the executive, unlike the drunk driver, never puts his/her own life at risk *and* stands to profit from his negligence (Pearce, 1993).) Some are simply incorrect—corporate crime is not victimless, it kills, injures and defrauds far more than traditional lower class crime (Coleman, 1989; Clarke, 1990; Snider, 1993). In the average break and enter $500 or $1000 is lost, $500 billion was looted by S&L executives. [...]

[...] Hearing and attending to neo-liberal truth claims has certainly set capital free. It has legitimized the elimination of national assets and public corporations[12] and facilitated the creation of oligopolies, massive agglomerations of capital larger than most nation-states which answer to no regulatory or democratic authority. The sovereign transnational corporation has claimed the right to maximize profits, downsize at will, destroy unions and hire the cheapest labour world-wide. The result has been massive growth in the size, power and profitability of the corporate sector. Fifty-one of the largest economies in the world belong not to countries, but to transnational corporations. Wal-Mart, at number 12, has gross revenues greater than the total wealth of 161 countries (Dobbin, 1998). Companies such as General Motors, Mitusi and Itoh have sales revenues over $100 billion, bigger than the GDPs of Denmark, Finland and Norway. 'The 200 largest corporations have more economic clout than the poorest four-fifths of humanity' (Dobbin, 1998: 74–5). Monopolistic markets are the norm in automotive, airline, computing, aerospace, electronics and steel (Miyoshi, 1993). Free trade has allowed nation-states to justify deregulation by arguing they no longer have the authority to regulate—the aforementioned ideology of globalization. Three trading blocks—Europe, the Americas and the Pacific Rim—control world export and trade and the dominance of the US economy, whose elites led the neo-liberal counter-revolution, has been reinforced (Dicken, 1992).[13] [...]

Notes

1 Of course traditional crime is similarly contingent on the definitional acts os a sovereign state. Buts its boundaries, far from disappearing, are exploding.

2 Corporate crime must not be confused with occupational crime because the former is committed on behalf of a corporation (although competing business may be victimized), the latter against it (Marshall, 1998: 122). Crimies against

business, occupational crimes such as embezzlement or expense account fraud, are flourishing conceptually and as policy (though still underenforced in comparison to traditional 'blue-collar' crime) (Hollinger and Clark, 1983; Weisburd et al., 1990).

3   Efficiency fell as well, as regulatory staff became little more than publicly funded consultants to the corporate sector, and the time required to register and assess each merger file expanded to two person-days minimum. The costs of enforcement rose (average expenditures went from $2,758,000 in 1971–5 under the Combines Investigation Act to $15,284,000 in 1986–8)

4   Thatcherism, as it has become known, is a dramtic case of a formerly generous welfare state using massive repression to remove workers' and citizens' rights (e.g. the strike of the coal mierns, the treatment of the Greenham Common protesters) and destroy resistance (Carlen, 1995; Tombs, 1996).

5   The US is perhaps the most extreme example, with variation by city as well as state. Los Angeles elected an official responsible for prosecuting occupational health, safety and environmental offences in 1985 (Grabosky and Braithwaite, 1993: 16). But even in the highly centralized UK, differences between agencies and regions are pronounced.

6   From 1988–93 20 percent of all deaths on the job in Canada were caused by exposure to harmful substances (poisons, chemicals, carcinogens, radiation), 19 percent by transport accidents and 18 percent by being struck or caught by an object (trees, machines, rock faces) (Statistics Canada, 1996).

7   Workers are also culpable. Smoking, abuse of legal and illegal drugs, carelessness and stupidity also cause illness and injury. Machismo subcultures—real men take risks, wimps wear safety helmets and wine about coal dust—prevent safety consciousness (Glasbeek and Tucker, 1992). National cultures are important too—in the US violent acts (shootings) cause 21 percent of work-related deaths (versus 2 percent in Canada, negligible percentages elsewhere).

8   This is not a unique case, nor one that has caused provincial or federal re-regulation. In 1997 the left-leaning government of British Columbia introduced a Bill giving workers more rights to refuse unsafe work. Business opposition was so virulent that Bill 44 was withdrawn six months later. Although British Columbia has the highest fatality rates in Canada, with on-the-job deaths per 100,000 in construction, forestry, and transportation more than double the rates of other provinces (Statistics Canada, 1996), mainstream media insisted this was a battle between small business and monolithic, all-powerful 'Big Labour'. Bill 44, thundered the *Globe & Mail*, was an attempt by the 'last surviving NDP crank government' to 'enslave the private sector' (*Globe & Mail*, 17 July 1997: B2).

9   Access to information is also a casualty, the 'real' figures may be lower still. The Canadian Institute for Environmental Law and Policy claims that fine levels actually totalled a mere $955,000.

10   This record is atypical only in its rapidity. In Alberta, the budget for Environment Protection Ministry dropped from $405 million in 1992–3 to

$275 million in 1996–7. Downsizing ocurred even in Quebec, where a strong state has historically been central to protecting French heritage (*Globe & Mail*, 27 May 1998: A1, 3).

11 The terminology is confusing. Neo-liberal ideas lead to conservative policies. But they are libertarian extensions of classic liberal thought championing the rights of the individual against the 'coercive state' (Marshall, 1998: 445).

12 By 1991 extensive public assets had been sold off in more than 88 countries (Pearce and Sinder, 1995: 25). by the mid-1990s downsizing and deregulation were ascendant in even the most stalwart of welfare states: between 1994 and 1998, public spending in Sweden fell from 68 percent of gross domestic product to 59 percent, a decline of 9 percent; in Denmark during the same period public spending was cut by 7 percent, 6 percent cuts were made in Finland and Canada; 5 percent in Italy, (another) 4 perecnt in Britain, 2 percent in Germany and .5 percent even in France (*Globe & Mail*, 25 April 1998: B2; from *The Economist* and the Swedish Ministry of Finance, OECD).

13 Indeed the only effective controls on transistional capital arise from conflicts between the blocks. The European Common Market, for example, has taken on the US over its domination of world culture, genetic engineering of plants, import duties on Caribbean bananas and 'illegal' subsides paid to French farmers or German auto workers (e.g. *Guardian Weekly*, 15 June 1997: 19).

37

Defenders of order or guardians of human rights?
Herman Schwendinger and Julia Schwendinger

[...] [I]f ruling classes and powerful interest groups are able to manipulate legislators to their own advantage, isn't it possible that there are instances of socially injurious behavior which have no legal precedents? Consider further the chance that there are practices by men of power which are highly injurious to most of mankind and which are neither defined nor sanctioned by civil or criminal laws, such as, for example, genocide and economic exploitation. Isn't it apparent, if Sutherland had consistently explored the use of ethical categories like social injury, that he would have concluded that there are, on one hand, socially non-injurious acts which are defined as crimes and, on the other, socially injurious acts which are nevertheless not defined as either civil or criminal violations?

It is in relation to these logical possibilities that the ideological function of legal sanctions (as a defining criterion) is fully exposed. If the *ethical* criteria of "social injury," "public wrong," or "anti-social behavior" are not explicated, then the existent *ethical standpoint of the State is taken as a given* when the criterion of sanctions by the State is also used in the definitions of crime. This is why the meanings of such categories as social injury are so critical for the definition of crime. [...]

[...] No scholar involved in the controversy about the definitions of crime has been able to avoid direct or indirect use of moral standards in a solution to this problem. In spite of this, the choices of defining criteria have been accompanied by a technocratic incapacity to confront the moral implications of this selection. It is not clear, for example, that the acceptance of procedural law as a defining criterion delegates personal responsibility to agents of the State. But this delegation is no less a moral act and therefore cannot avoid complicity in the actual definitions made by official agents. Just as moral is the explicit use of sanctions or the implicit use of other defining criteria,[1] derived from functional imperatives of established institutions or political economies. In light of this, the claim that value judgments have no place in the formulation of the definition of crime is without foundation.

An alternative solution to the definition of crime should openly face the moral issues presented by this definitional dilemma. Traditionally, these issues have been inadequately represented by such unanalyzed terms as "social injury," "anti-social act," or "public wrongs." But how does one confront the problem of explicating "social injury" or "public wrongs"? Is this done by reference to the functional imperatives of social institutions or by the historically determined rights of individuals? In our opinion, the latter is the only humanistic criterion which can be used for this purpose.

There has been an expansion of the concept of human rights throughout history. And political events have made it possible, at this time, to insist on the inclusion of standards clustered around modern egalitarian principles, as well as enduring standards such as the right to be secure in one's own person, the right to speak one's mind, and the right to assemble freely. We refer to these ideas as modern because they are to be distinguished from those fashioned in the eighteenth century when a rising middle class formulated a challenge to the economic prerogatives of feudal aristocracies. At that time, the functional imperatives of the patriarchal family, price-making market, and political state were reified, by recourse to natural law, as basic human needs. In this reified form, equality was primarily perceived as the immutable right to compete *equally* with others for a position in social, economic and political spheres of life. In the context of our modern political and economic institutions, however, competitive equality has not had, as an empirical outcome, the furtherance of human equality. Instead, it has been used to justify inequalities between the sexes, classes, races and nations. [...]

[...] In opposition to the ever increasing demand for equalitarianism, elitist social scientists have formulated theoretical justifications for social inequality.[2] We deny the ethical and empirical validity of these theoretical justifications! Irrespective of claims to the contrary (Warner, 1949; Moore, 1963), there is no universal moral rule or empirical property which is inherent to man or society which makes social inequality a functional necessity. Above all, there is no valid moral or empirical justification for the outstanding forms of social inequality in existence today including economic, racial and sexual inequality. If the traditional egalitarian principle that *all* human beings are to be provided the opportunity for the free development of their potentialities is to be achieved in modern industrial societies, then persons must be regarded as more than objects who are to be "treated equally" by institutions of social control. All persons must be guaranteed the fundamental prerequisites for well-being, including food, shelter, clothing, medical services, challenging work and recreational experiences, as well as security from predatory individuals or repressive and imperialistic social elites. These material requirements, basic services and enjoyable relationships are not to be regarded as rewards or privileges.[3] They are rights! [...]

[...] Perhaps there are no statements more repugnant to traditional legal scholars than those which define social systems as criminal. But this repugnance reflects the antiquarian psychologistic and technocratic character of the legal tradition. This tradition is blind to the fact that extensive social planning makes it possible to evaluate, mitigate or eliminate the *social* conditions which generate criminal behavior. It is no longer sufficient to justify the restriction of criminology to the study of those institutions which define, adjudicate and sanction *individual* criminals. It has become evident that any group which attempts to control or prevent criminal behavior by the activity of the traditional institutions of criminal justice alone is incapable of accomplishing this end.

As a rule, criminal behavior *does* involve individual moral responsibility and the assessment of psychological relationships, such as the motivated character of the criminal act. However, the science of crime has gone beyond the centuries old notion that crime can be conceived as a function of the properties of atomistic individuals alone.[4] Social scientists today are intensely involved in scrutinizing social relationships which generate criminal behavior. This activity is reflected in the *real definitions* of crime which have been and are being developed by sociologists, economists, anthropologists and political scientists.

The logical strictures on the definition of social systems or relationships as criminal are removed when it is realized that real definitions by social scientists establish a diachronic relationship between the notion of criminal rates, for example, and the *socially* necessary and sufficient conditions for these rates.

If crime is defined by scientists in terms of the *socially* necessary and sufficient conditions for its existence, what would be more logical than to call these social conditions criminal? After all, crime has been traditionally defined by legalists on the basis of nominalist definitions or descriptive definitions which refer to the ways in which agents of the State react to criminal behavior. To be sure, some legalists have used ethical terms such as "public wrongs" or "social injury" in earmarking criminal behavior. But isn't a real definition of crime vastly superior to a nominalist definition or a definition which does not even define crime but merely refers to how the State reacts to it? And isn't a scientist justified in making a logically implied, normative evaluation of what he considers to be the cause of crime? And given the acceptance of criminal institutions and socialeconomic relationships as real definers of crime, what more ultimate claim can social-scientists use to justify their unique role as criminologists, than to use the term crime to identify social systems which can be regulated or eliminated in order to control or prevent crime? What better term than crime can be used to express their *normative* judgments of the conditions which generate criminal behavior? [...]

[...] Once human rights rather than legally operative definitions are used to earmark criminal behavior, then it is possible to ask whether there are violations of human rights which are more basic than others and to designate these rights as most relevant to the domain of criminology.[5] Basic rights are differentiated because their fulfillment is absolutely essential to the realization of a great number of values. Although the lower boundary of this number is not specified here, the sense of what is meant can be ascertained by considering security to one's person as a basic right. Obviously a danger to one's health or life itself endangers all other claims: A dead man can hardly realize *any* of his human potentialities.

Similar assessments can be made of the right to racial, sexual and economic equality. The abrogation of these rights certainly limits the individual's chance to fulfill himself in many spheres of life. These rights therefore are basic because there is so much at stake in their fulfillment. It can be stated, in light of the previous argument, that individuals who deny these rights to others are criminal. Likewise, social relationships and social systems which regularly cause the abrogation of these rights are also criminal. If the terms imperialism, racism, sexism and poverty are abbreviated signs for theories of social relationships or social systems which cause the systematic abrogation of basic rights, then imperialism, racism, sexism, and poverty can be called crimes according to the logic of our argument.

It is totally irrelevant, in this light, to consider whether leaders of imperialist nations are war criminals by virtue of legal precedent or decisions by war tribunals.[6] Nor is it relevant to make note of the fact that property rights which underlie racist practices are guaranteed by law. It is likewise unimportant that sexual inequality in such professions as sociology is maintained by references to the weight of tradition. Neither can persistent unemployment be excused because it is ostensibly beyond the control of the State. [...]

Notes

1   These other criteria usually deline crime as a departure from "normal" states, when may be vaguely signified by exceedingly formal terms as "the mores," "the group," "the political group," "superordinaces," "the public," or "society."

2   For a classic debate on this issue, see the discussion between Davis (1953), Moore (1953) and Tumia (1953a, 1953b).

3   The degree to which the fullfillment of basic human needs is equated with dollars in our society is revealed in the American Medical Association's persistent denial of the right of all persons to medical services. As John H. Knowles (1970: 74) states "... a significant group of doctors has the attitude as stated by a past AMA president, that health is privilege, not a right. I think that health is as much a right as the right to schooling or decent housing or food, and the people have begun to perceive it as a right."

4   The science of crime has gone beyond this even though the legalists may not have progressed thisfar. It is vital, however, that legalists be informed that social scientists are formerely in isolated criminal acts but in personality relationships, social relationships and systems of social relationships which generate a succession of criminal acts on the part of distinct individuals, on one hand, and socially distributed instances of criminal acts by many individuals on the other hand. The psychiatrist, for example, interested in the moral careers of individuals, has moved beyond the emperial issues which were traditionally addressed by legal scholars and which are still reflected in the way in which the criminal law is fashioned today.

5   The basic human rights. It should be reiterated, that are not being referred to here are those alleged rights which are intrinsic to the nature of man, or which are functionally imperative for social stability and order. A prime example of the reification of social imperatives is Garafolo's depiction of "natural crimes" on the basis of basic moral sentiments of *pity* (involving empathic feelings) and *probity* (involving the respect for rights of private property). These "basic moral sentiments" are functionally necessary for the maintenance of "modern

societies." Garafolo's theory was in the *reform* Darwinist tradition initiated by early corporate liberals. This tradition was used to justify the expansion the political power of the State in order to regulate the uncontrolled competitive processes represented by laissezfaire capitalism.

38

State crime, human rights, and the limits of criminology
Penny Green and Tony Ward

[...] [T]he term "state crime" (as applied to contemporary states) should be restricted to the area of overlap between two distinct phenomena: (1) violations of human rights and (2) state organizational deviance. We define human rights, following Gewirth and the Schwendingers, as the elements of freedom and well-being that human beings need to exert and develop their capacities for purposive action. The exact scope of such rights (or needs) is debatable, but it is a debate to which social scientists can and should contribute. State organizational deviance is conduct by persons working for state agencies, in pursuit of organizational goals, that if it were to become known to some social audience would expose the individuals or agencies concerned to a sufficiently serious risk of formal or informal censure and sanctions to affect their conduct significantly (for example, by inducing them to conceal or lie about their activities). Such censure or sanctions may originate "from above" (formal legal or disciplinary sanctions), "from below" (delegitimation, i.e., conduct manifesting a withdrawal or erosion of consent, see Beetham, 1991), "from within" (informal norms of the organizational culture), or "from without" (international pressures).

Our definition reserves the label "crime" for behavior that is both "objectively" illegitimate (albeit according to an intensely value-laden criterion) and "subjectively" deviant. We do not consider it morally or semantically appropriate to apply the word "crime" either to deviations from other value systems (for example, Islam, free trade, or socialism) to which particular states claim to subscribe, or to practices that the critical social scientist may justifiably perceive to be illegitimate, but which are generally accepted as part of the routine, legitimate activity of the state (or at least as within the fair range of party-political disagreement). The obvious example of the latter is the maintenance of a capitalist economy. The contradiction between the gross inequities in the distribution of wealth and power under capitalism, and ideologies of human rights and democracy call into question the legitimacy of any capitalist state, but by no stretch of the term is this contradiction an example of organizational deviance. It is debasing the currency of criminology to label failures to pursue radical egalitarian policies as "crimes" (*pace* the ingenious arguments of Henry, 1991) Such general sociopolitical questions underpin all critical social science, but we must be clear that criminology is an inappropriate vehicle for addressing them politically.

It is also necessary (as in the field of corporate and white-collar crime) to distinguish between individual deviant acts committed by state agents in the course of their employment and acts committed in pursuit of organizational goals. The organizational goals of state agencies are not necessarily those publicly prescribed for them. For example, if police forces in practice pursue a goal of "social discipline" rather than law enforcement as Choongh (1997) has argued, the use of violence in pursuit of that goal (assuming there is a risk of sanctions if it becomes known to lawyers, the media, etc.) will constitute a state crime. Because the goals of state agencies are more various than those of commercial organizations, the boundary between organizational and individual deviance by state agents is less clearly defined than it generally is for corporate employees. Bribery, for example, is sometimes, like embezzlement, a straightforward crime of individual enrichment at the expense of organizational goals. Yet exchanges of gifts, information, or favors with business contacts or criminal informants may be a means of advancing legitimate organizational goals (e.g., Hobbs, 1988; Smart, 1999); bribery may be tacitly condoned by states as an economical way of paying their work forces; particular state agencies (such as some U.S. police forces in the 1960s and 1970s) may adopt corruption and extortion as informal organizational goals (Sherman, 1978); and whole states ("kleptocracies") may exist primarily to enrich their officials.

Implicit in the human-rights-based definition of state crime is the inclusion not only of active violations of human rights, but also of passive failures to protect individuals against violations of their rights by other individuals or corporations. There is a continuum here between crimes that are plainly instigated and condoned by state agencies (such as the activities of anti-independence militias in East Timor), through the "capture" of regulatory agencies by the bodies they are supposed to regulate, through negligent policing that reflects institutionalized race, class, or gender bias, to errors of judgment that may be apparent only in hindsight. Such definitional problems should not, however, preclude the recognition of crimes of complicity or omission as an important dimension of state crime.[1] [...]

[...] We have attempted to develop here an approach to state crime that retains at its essence the concept of deviance. Relying solely on a human rights discourse leaves us with the borderless condition of "social harm" — politically valid, but criminologically less satisfactory. However, when a human rights analysis is used within a framework of deviance and legitimacy and the audience for whom state norms are breached is extended beyond that of the powerful to those from "below," then we have a conceptually coherent definition of state organized crime. One of the virtues of this perspective, as we have shown, is that it allows us to systematically explore state crime in very different political contexts. [...]

Note

1 The catastrophic consequences of the Turkish earthquakes in August and November 1999 may very usefully be analyzed from within the framework of our definition.

39

The World Bank and crimes of globalization: a case study
David O. Friedrichs and Jessica Friedrichs

[...] The World Bank has been criticized for being paternalistic, secretive, and counterproductive in terms of any claimed goal of improving people's lives. Specifically, it has been charged with being complicit in policies with genocidal consequences, with exacerbating ethnic conflict, with increasing the gap between rich and poor, with fostering immense ecological and environmental damage, and with the callous displacement of vast numbers of indigenous people in developing countries from their original homes and communities (Rich, 1994: *xii*, 16, 30, 93, 151). Critics claim that many of the less-developed countries that received World Bank loans are worse off today in terms of poverty, and that the severe austerity measures imposed on borrowing countries, deemed necessary to maximize the chances of Bank loans being repaid, most heavily affect the poorest and most vulnerable segments of the population (Johnson, 2000).

The most favored World Bank project has been the building of dams, but even its own experts concede that millions of people have been displaced because of these projects (Caufield, 1996: 12, 73). In many of these projects, resettlement plans have been nonexistent — violating the Bank's own guidelines — or have been inadequately implemented. In a notorious case from the 1970s, in which anti-dam protesters in Guatemala were massacred by the military, the World Bank report on the project failed to directly mention the atrocity (*Ibid.*: 207–208; 263). Given such circumstances, claims of criminality have been leveled against the World Bank. At a 1988 World Bank meeting in Berlin, protesters called for the establishment of a Permanent People's Tribunal to try the World Bank (and the International Monetary Fund) for "crimes against humanity" (Rich, 1994: 9). An American anthropologist characterized the forced resettlement of people in dam-related projects as the worst crime against them, short of killing them (Caufield, 1996: 262). An American biologist characterized the World Bank's report on the environmental impact of one of its dam projects in a developing country as "fraudulent" and "criminal" (Rich, 1994: 11–12). [...]

[...] The World Bank's complicity in the crimes outlined above is best understood in terms of its criminogenic structure and organization. The historical charge of its charter called upon it to focus on economic developments and considerations, not the other consequences of its policies and practices (*Ibid*.: 199). Throughout its history, it has thus avoided addressing or taking a strong stand on human rights issues (Caufield, 1996: 206). Its focus on a less than well-defined mission of promoting "long-term sustainable growth" has served as a rationale for imposing much short-term suffering and economic losses (Rich, 1994: 189). This orientation has led the World Bank to adopt and apply somewhat one-dimensional economic models to its project-related analyses, with insufficient attention to many other considerations and potentially useful insights from other disciplines (*Ibid*.: 195). Once the projects are initiated, they tend to develop a momentum of their own that often marginalizes or negates any real adjustments in response to reports indicating negative environmental or social effects (Vallabhaneni, 2000: 11). The underlying incentive structure at the Bank encourages "success" with large, costly projects. Bank employees are pressured to make the environmental (as well as social) conditions fit. Like other international financial institutions, the World Bank is structured so that it rewards its personnel for technical proficiency rather than for concerning themselves with the perspectives and needs of the ordinary people of developing countries (Bradlow, 1996: 75).[1]

In terms of their career interests, World Bank officials are rewarded for making loans and moving large amounts of money, rather than relative to any human consequences of these loans. Furthermore, World Bank personnel have not been held accountable for the tragic human consequences of their projects (Rich, 1994: 91, 307). All of these institutional factors contribute to a criminogenic environment.

Insofar as the World Bank is not a signatory to international human rights treaties, it has manifested relatively little concern with human rights abuses (Bradlow, 1996: 63). International financial institutions are, however, subject to the imperatives of international law, and at a minimum are obliged to insure that they do not exacerbate conditions impinging on human rights, Most of the countries with which they have dealings have ratified the U.N.'s Economic Covenants, and accordingly should be bound by its provisions.

Our claim is not that the World Bank adopts policies or makes loan-related decisions with the intent or objective of causing harm. The case can be made that at least some World Bank policymakers sincerely hope to achieve positive results, to foster development and reduce the scope of poverty (Caufield, 1996; Rich, 1994). Furthermore, voices within the World Bank during the recent era have questioned or challenged some World Bank policies and practices that appear to have had harmful consequences. Policies are being examined now through the Bank's internal departments that will more clearly define the Bank's influence (or lack of it) after a project has been completed. This influence may be monetary, such as providing compensation for mistakes made. It may also be based on leverage to pressure governments to take responsibility for a project, leverage that propelled these projects from the start. However, many critics — and even the former chief economist of the World Bank, Joseph Stiglitz (2000; 2001) — contend that the policies and practices of the World Bank and other international financial institutions have adopted the interests of the advanced industrialized nations and the Wall Street financial community as their highest priority. Without checks in the Bank's procedures, it can continue to encourage, fund, and assess development projects that do not support the goals of a country's people (yet continuously prop up powerful government and big business). Ideologically, the World Bank creates and contributes to the general concept of "development" by funding only a certain kind of development. For the past 50 years, the World Bank has invested in large, export-oriented projects such as pipelines and dams that cause severe environmental upheaval and penalize the very people they claim they wish to help: the poor.

A characteristic of significant forms of white-collar crime (including much corporate crime) is that the harm involved is a consequence, not a specific objective, of certain policy choices and practices. As with other forms of white-collar crime, the harmful (or illegal) activity associated with the crimes of international financial institutions occurs within the context of productive, legal activity; it is a byproduct of efforts to achieve gain, avoid loss, or advance some other legitimate organizational objective, with such objectives taking precedence over other considerations. Legitimate organizations do respond at times to claims that they are engaging in harmful (or illegal) activities, as in the case of the World Bank. Yet such responses may simply be cynical (purely for public relations purposes), strategic (to maximize chances of achieving major objectives), political (in deference to internal coalitions, or as necessary compromises), or sincere (authentically concerned with pursuing the most morally and ethically defensible policies). With organizations such as the World Bank, a complex combination of responses is surely involved.

In sum, we do not contend that the specific intent and purpose of the policies of the World Bank is to do harm. However, we hold that the World Bank's mode of operation is intrinsically criminogenic and that it functions undemocratically; its key deliberations are carried out behind a veil of secrecy and it is insufficiently accountable to any truly independent entity. At a minimum, the World Bank is criminally negligent when it: (1) fails to adequately explore or take into account the impact of its loans for major projects on indigenous peoples; (2) adopts and implements policies specifically at odds with the protocols of the *Universal Declaration of Human Rights* and subsequent covenants; or (3) operates in a manner at least hypothetically at odds with international and state law. [...]

Note

1   In the case of Thailand, the government elite adopted a policy to deliberately undermine rural peasants. "The World Bank supported this strategy with development loans to finance infrastructure — roads, dams, electrical generation — and the industrialization of agricultural production" (Greider, 1997: 352).

SECTION 7:

The problem of criminalisation

The power to break the law

As we have seen in previous sections of this book, the relative power held by members of the ruling class, by privileged corporate 'persons' and by government institutions places limits upon the extent to which domestic and international law can be effective. Together, the extracts in this chapter reveal three types of power. The first is power as it is expressed directly, as a form of 'power over', whereby a powerful group imposes its will upon those who create or enforce the law (for example, by lobbying policy-makers and regulators). This form of power enables us to see how power operates in a relatively naked and visible way. However, power cannot be represented too simplistically or reduced to the idea that powerful institutions simply do as they like. As we have seen, legal accountability mechanisms for state and corporate crime tend to arise from moments of crisis or exposure for the state and the continuing zeal of those mechanisms is dependent upon ongoing struggles around enforcement. Power, then, does not merely operate in a one-dimensional sense, in a way that allows the powerful to demand that the law always works in their favour. Therefore we need a more subtle understanding of how the power to shape decisions works.

A second approach to power begins from the point that not all power is immediately visible. Policy decisions can be influenced by relatively hidden assumptions and underlying precepts that shape such decisions. So, for example, law-makers and criminal justice institutions may be persuaded against taking a particular form of punitive action because it is cast as being not in the general or public interest. Often, as we shall see in this section, this brings ideology into play. The desirability or feasibility of pursuing criminalization strategies is often grounded in particular sets of ideas about what the corporation is and how it can most easily be made to comply with the law.

Thirdly, power operates in a way that pre-empts and short-circuits choices and decisions. This roughly approximates to what Lukes (1974) has called a three-dimensional view, whereby power is exercised in a way that is derived from "socially structured and culturally patterned behaviour" (1974: 22). And law plays a central role here by establishing a general pattern that appears as the natural order of things. It seems natural that violent individuals and not corporations commit crime; and it seems natural that the development of international law is a process that promotes harmony and equality. This dimension of power, what we might call 'the pre-emptive power of law' keeps at bay the prospects for imagining alternative means of accountability for state and corporate crime.

This section begins with a second extract from Marx's *Capital*. In this extract, the problem of criminalisation is considered through a focus upon some of the earliest laws that were designed to protect workers. The factories inspectors of mid-nineteenth-century Britain faced considerable difficulties when they tried to enforce the law against a relatively powerful elite. Marx here is describing the various dodges used by factory masters to maintain a 'relay system' and circumnavigate the legal limits on the working day by employing workers concurrently across different shifts. The introduction of the relay system was characterised as the manufacturers' "revolt" against government. In response to this revolt, workers held protest meetings across Yorkshire and Lancashire, creating a 'counter-revolt' so ferocious that the Factory Inspectorate 'urgently warned the government that the antagonism of classes had arrived at an incredible tension' (Marx, 1954: 276). Determination to enforce the law under very difficult conditions, indicated here by Marx's description of the determined efforts of Leonard Horner, was by no means replicated across the Inspectorate. Later on in this section of *Capital,* Marx notes how the Home Secretary appealed, via a Home Office circular, to the Inspectorate to treat factory owners more leniently for breaches of the 1844 Act. Some, like Horner, resisted. But another factory inspector, J. Stuart, is singled out for allowing illegally long working hours to flourish within his jurisdiction in Scotland.

Although the law had never been framed in a particularly punitive way (proposals for imprisonment as punishment for the most serious offences had been rejected in the framing of the 1833 Act), the coincidence of interests across the judicial and factory-owning sections of the ruling class meant that the Factory Inspectorate was always going to encounter resistance to criminalisation in the courts. The unwillingness of magistrates to convict respectable members of society for their crimes was to dampen the Factory Inspectorate's initial punitive zeal. And the courts from an early point used their prerogative to avoid conviction where it could be shown that the offence was not willfully or grossly negligent. They also tended to impose the minimum penalties. As Carson (1979: 50) noted, just over two-thirds of convictions between 1836 and 1842 resulted in a minimum £1 fine. With the courts in the main unwilling to embark upon a collective criminalisation of this respectable class of factory owners, the Inspectorate began to apply the law in a highly selective manner. Inspectors exercised a high degree of discretion and were given limited powers to devise regulations. The latter might include the imposition of a particular administrative responsibility upon employers (keeping time-books, certificates of employees' age and so on). This is the origin of 'a strategy of last resort prosecution' (Norrie, 2001: 85).

Another important development at this time was the dilution in the 1844 Factory Act of the normal *mens rea* requirement in the criminal process (see the extract by Glasbeek in Section 4). The 1844 Act enabled the *mens rea* requirement to be sidestepped by allowing an employer to be found 'guilty in the first instance'. Using this concept of 'strict liability' (see the extract by Wells in

Section 4), the employer was required to prove that due diligence had been exercised to comply with the law (Carson, 1980: 164). An employer who could not demonstrate due diligence would be found guilty of an offence. Thus, there was no need to demonstrate *mens rea* in such cases. Whilst this concept of liability made it easier to prosecute factory owners, it also ensured that breaches of the Factory Act would be seen as less serious. And this offence – since it did not require a state of mind to be demonstrated and since it carried low-level administrative penalties in the first instance – was categorised as an 'administrative' or 'technical' offence, rather than an unambiguously *criminal* offence. The penalties triggered by this type of offence were also relatively low and mostly dealt with by fines. This is essentially why strict liability offences came to be regarded as a different class of offence and generally not regarded as 'real crimes'. From this brief history we can see not only that the power of the factory owner class was important in shaping the leniency of the courts, but in fact was a formative influence on the development of the legal categories that were to apply to its members.

The introduction to the previous section identified an enduring paradox in capitalist social orders. This paradox is captured by the tendency of states to simultaneously encourage and control potentially harmful corporate activity. So at the same time as the law provides a basic structure of rules that enable corporations to act, to make profits and so on (law's enabling function), the law is also required to intervene to impose a regulatory structure on corporations that limits their activities (law's controlling function). As it applies to corporate crime, then, the law can be said to have a simultaneously enabling and controlling function. Indeed, it is important not to underestimate the formal powers that are retained by the criminal justice system. For very often the powers given to criminal justice authorities to investigate white-collar crime are more extensive than powers provided for any other form of crime (Levi, 1995). If there are indications that the capacity for criminal justice agencies to deal with corporate crime is very great indeed in some jurisdictions, this is not to say that this capacity has much of an impact. For even where clear legal and political rationales exist to allow – even insist upon – the criminalization of corporations, the enforcement and punishment of corporate crime remains relatively peripheral in criminal justice systems. 'Regulatory agencies' that are given the responsibility of dealing with corporate crime tend to be allocated resources that appear negligible when compared with mainstream law enforcement agencies; ongoing surveillance and inspection are barely executed – in the UK, companies can expect an inspection from the Field Operations Directorate of the Health and Safety Executive much less than once every 10 years (Tombs and Whyte, 2007); and prosecutions are infrequent – between 2000 and 2007, the Environment Agency in the UK only prosecuted 99 process industry pollution offences, certainly a function of their lack of resources rather than the lack of prosecutable cases (Tombs and Whyte, forthcoming).

The underenforcement of corporate crime results from a combination of a general lack of political priority afforded to regulation, and the dominant ideological assumptions that underpin the regulation of business. Regulatory agencies in liberal democratic societies typically use 'compliance' strategies of regulation. Agencies charged with controlling corporate harms, including food and consumer safety, environmental offences and worker health and safety, tend to seek *negotiated* settlements rather than strict enforcement strategies (Hutter, 1997). In practice this means that, in contrast with many categories of 'street' crime or 'mainstream' crime, prosecution is used as a strategy of last resort (Hawkins, 2002). Instead, corporations are encouraged to comply with the law through a process of bargaining or consensual agreement. Compliance approaches are based upon a series of assumptions about the nature of corporate offending and the levers that are most likely to ensure legal compliance. The first assumption is that, in general, corporations are inclined towards acting as law-abiding citizens. In other words, the corporate personality is one that *can* be appealed to on moral grounds. The second is that corporations will respond positively to a business case for offending in order to avoid losses in insurance premiums, losses in production, loss of market share and so on. Third, they are more likely to be encouraged into compliance by indirect commercial pressure from stakeholder groups, consumers, publics, non-governmental organisations, and even their industrial client and peer groups. Compliance theories are therefore very easily reducible to support for a form of market – as opposed to government – regulation.

If the process of de(c)riminalisation described by Marx can be understood as a direct expression of the class power of those the law sought initially to criminalise, and the preceding discussion described an indirect (but by no means less effective) means of bringing class power to the politics of regulation the readings in the rest of this section turn to look at problems for criminalisation that are rooted in the deeper structure of law. The extract by Anne Alvesalo is a reflection upon her research on the enforcement of corporate crime in Finland by regular police officers (Alvesalo, 2003; Alvesalo and Tombs, 2001). This research is of particular interest given the argument, noted above, that regulatory agencies are often underresourced. In Finland, some forms of corporate crime are dealt with by regular police forces, and it is this peculiar feature of the criminal justice system that allows Alvesalo to raise questions about the extent to which ideological construction of corporate crimes as 'not real crimes' is rooted in a process of differentiating separate enforcement agencies and separate bodies of law. In asking such questions, Alvesalo reveals a more fundamental aspect of law that is significant here. For it is not just in the construction of the criminal that the problem of criminalization arises, but in the construction of the crime. This, as Alvesalo notes, is not merely a procedural question, but also an ideological question of how prepared police officers are able to conceptualise and then act upon crime. But it is also a question that is related to the way that 'crimes' are constructed as events. We cannot fully understand corporate crimes as one-off incidents in which the criminal 'event' is contained within a relatively narrow time frame. Corporate crimes have a history. In corporate crimes, a concept of a criminal 'event' is also of limited value precisely because the relationship between the victim and the offender is also based upon an ongoing relationship of unequal power.

The extract by Raymond Michalowski and Ronald Kramer also focuses upon the 'deep' problems of criminalisation that arise in the regulatory spaces that exist as part of the global economy. Writing in 1987, a point at which a literature on 'globalisation' was beginning to expand rapidly, they note that the growing number of transnational corporations (TNCs) operating in developing countries has exposed the citizens of those countries to a growing range of corporate harms. For Michalowski and Kramer, because the largest TNCs have production facilities in the developing world, this creates the possibility that all corporate activities (including the most harmful activities) can be relocated. At the same time, the growth of exports of consumer goods to the developing world has generated consumer safety problems. The lack of public and regulatory pressure to monitor, regulate and recall products amplifies the dangers to consumer populations in relatively poor countries. Those problems in production and consumer standards are made potentially more harmful given the fact that developing nations have less developed laws in relation to workplace, environmental and consumer hazards than are found in developed countries. At the same time, international law has so far failed to develop universal legal standards for corporations. It is this 'space between the laws' that encourages the export of hazards. Thus, for Michalowski and Kramer, the problem of criminalisation arises from the 'space' between the regulatory standards that are applied to TNCs in relatively developed countries and the lack of appropriate legal standards in international law. In sum, the problem of criminalisation that is being identified here arises where a globalised market permits capital investment in locations where there are relatively low or ineffective legal standards (Brecher and Costello, 1994; Jeffcott, 2007; Tonelson, 2002) that in some contexts allow companies to act with impunity. If we understand those trends in the context of neo-liberalism, then, as Snider noted in the previous section, spaces between the laws are encouraged by the dominant political and economic logic not only in developing nations, but also in advanced capitalist nations.

The space that exists at the level of international law is important for thinking about the last three readings here. Each of these readings considers the problem of criminalizing state crimes under international law. Catherine MacKinnon's feminist perspective on international law opens up a new terrain for thinking about state crime. She notes how torture in the form of rape, battering and pornography are generally excluded from human rights law. This raises important questions about the complicity of states since she identifies forms of torture for which states are generally not held accountable. Yet they are very often used by military forces in the knowledge that they are unlikely to be held accountable (see also Stiglmayer, 1993; Jamieson, 1999). They are therefore crimes that are facilitated by the state's active intervention or passive non-intervention. This is a point that is concisely summed up by MacKinnon as follows: '[t]he abuse is systematic and known, the disregard is official and organized, and the effective government tolerance is a matter of law and policy' (extract: 25). And those examples of torture cited by MacKinnon include violations of rights and violations of state responsibilities that are established in international law. Yet they are humanitarian and human rights violations that have yet to be used to justify the positive intervention of UN peace-keeping forces. The difference, MacKinnon argues, is that the law fails to act to protect women in cases where men do not require the same protection. In this sense, she raises fundamental issues in relation to the gendered structure of the law and its impact upon criminalisation.

The readings by Bill Bowring and Noam Chomsky together demonstrate the fragility of a rule of law that purports to guide the conduct of states. Bowring's account is organized around the relationship between the legality of the use of military force by states and its sanction by the UN Security Council. In this context, we should recall the reasoning behind the emergence of a new system of international law following the Second World War discussed briefly in Section 1. The Nazi Holocaust, defined as it was as a crime against humanity, invalidated the Third Reich's legitimacy as a sovereign state. Yet despite this important precedent, states and state officials today retain a high degree of immunity from legal interference under international law. Sovereign and diplomatic immunity are only seriously challenged by international law where the state can invoke Chapter VII of the UN Charter. This is the rule that permits states to take military action against other states to prevent a threat to peace, a breach of the peace or an act of aggression. Chapter VII interventions depend upon UN Security Council approval.

However, as Bowring clearly illustrates, since 1986 there has been a precarious relationship between Security Council approval and US-led military intervention, a relationship that he characterizes as 'the degradation of international law'. The key military interventions described by Bowring reveal a range of justifications offered by the US, which together indicate an undermining of the authority of the UN Security Council. The extract starts with the 1986 attack on Libya justified by the 'Schulz doctrine', with echoes of the justification of self-defence offered for the attacks on Afghanistan and Iraq, 15 and 17 years on respectively. The extract then goes on to show how the 1991 Gulf War marked a point when, under the influence of the US, the Security Council began to replace its peace-keeping strategy with a strategy of 'vigilante violence'. Following this point, the US began to view UN Security Council approval as an add-on, a politically advantageous but unnecessary support for its military adventures. The war against Serbia was not directly authorised by the Security Council, but the relevant resolution, UNSCR 1244, was selectively interpreted and contorted to suit NATO's claim of legality. By the time of the Afghanistan invasion in 2001, the US and UK did not even bother to seek the approval of the UN Security Council.

A slightly different interpretation of the trajectory of post-war international law is offered by Zolo (2006). He argues that history shows that international law has always been imposed selectively and arbitrarily. From Nuremberg to Baghdad, international law 'produces an asymmetrical and retributive form of justice from which consideration of the winners' crimes is systematically excluded' (Toscano, 2008: 129–30). In fact, international law has provided a means of extending the power and influence of the most powerful states. He argues that selective criminalisation of war legitimates the low-intensity conflict and humanitarian wars of the victors, and that if there is a principle at the core of international law, it is the 'normalization of the great-power aggression' (Toscano, 2008: 133).

The reassertion of US military hegemony then, can be understood primarily as a question of power and sovereignty as opposed to law. As we saw in this section[1], in order for a state to retain its sovereignty, no other state can sit in judgement over it. Indeed, ceding the right to approve or disapprove military action to the UN Security Council involves a surrender of sovereignty, and, in consequence, a surrender of the power to intervene militarily. International law depends upon the willingness of the most powerful states to cede sovereign authority to an international sovereign body such as the Security Council. But by acting with impunity and with distain for an international rule of law in the way that Bowring outlines, the US has effectively jettisoned the UN Charter and customary international law in the name of a war on terror.

The Chomsky reading, written in the aftermath of the 2003 attack on Iraq, picks up where Bowring left off. For Chomsky, the attack on Iraq represents the 'supreme crime'. Here he is alluding to the term used in the trial of the Third Reich command at Nuremberg to describe their crimes of aggression. The concept of the 'supreme crime' of aggression was applied by the American jurist, Robert H. Jackson, to describe 'preventive' wars that have the aim of capturing territory, or controlling a population, as opposed to wars fought in self-defence. It is worth remembering in this context that Hitler had also produced humanitarian and self-defence arguments to justify the invasion of Poland and Czechoslovakia (the humanitarian protection of the German minority) and the aggressive war against the Soviet Union (to prevent imminent attack on Germany). As Chomsky points out, there are very clear similarities in law in the case of the Anglo-American attack on Iraq, and it is both legitimate and appropriate to use the same terms coined at Nuremberg to describe the 2003 invasion of Iraq. The view that this war constituted a crime of aggression remains widespread amongst international lawyers (for example, Sands, 2006; Simpson, 2005).

The extracts by Bowring and Chomsky therefore point to the predominance of political will and military strength above the rule of international law. The lack of a developed international law or international enforcement structure are less obstructive stumbling blocks to the prosecution of Blair/Brown and Bush for this crime of aggression than the naked political power of the US and UK governments. We have an International Criminal Court now. But we might seriously ask who would dare to act as prosecutor, judge and jury in such a prosecution. In any case, the US has invoked its own 'state of exception' and exempted its own nationals from prosecution in the International Criminal Court (Robertson, 2002: Chapter 9). The factors that impede the development of an enforceable body of international law are therefore complex and reside both in the complex sovereignty trade-offs that are involved and in the ability of a fledgling international legal infrastructure to establish autonomy from its most powerful member, namely the US.

Belgium's attempt to introduce an 'anti-atrocity' law with universal jurisdiction in 1993 highlights those difficulties very clearly. The law enabled persons accused of genocide, crimes against humanity or war crimes to be tried in Belgium, regardless of the nationality of the accused or the location of the crimes. Amongst those indicted at the court were Henry Kissinger, George H. W. Bush,

Dick Cheney, Colin Powell, Fidel Castro and Ariel Sharon. In June 2003, the US Defense Secretary, Donald Rumsfeld, responded to Belgian lawsuits citing US generals Tommy Franks and Norman Schwartzkopf for their role in US war crimes in Iraq and Afghanistan by pointing out that 'Belgium appears not to respect the sovereignty of other countries' (Jelinek, 2003).

In some ways, Rumsfeld's comment sums up the indivisibility of the relationship between state sovereignty and the right to invoke a state of exception more concisely than any of the contributors here. The statement was accompanied by a threat to move NATO headquarters from Belgium and to ban Americans from attending NATO meetings in Belgium. The newly elected Prime Minister of Belgium responded by promising to scrap the law. In September 2003, the Belgian Supreme Court threw out the cases of US and Israeli citizens ruling against Belgian's right to apply the principle of universal jurisdiction. The rule of law being applied in Belgium very quickly yielded to the sovereign right of the US to conduct its relations with other states outside the law. Belgium in effect had attempted to identify the crimes that invalidate state-of-exception claims to sovereignty – genocide, crimes against humanity and war crimes – in order to invoke universal jurisdiction.

It is the legitimacy of an international system of law that is at stake when we discover that the principle that lies at the foundation of the problem of criminalising crimes of the powerful is not a legal or moral principle, but a principle of naked power that needs no more sophisticated an expression to describe it than 'might is right'. Belgium's attempt to confront the state of exception and offer a possibility for a new form of international law failed. But the attempt is nonetheless significant because it raises fundamental questions about the *legitimacy* of legal structure that permits – and indeed is based upon – the right to commit state crime with impunity.

So what does all of this mean for how we think about the relationship between power and the law? The opening comments in the introduction to this section set out a distinction between three types of power: direct power; indirect power; and pre-emptive power. Clearly the position enjoyed by powerful institutions in modern hierarchical societies gives them some leverage in terms of their ability to influence policy and law both directly and indirectly. And they use their power to routinely avoid legal responsibilities, through law avoidance and creative compliance strategies (McBarnet, 1988). But, as the extracts in this section (see also Section 4) demonstrate, it is the deep structure of the law that preserves corporate immunity. This is the case in the form of the corporation, an institution that is by and large exempt from the rule of law as it applies to individuals. It is similarly the case in the international state system where a very peculiar rule of law can be invoked to defend sovereignty and the 'state of exception'.

If there is any conclusion to this section, then it is one that is also a fitting conclusion to the text: power is derived both from the form that the law takes and from the ability of powerful institutions to influence and even create the law. Together those elements of 'law as power' demonstrate something that is often treated as peripheral in criminology and in socio-legal studies: that power is derived from the ability of the powerful to break the law. The readings in this book allow us to begin to see how their mediated ability both to make and to break the law remains a key source of power for state institutions and corporations.

References

Alvesalo, A. (2003) 'Economic Crime Investigators at Work', *Policing and Society*, 13(2).

Alvesalo, A. and Tombs, S. (2001) 'Can Economic Crime Control be Sustained? The case of Finland', *Innovation*, 14(1).

Brecher, J. and Costello, T. (1994) *Global Village or Global Pillage? Economic reconstruction from the bottom up*. Cambridge, MA: South End Press.

Carson, W.G. (1979) 'The Conventionalisation of Early Factory Crime', *International Journal of the Sociology of Law*, 7(1): 37–60.

Carson, W.G. (1980) 'The Institutionalisation of Ambiguity: Early British Factory Acts' in G. Geis and E. Stotland (eds) *White-Collar Crime. Theory and research*. London: Sage.

Hawkins, K. (2002) *Law as Last Resort: Prosecution decision-making in a regulatory agency*. Oxford: Oxford University Press.

Hutter, B. (1997) *Compliance, Regulation and the Environment*. Oxford: Clarendon Press.

Jamieson, R. (1999) 'Genocide and the social production of immorality', *Theoretical Criminology*, 3(2).

Jeffcott, B. (2007) 'Sweat, Fire and Ethics: The sweatshop is back', *New Internationalist*, no. 399, April.

Jelinek, P. (2003) 'US Pressures Belgium to Change War Crime Law', *Associated Press*, 13 June.

Levi, M. (1995) 'Serious Fraud in Britain: criminal justice versus regulation' in F. Pearce and L. Snider (eds) *Corporate Crime: Contemporary debates*. Toronto: University of Toronto Press.

Lukes, S. (1974) *Power: A radical view*. Basingstoke: Macmillan.

McBarnet, D. (1988) 'Law, Policy and Legal Avoidance', *Journal of Law and Society*, 15(1).

Marx, K. (1954) *Capital: Volume 1*. London: Lawrence and Wishart.

Norrie, A. (2001) *Crime, Reason and History: A critical introduction to criminal law*, 2nd edn. London: Butterworths.

Robertson, G. (2002) *Crimes Against Humanity*, 2nd edn. London: Penguin.

Sands, P. (2006) *Lawless World*. London: Penguin.

Simpson, G. (2005) 'The War in Iraq and International Law', *Melbourne Journal of International Law*, no. 7.

Stiglmayer, A. (1993) *Mass Rape: The war against women in Bosnia-Herzegovina*. Lincoln: University of Nebraska Press.

Tombs, S. and Whyte, D. (2007) *Safety Crimes*. Cullompton: Willan.

Tombs, S. and Whyte, D. (forthcoming) 'Corporate crime? Theft, violence and harm' in J. Muncie, D. Talbot and R. Walters (eds) *Crime: Local and Global*. Maidenhead: Open University Press.

Tonelson, A. (2002) *The Race to the Bottom: Why a worldwide worker surplus and uncontrolled freetrade are sinking American labor standards*. New York: Basic Books.

Toscano, A. (2008) 'Sovereign impunity', *New Left Review*, no. 50, March/April.

Zolo, D. (2006) *La Giustizia dei Vincitori: Da Norimberga a Baghdad*. Rome: Editori Laterza.

40

Capital: a critical analysis of capitalist production, Volume 1
Karl Marx

[...] We have hitherto considered the tendency to the extension of the working-day, the were-wolf's hunger for surplus-labour in a department where the monstrous exactions, not surpassed, says an English bourgeois economist, by the cruelties of the Spaniards to the American red-skins,[1] caused capital at last to be bound by the chains of legal regulations. Now, let us cast a glance at certain branches of production in which the exploitation of labour is either free from fetters to this day, or was so yesterday.

Mr. Broughton Charlton, county magistrate, declared, as chairman of a meeting held at the Assembly Rooms, Nottingham, on the 14th January, 1860, "that there was an amount of privation and suffering among that portion of the population connected with the lace trade, unknown in other parts of the kingdom, indeed, in the civilised world ... Children of nine or ten years are dragged from their squalid beds at two, three, or four o'clock in the morning and compelled to work for a bare subsistence until ten, eleven, or twelve at night, their limbs wearing away, their frames dwindling, their faces whitening, and their humanity absolutely sinking into a stone-like torpor, utterly horrible to contemplate .... We are not surprised that Mr. Mallett, or any other manufacturer, should stand forward and protest against discussion ..... The system, as the Rev. Montagu Valpy describes it, is one of unmitigated slavery, socially, physically, morally, and spiritually. ... What can be thought of a town which holds a public meeting to petition that the period of labour for men shall be diminished to eighteen hours a day? .... We declaim against the Virginian and Carolinian cotton-planters. Is their black-market, their lash, and their barter of human flesh more detestable than this slow sacrifice of humanity which takes place in order that veils and collars may be fabricated for the benefit of capitalists?"[2]

The potteries of Staffordshire have, during the last 22 years, been the subject of three parliamentary inquiries. The result is embodied in Mr. Scriven's Report of 1841 to the "Children's Employment Commissioners," in the report of Dr. Greenhow of 1860 published by order of the medical officer of the Privy Council (Public Health, 3rd Report, 112–113), lastly, in the report of Mr. Longe of 1862 in the "First Report of the Children's Employment Commission, of the 13th June, 1863." For my purpose it is enough to take, from the reports of 1860 and 1863, some depositions of the exploited children themselves. From the children we may form an opinion as to the adults, especially the girls and women, and that in a branch of industry by the side of which cotton-spinning appears an agreeable and healthful occupation.[3]

William Wood, 9 years old, was 7 years and 10 months when he began to work. He "ran moulds" (carried ready-moulded articles into the drying-room, afterwards bringing back the empty mould) from the beginning. He came to work every day in the week at 6 a. m., and left off about 9 p. m. "I work till 9 o'clock at night six days in the week. I have done so seven or eight weeks." Fifteen hours of labour for a child 7 years old! J. Murray, 12 years of age, says: "I turn jigger, and run moulds. I come at 6. Sometimes I come at 4. I worked all night last night, till 6 o'clock this morning. I have not been in bed since the night before last. There were eight or nine other boys working last night. All but one have come this morning. I get 3 shillings and sixpence. I do not get any more for working at night. I worked two nights last week." Fernyhough, a boy of ten: "I have not always an hour (for dinner). I have only half an hour sometimes; on Thursday, Friday, and Saturday."[4]

Dr. Greenhow states that the average duration of life in the pottery districts of Stoke-on-Trent, and Wolstanton is extraordinarily short. Although in the district of Stoke, only 36.6% and in Wolstanton only 30.4% of the adult male population above 20 are employed in the potteries, among the men of that age in the first district more than half, in the second, nearly 2/5 of the whole deaths are the result of pulmonary diseases among the potters. Dr. Boothroyd, a medical practitioner at Hanley, says: "Each successive generation of potters is more dwarfed and less robust than the preceding one." In like manner another doctor, Mr. M'Bean: "Since he began to practise among the potters 25 years ago, he had observed a marked degeneration especially shown in diminution of stature and breadth." These statements are taken from the report of Dr. Greenhow in 1860.[5]

From the report of the Commissioners in 1863, the following: Dr. J. T. Arledge, senior physician of the North Staffordshire Infirmary, says: "The potters as a class, both men and women, represent a degenerated population, both physically and morally. They are, as a rule, stunted in growth, ill-shaped, and frequently ill-formed in the chest; they become prematurely old, and are certainly short-lived; they are phlegmatic and bloodless, and exhibit their debility of constitution by obstinate attacks of dyspepsia, and disorders of the liver and kidneys, and by rheumatism. But of all diseases they are especially prone to chest-disease, to pneumonia, phthisis, bronchitis, and asthma. One form would appear peculiar to them, and is known as potter's asthma, or potter's consumption. Scrofula attacking the glands, or bones, or other parts of the body, is a disease of two-thirds or more of the potters .... (That the 'degenerescence' of the population of this district is not even greater than it is, is due to the constant recruiting from the adjacent country, and intermarriages with more healthy races."[6]

Mr. Charles Parsons, late house surgeon of the same institution, writes in a letter to Commissioner Longe, amongst other things: "I can only speak from personal observation and not from statistical data, but I do not hesitate to assert that my indignation has been aroused again and again at the sight of poor children whose health has been sacrificed to gratify the avarice of either parents or employers." He enumerates the causes of the diseases of the potters, and sums them up in the phrase, "long hours." The report of the Commission trusts that "a manufacture which has assumed so prominent a place in the whole world, will not long be subject to the remark that its great success is accompanied with the physical deterioration, widespread bodily suffering, and early death of the work-people ... by whose labour and skill such great results have been achieved."[7] And all that holds of the potteries in England is true of those in Scotland.[8]

The manufacture of lucifer matches dates from 1833, from the discovery of the method of applying phosphorus to the match itself. Since 1845 this manufacture has rapidly developed in England, and has extended especially amongst the thickly populated parts of London as well as in Manchester, Birmingham, Liverpool, Bristol, Norwich, Newcastle and Glasgow. With it has spread the form of lockjaw, which a Vienna physician in 1845 discovered to be a disease peculiar to lucifer-matchmakers. Half the workers are children under thirteen, and young persons under eighteen. The manufacture is on account of its unhealthiness and unpleasantness in such bad odour that only the most miserable part of the labouring class, half-starved widows and so forth, deliver up their children to it, "the ragged, half-starved, untaught children."[9]

Of the witnesses that Commissioner White examined (1863), 270 were under 18, 50 under 10, 10 only 8, and 5 only 6 years old. A range of the working-day from 12 to 14 or 15 hours, night-labour, irregular meal-times, meals for the most part taken in the very workrooms that are pestilent with phosphorus. Dante would have found the worst horrors of his Inferno surpassed in this manufacture. [...]

[...] The incredible adulteration of bread, especially in London, was first revealed by the House of Commons Committee "on the adulteration of articles of food" (1855–56), and Dr. Hassall's work, "Adulterations detected."[10] The consequence of these revelations was the Act of August 6th, 1860, "for preventing the adulteration of articles of food and drink," an inoperative law, as it naturally shows the tenderest consideration for every Free-trader who determines by the buying or selling of adulterated commodities "to turn an honest penny."[11] The Committee itself formulated more or less naïvely its conviction that Free-trade meant essentially trade with adulterated, or as the English ingeniously put it, "sophisticated" goods. In fact this kind of sophistry knows better than Protagoras how to make white black, and black white, and better than the Eleatics how to demonstrate *ad oculos* that everything is only appearance.[12]

At all events the committee had directed the attention of the public to its "daily bread," and therefore to the baking trade. At the same time in public meetings and in petitions to Parliament rose the cry of the London journeymen bakers against their over-work, &c. The cry was so urgent that Mr. H. S. Tremenheere, also a member of the Commission of 1863 several times mentioned, was appointed Royal Commissioner of Inquiry. His report,[13] together with the evidence given, roused not the heart of the public but its stomach. Englishmen, always well up in the Bible, knew well enough that man, unless by elective grace a capitalist, or landlord, or sinecurist, is commanded to eat his bread in the sweat of his brow, but they did not know that he had to eat daily in his bread a certain quantity of human perspiration mixed with the discharge of abscesses, cobwebs, dead black-beetles, and putrid German yeast, without counting alum, sand, and other agreeable mineral ingredients. Without any regard to his holiness, Free-trade, the free baking-trade was therefore placed under the supervision of the State inspectors (Close of the Parliamentary session of 1863), and by the same Act of Parliament, work from 9 in the evening to 5 in the morning was forbidden for journeymen bakers under 18. The last clause speaks volumes as to the over-work in this old-fashioned, homely line of business.

"The work of a London journeyman baker begins, as a rule, at about eleven at night. At that hour he 'makes the dough,'—a laborious process, which lasts from half an hour to three quarters of an hour, according to the size of the batch or the labour bestowed upon it. He then lies down upon the kneading-board, which is also the covering of the trough in which the dough is 'made;' and with a sack under him, and another rolled up as a pillow, he sleeps for about a couple of hours. He is then engaged in a rapid and continuous labour for about five hours—throwing out the dough, 'scaling it off,' moulding it, putting it into the oven, preparing and baking rolls and fancy bread, taking the batch bread out of the oven, and up into the shop, &c., &c. The temperature of a bakehouse ranges from about 75 to upwards of 90 degrees, and in the smaller bakehouses approximates usually to the higher rather than to the lower degree of heat. When the business of making the bread, rolls, &c., is over, that of its distribution begins, and a considerable proportion of the journeymen in the trade, after working hard in the manner described during the night, are upon their legs for many hours during the day, carrying baskets, or wheeling hand-carts, and sometimes again in the bakehouse, leaving off work at various hours between 1 and 6 p. m. according to the season of the year, or the amount and nature of their master's business; while others are again engaged in the bakehouse in 'bringing out' more batches until late in the afternoon.[14] ... During what is called 'the London season,' the operatives belonging to the 'full-priced' bakers at the West End of the town, generally begin work at 11 p. m., and are engaged in making the bread, with one or two short (sometimes very short) intervals of rest, up to 8 o'clock the next morning. They are then engaged all day long, up to 4, 5, 6, and as late as 7 o'clock in the evening carrying out bread, or sometimes in the afternoon in the bakehouse again, assisting in the biscuit-baking. They may have, after they have done their work, sometimes five or six, sometimes only four or five hours' sleep before they begin again. On Fridays they always begin sooner, some about ten o'clock, and continue in some cases, at work, either in making or delivering the bread up to 8 p. m. on Saturday night, but more generally up to 4 or 5 o'clock, Sunday morning. On Sundays the men must attend twice or three times during the day for an hour or two to make preparations for the next day's bread. ... The men employed by the underselling masters (who sell their bread under the 'full price,' and who, as already pointed out, comprise three-fourths of the London bakers) have not only to work on the average longer hours, but their work is almost entirely confined to the bakehouse. The underselling masters generally sell their bread. ... in the shop. If they send it out, which is not common, except as supplying chandlers' shops, they usually employ other hands for that purpose. It is not their practice to deliver bread from house to house. Towards the end of the week. ... the men begin on Thursday night at 10 o'clock, and continue on with only slight intermission until late on Saturday evening."[15]

Even the bourgeois intellect understands the position of the "underselling" masters. "The unpaid labour of the men was made the source whereby the competition was carried on."[16] And the "full-priced" baker denounces his under-selling competitors to the Commission of Inquiry as thieves of foreign labour and adulterators. "They only exist now by first defrauding the public, and next getting 18 hours' work out of their men for 12 hours' wages."[17] [...]

Notes

1   "The cupidity of mill-owners whose cruelties in the pursuit of gain have hardly been exceeded by those perpetrated by the Spaniards on the conquest of America in the pursuit of gold." John Wade, "History of the Middle and Working Classes," 3rd Ed. London, 1835, p. 114. The theoretical part of this book, a kind of hand-book of Political Economy, is, considering the time of its publication, original in some parts, *e.g.*, on commercial crises. The historical part is, to a great extent, a shameless plagiarism of Sir F. M. Eden's "The State of the Poor," London, 1797.
2   *Daily Telegraph*, 17th January, 1860.
3   Cf. F. Engels' "Lage, etc." pp. 249–51.
4   Children's Employment Commission. First report, etc., 1863. Evidence, pp. 16, 19, 18.
5   Public Health, 3rd report, etc., pp. 102, 104, 105.
6   Child. Empl. Comm. I. Report, p. 24.
7   Children's Employment Commission, p. 22, ans xi.
8   l. c., p. xlvii.
9   l. c., p. liv.
10   Alum finely powdered, or mixed with salt, is a normal article of commerce bearing the significant name of "bakers' stuff."
11   Soot is a well-known and very energetic form of carbon, and forms a manure that capitalistic chimney-sweeps sell to English farmers. Now in 1862 the British juryman had in a law-suit to decide whether soot, with which, unknown to the buyer, 90% of dust and sand are mixed, is genuine soot in the commercial sense or adulterated soot in the legal sense. The "amis du commerce" decided it to be genuine commercial soot, and non-suited the plaintiff farmer, who had in addition to pay the costs of the suit.
12   The French chemist, Chevallier, in his treatise on the "sophistications" of commodities, enumerates for many of the 600 or more articles which he passes in review, 10, 20, 30 different methods of adulteration. He adds that he does not know all the methods, and does not mention all that he knows. He gives 6 kinds of adulteration of sugar, 9 of olive oil, 10 of butter, 12 of salt, 19 of milk,

20 of bread, 23 of brandy, 24 of meal, 28 of chocolate, 30 of wine, 32 of coffee, etc. Even God Almighty does not escape this fate. See Rouard de Card, "On the Falsifications of the Materials of the Sacrament." ("De la falsification des substances sacramentelles," Paris, 1856.)

13 "Report, &c., relative to the grievances complained of by the journeymen bakers, &c., London, 1862" and "Second Report, &., London, 1863."
14 1. c. First Report, &c., p. vi.
15 1. c., p. lxxi.
16 George Read, "The History of Baking," London, 1848, p. 16.
17 Report (First) &c. Evidence of the "full-priced" baker Cheesman, p. 108.

41

Downsized by law, ideology, and pragmatics – policing white-collar crime
Anne Alvesalo

[...] Despite the fact that legislative changes happen, the traditional ideas such as criminal liability as a system of personal accountability, and crimes as incidents that happen at a certain time in a certain place, are built-in to criminal law and doctrine as a whole, and have their implications on the pragmatics of enforcement.

The units or squads and the areas of responsibilities within the police are often divided on the basis of the criminal law, either using the concept of the legal goods or crimes, such as property offences, violent crime, robbery, drugs, or homicide. Especially in the local police districts, it is not always clear whose responsibility it is to investigate different forms of white-collar crime. Even if there are specialized units for white-collar crime, the types of crimes investigated vary enormously, and division of labor between other units of different crimes are not obvious. In Finland, for example, environmental crimes are investigated in white-collar crime and violent crime units; in both they are rare and considered oddities.[1] It is likely that the unclear duties and "enemies" of white-collar crime investigators make it difficult for them to create an identity, subculture or working culture within the police, and to illustrate their importance in "fighting crime." It is difficult enough, because the daily work of white-collar crime investigation itself is commonly not considered as "real police work" within the police;[2] investigators have nicknames such as "cardigan soldiers" or "sandal men," and their cases are called "paperclip cases" or "piles of appendices."[3]

Studies on policing demonstrate how much of detective work is to transform an incident into a case and an individual into a defendant by the collection, categorization, and presentation of evidence.[4] Looking at the instructions for victims of "useful information to the police when a crime has been committed" in the beginning of this article, one should note that the problems in attaining useful information begin before one gets as far as to the first tip: in most cases it is not clear whether a crime – or which crime – is in question in the first place. In traditional crime it is usually easy to construct the course of events and the criminalized conduct, and many standard practices, processes, and legal rules defining the use of police powers are evolved from this standpoint. In their analysis of the Ford Pinto case, Cullen et al. have demonstrated how, at each stage of the criminal justice system, even if existing legal statutes would allow, circumstances exist that limit the practicality of using the criminal law in cases of corporate crime.[5]

In policing white-collar crime, the essential point is to separate illegal business activities from legal ones; business per se is not criminal. The police need various forms of professional expertise and knowledge that are not required in traditional policing. In fact, the investigation of white-collar crime is hardly possible without using expertise and powers of other officials.[6] One significant feature of investigation is that law is an important daily tool for white-collar crime investigators.[7] This is naturally the case in all policing, but the use of law has different dimensions than in traditional crime. During investigation, white-collar crime investigators are constantly reading the criminal code in order to recall the exact rubrics of criminalizations. Also, knowledge of laws concerning business operations is necessary.[8] The problem is figuring what the crime is, even if one knows – or has an idea – who the offender is. As an investigator said, "In traditional crime investigation, the police are searching for the *criminal,* but in cases of white collar crime they are searching for the *crime.*"[9] As an "incident" or "act," white-collar crime differs totally from traditional crime; the basic activity that is happening is legal and even considered desirable; white-collar crime could be defined as exaggerated business. Though some criminologists have defined *all* crime as "merely the exaggerated form of common practices,"[10] there is a difference between traditional and white-collar crime, when one looks at how the *criminalizations in law texts* are formed. In traditional crime, the starting point is that the activity is forbidden as such, whereas in white-collar crime they are connected to activity that is encouraged as such. The ways of conducting business are regulated outside the criminal law, and only certain ways of doing business activities are criminalized. This leads to the fact that the *criminal act itself finds its definition often with the support other legislation* or even business practices, through concepts such as "good book-keeping practice" or "permissible risk," "insolvency," "careful management" or "economically reasonable behavior."[11] The result is that those whose conduct is criminalized are able to define the borders of the criminalizations. [...]

[...] Police seldom detect white-collar crimes themselves, but get the report from other officials, usually months or years after the crime has been committed.[12] This is due to many reasons, but one important reason is that there is no "exact time and place of the crime." Thus, it is very difficult to make a "description of what has happened and where." The difficulty of defining the exact time of the offence leads to many pragmatic problems. For example, the periods of limitation to prosecute are mostly calculated from the day the crime was committed, and the uncertainty of whether the crime has fallen under the statutes of limitations may lead to a decision not to proceed in the investigation. The *forum delicti* rule – the principle that crimes should be investigated and prosecuted by the authorities in the locality where the crime has been committed – causes problems in deciding where the case should be investigated and prosecuted. In order for a crime to be formulated, all the essential elements of the crime have to be constructed. In cases of white-collar crime, the crime described in the law text does not mean that the elements have happened at the same time, but some act can be committed long before another and the separable acts are not usually crimes. This has its implications in constructing the incidents as crimes. Kelman's analysis on *narrow and broad time frames*[13] in legal argumentation demonstrates well the problems that follow from the fact that white-collar crimes are not incidents that "happen" at a certain time in a certain place. Particular acts are construed as crimes and prosecuted. However, these incidents have a history: things occur before and after incidents that are *considered relevant,* things such as events preceding or post-dating the criminal incident. Narrow time frames – to focus solely on the isolated criminal incident – buttress the traditionally asserted intentionalism of the criminal justice system. In white-collar crime the use of narrow time frames hamper the construction of crime because the relevant acts that constitute the crime are spread, i.e., happen at different times. Kelman points out, for example, how commentators who attack the use of strict liability invariably use narrow time frames.[14] [...]

[...] In understanding the particularity of white-collar crime and its control, it is crucial to note that the "ontology" of the organization, what they are doing and crimes committed in or by them – their legal existence – is established through documentation such as contracts, bookkeeping, entries in the trade register, or in the records of the board of directors. The possibility of creating "paper reality" offers many possibilities to commit many types of offences behind the veil of seemingly legitimate business; crimes which would not even be possible without using an economic organization. Incidents that constitute the crime are usually legal constructions which have "happened" through documentation, and the police's task is to show that this "paper reality" is untrue.[15] This creates a particularly heavy burden of proof for the police; the white-collar crime defendants have an exceptional possibility to create "reality," which is true until proven otherwise. The tools needed in the collection of evidence – e.g., home searches – can be used if there is reasonable suspicion of both a crime and a suspect. The problems that lie in the "search of the crime" derail the possibilities to conduct an effective investigation on the whole. The vicious circle in the investigation of white-collar crime is that, without a crime, the police cannot collect evidence, but without evidence they are unable to construct the crime. [...]

Notes

1   Laitinen and Alvesalo, 1994:21; Alvesalo (unpublished manuscript).
2   See e.g., Levi, 1995:38; Korander (unpublished manuscript) and Honkonen, 1999:180 have noted how within especially the uniformed police the way of thinking is that [police]man is not supposed to degrade himself in the "feminine" role of the ridiculous 'clerk' who has to do foul paperwork, keep indoors and study legal technicalities. Even 'normal' detective work is perceived to some extent as not being real "policeman work."
3   Alvesalo (unpublished manuscript).
4   Dixon, 1997:270.
5   Cullen, Maakestad, and Cavender, 1987:319-334.

6　Alvesalo (unpublished manuscript). The police conduct investigation with e.g., tax-authorities, customs, bailiffs, and officials of the bankruptcy ombudsman's office.

7　Alvesalo, 1999:6.

8　Salminen, 1998:15; Alvesalo (unpublished manuscript).

9　Alvesalo (unpublished manuscript); Pontell, Calavita and Tillman, 1994:402; Slapper and Tombs, 1999:98.

10　E.g., Box, 1983, drawing from Durkheim.

11　See e.g., Nuutila, 1996:147, 160-172 and his analysis on how the "operational environment," e.g., arranging safety at the workplace, is used as a model to connect norms and facts in the process of "finding the crime." Häyrynen, 1998:35 has pointed out how the borders of criminalizations in security market crimes are influenced by the rules of the Stock Exchange.

12　Pontell, Calavita, and Tillman, 1994:403.

13　Kelman, 1981:600.

14　Kelman, 1981:605.

15　Alvesalo (unpublished manuscript). See also Benson and Cullen, 1998:174; Talvela, 1998:136-140.

42

The space between laws: the problem of corporate crime in a transnational context
Raymond Michalowski and Ronald Kramer

[...] TNCs and the Relocation of Corporate Hazards

Over the last quarter century, foreign investment by TNCs has expanded dramatically (United Nations, 1978:36). In the 20 years from 1960 to 1980, the revenues of TNCs grew tenfold—from 199 billion dollars to 2,155 billion dollars—with U.S. based corporations accounting for 50 percent of this growth (Cavanaugh and Clairmonte, 1983:17). By 1983, the worldwide profits of TNCs had reached a record high of 130 billion dollars (*Multinational Monitor*, 1984:11). This internationalization of corporate activity necessitates an expansion of corporate crime research beyond its dominant focus on offenses by corporations in their home countries.[1]

While, on a dollar basis, foreign investment in developed nations exceeds that in developing nations (Hamilton, 1983:3; United Nations, 1978:40; U.S. Department of Commerce, 1984:8), it is transnational investments *in developing nations* that pose the greatest likelihood of injurious corporate activity, and which raise the most perplexing problems for the definition and study of corporate crime. There are several reasons for this.

First, the most significant change in patterns of foreign investment since the Second World War has been the increased location of TNC industrial facilities in developing nations (United Nations, 1978:40–41). Three-fourths of all U.S. companies with sales over 100 million dollars had manufacturing facilities in other countries by 1975 (United Nations, 1978:222). By 1977, developing nations had surpassed developed ones in dollar value as locations for manufacturing by U.S. industries (U.S. Department of Commerce, 1981:159). Reimportation of overseas assembly by U.S. companies increased five-fold between 1969 and 1983, and in the textiles and electronics industries more than half of all current sales by U.S. corporations are now assembled abroad (Grunwald and Flamm, 1985:12–13). As TNCs export their industrial operations to developing nations, many of the hazards of industrial production and the associated possibilities for corporate crime are relocated from developed to developing countries. Moreover, as the fatal poisoning of over 2,000 residents of Bhopal, India dramatized (Hazarka, 1984:1), the settlement patterns, population density, and limited disaster preparedness of developing nations means that, when problems do occur, the human and environmental costs are likely to be greater than those resulting from similar incidents in developed countries.

Second, the growth in consumer exports to the Third World, as well as the increased local production of consumer goods by TNCs in developing nations, has generated significant consumer safety issues. Differences in marketing practices of TNCs in home versus host nations, variations in the provision of information by TNCs regarding product hazards, and variations in cultural practices regarding product usage has led to unnecessary injury, illness, and death for Third World consumers of TNC products (Mattelart, 1983).

Finally, in comparison to developed nations, developing nations frequently have fewer legal controls over workplace, environmental, and consumer hazards of industrial production (Braithwaite, 1984; Castleman, 1975; Dewar, 1978; Vieira, 1985). Therefore, the potential for corporations to behave in socially-injurious ways in developing nations is greater. For these reasons the growing internationalization of business points to developing nations as a significant emerging arena for injurious corporate activity.

TNCs and Corporate Deviance in the Third World

In recent years corporate injuries to workers, physical environments, and consumers in developing nations have revealed significant problems with respect to the control of corporate activity in these countries. We will explore each of these arenas, with particular attention to injurious actions that arise in the space between legal systems—actions which were prohibited in home nations, but permissible in the host countries where they occurred.

Working Conditions

According to the International Labor Organization (1985:55), industrial workers in TNCs in developing nations "suffer from more safety and health problems than similar workers in the developed countries." While in some cases TNC manufacturing operations provide better working conditions than locally-owned factories (Blake, 1980; International Labor Organization, 1985:44), it is the comparison between TNC operations in home and host countries, rather than between TNCs and local conditions, that raises the most perplexing questions for the study of injurious corporate activities.

In a number of instances, occupational safety and other working conditions in TNC operations have been found to fall below those mandated by law in more developed countries. The exposure of workers in electronics assembly plants to levels of carcinogens and other toxic materials beyond those allowed in the United States, for instance, has been one of the consequences of the exportation of this "clean" industry (LaDou, 1984). In the more obviously "dirty" industries such as asbestos and chemical production, foreign workers in U.S. subsidiaries have been knowingly exposed to toxic levels that were illegal in the United States. In 1972 for instance, Amatax, a Pennsylvania asbestos yarn mill, moved its entire production facility to Mexico to take advantage of the fact that Mexico had no laws regulating exposure of workers to asbestos fibers. Similarly, in 1974 Raybestos-Manhattan acquired 47 percent of the stock in a Venezuelan asbestos plant in order to take advantage of Venezuelan law which allows higher levels of airborn asbestos fibers than does the Occupational Safety and Health Administration (OSHA) in the United States (Castleman, 1979). In a similar case, Arasco, the only U.S. producer of arsenic, moved its entire operation to Mexico when OSHA lowered the U.S. limit for exposure to airborne arsenic from 500 to 4 micrograms per cubic meter of air (Mattelart, 1983:102). In the electronics industry, Third World workers in U.S. subsidiaries have been found to suffer eye strain and eye failure due to constant peering into microscopes without the benefit of rest breaks on company time required by law in the United States (Fuentes and Ehrenreich, 1983:6).

Industrial operations by some TNCs in developing host countries have used wage and employment practices prohibited in their more developed home nations. In some cases, work is contracted out to home workers at piece rates which require a level of effort comparable to nineteenth-century garment sweatshops. These contract workers enjoy no benefits in terms of holidays, health insurance, sick leave or pensions—all of which are legally-protected worker rights in more developed nations (Fernandez-Kelly, 1983:118). Likewise, the practice of using extended "probationary" periods during which workers (often women) are paid a lower wage rate and then "laid off" just prior to completing this period would be illegal under U.S. labor law (Fuentes and Ehrenreich, 1983:9–10). As Fernandez-Kelly (1983:114) found in the "maquiladoras" factories of the Mexican border, a variation on this theme is to bring prospective workers in for a "test" during which they spend a day or more sewing garments for no pay in the hopes of possible employment. Ong (1983:431) suggested that employers also deliberately keep workers on "temporary status" for prolonged periods to minimize the risks of unionization. This strategy makes it easy to fire workers who organize or join unions.

Environmental Pollution

In some instances TNCs have located and/or relocated high-pollution industries in less-developed countries in order to escape the pollution control costs imposed by environmental protection laws in their home nation. Blake and Walters (1976:159) have suggested that TNCs "will be very sensitive to disparities among various [national] pollution control standards which affect production costs and competitiveness in international trade" as a means of expanding or protecting profit margins. This sensitivity reflects the fact that pollution control costs in the United States are higher than in most other countries (Pearson and Pryor, 1978:170). Robert Strauss (1978:451), President Carter's chief trade negotiator, warned in 1978 of a developing "pattern of flight" as U.S. companies are drawn to developing nations with less costly pollution control laws. Castleman (1978:3) similarly noted that "hazard export is emerging as a driving force in new plant investment in many hazardous and polluting industries." In some cases entire industries involving highly toxic substances such as asbestos, arsenic, mercury, and benzidene dyes have been exported to rapidly developing nations such as Korea, Mexico, Brazil, India, and Ireland (Leonard and Duerksen, 1981:55). Even computer and electronics assembly, once thought to be "clean" industries, often expose the environments of developing nations to a wide range of toxic substances that are more closely regulated in the United States (*Cultural Survival*, 1981; *Dollars and Sense*, 1984:6).

There has been some disagreement over whether pollution control costs actually play a significant role in location decisions (Flamm, 1985:77–78; Randall, 1977:v). However, the debate over the relative importance of pollution regulations for location decisions speaks only to the question of corporate motivation, not the consequences of corporate behavior. Even if they are not actively seeking "pollution havens," in many developing nations TNCs remain legally free to expose the water, air, soil, and bodies of workers to hazardous substances at rates higher than those allowed in their home countries (Vieira, 1985).

In addition to the problem of pollutants produced by TNCs operating in host countries, hazardous waste produced *in developed countries* has begun to find its way into developing nations. Some TNCs have sought to avoid the costs of mandated controls on hazardous waste storage in their home nation by transporting wastes to countries which have few or no legal controls on hazardous waste disposal (Centre on Transnational Corporations, 1985:59–60). In these cases, the TNCs involved are clearly acting to circumvent laws in their home nations rather than simply being passive beneficiaries of the difference in laws between home and host nations.

Consumer Safety

According to the U.N. Centre on Transnational Corporations (1985:58) "the one issue that has generated the greatest emotion and controversy in the 1980s regarding transnational corporations ... is the exportation of products deemed to be harmful to health and the environment." Several cases in recent years have dramatized the kinds of hazards consumers in developing nations face when TNCs circumvent product regulations in their home nations.

The export of children's sleepwear treated with the carcinogenic flame retardant Tris, after the sale of such sleepwear was banned in the United States, was one of the first cases of knowingly-exported consumer hazards to receive widespread attention (*New York Times*, 1978:26). In the late 1970s, A.A. Robbins company arranged (with the help of United States Agency for International Development) for the distribution of the Dalkon Shield intrauterine device in a number of developing countries. This overseas market was sought after Robbins already knew that the Shield was responsible for 20,000 cases of serious uterine infection, that it had resulted in several thousand hysterectomies among its users in the United States, and that the product would soon be banned at home (Dowie and Johnston, 1976; Mintz, 1985). In another case, Parke-Davis, a U.S.

pharmaceutical company, successfully promoted the drug chloramphenicol on a non-prescription basis in 39 nations but provided no information concerning its dangerous and sometimes fatal side effects—even though the drug was banned in the United States and Japan (Mattelart, 1983:100–101).

In addition to the hazards posed by consumer goods, it is estimated that annually 375,000 people in the developing world are poisoned—10,000 of them fatally—through the misuse of industrial and agricultural chemicals exported from developed nations. There is evidence that much of this poisoning results from the failure of TNCs to provide adequate information on the hazards of their chemical exports, and from their active attempts to find markets for chemicals banned at home (Bull, 1982; Weir and Schapiro, 1981). In one such instance, paraquat was successfully promoted for use as a marijuana defoliant in Latin America after it was banned for that purpose in the United States (del Olmo, 1986).

Most of the injurious corporate actions described above were not prosecutable as crimes or regulatory violations in the nations where they occurred. Yet to omit them from the study of corporate crime on this basis does little to help us understand either the organization and causation of injurious actions by TNCs, or the definitional process by which these actions have been rendered legal in host nations. Moreover, as we argue in the next section, the ability of TNCs to influence regulatory climates in host nations may play a crucial role in keeping injurious actions by TNCs from being defined and prosecuted as crimes.

TNCs and Regulatory Climates

TNCs can influence the regulatory climates of developing host nations in indirect and direct ways. The logic of development in the free-market world necessitates that developing nations create hospitable environments for foreign investment. Simply by holding the economic keys to development, TNCs indirectly limit the political willingness of developing nations to establish strict controls over potential or actual corporate harms. At times, TNCs have also exerted pressure in more direct ways to forestall legislation contrary to their interests, and in some cases to subvert political movements or leaders deemed inhospitable to these interests. We now examine this relationship between TNCs and regulatory climates in closer detail, with a particular focus on labor policies.

Indirect Influences

Free-market nations that have followed a capitalist model of development based on foreign investment find their potentials for economic growth closely linked to their ability to attract TNCs. Domestic elites in developing nations frequently find that general economic improvement and political stability in their countries, as well as their own economic and political success, depend upon creating hospitable environments for investment by foreign TNCs. The deepening need for inflows of foreign investment in developing nations, and the pressures this places on domestic policy, have been extensively examined by a number of dependency theorists.[2] The specific regulatory adaptations that have been made to attract TNCs have been examined in less detail. However, there is some evidence that the existence of a profitable double-standard which allows TNCs in host countries to do what they are prohibited from doing in their home nations is related to the desire of host nations to attract foreign investment by creating regulatory climates hospitable to the interests of TNCs.

Controls over the rights of workers to organize for improved wage and working conditions is a good example of how TNCs become the passive beneficiaries of policies designed to attract them. Labor costs represent one of the most significant factors in the location of manufacturing plants (Burns, 1984). For instance, assembly line workers in the United States often earn per hour what assembly workers in developing nations earn per day (Fuentes and Ehrenreich, 1983:5). The desire to take advantage of significant differentials in national wage rates has been the primary stimulus for the location of TNC production facilities in developing nations (Grunwald and Flamm, 1985:3–9). Leaders in some developing nations have used limitations on worker rights as a strategy to convince foreign companies that, if they do invest, they will enjoy continued benefits from lower labor costs. The belief that this will attract foreign investment has received a degree of confirmation from investment practices of TNCs.[3] For instance, investment in Thailand by the U.S. semiconductor industry did not reach significant levels until 1977, the year following the installment of a military junta that ended a period of democratic government characterized by strikes and other movements for increased popular control over the economy. Similarly, foreign direct investment in semiconductor assembly in the Phillipines entered a period of significant growth beginning in 1972, the year Marcos declared martial law (Grunwald and Flamm, 1985:77). In 1982, Marcos continued his efforts to create a profitable climate for these TNCs by issuing a decree banning all strikes in the semiconductor industry as being against the "national interest" (O'Connor and Wong, 1983).

Another strategy used in developing nations to attract foreign investment at the expense of labor rights protected by law in developed nations is the creation of *economic free zones* (EFZs). In some cases these zones are little more than labor camps "where trade unions, strikes and freedom of movement are severely limited, if not forbidden" (Fuentes and Ehrenreich, 1983:5). For example, advertisements for Carribean Assemblies, a set of EFZs in Haiti and the Dominican Republic, promise foreign companies a "large, urbanized, low-cost labour pool" and "strict anti-strike and labour regulation laws" (Matellart, 1983:106). A promotional document by the South Korea government offers this description of its EFZ:

> The zone has the characteristics of a reserved territory in which the application of laws or relevant regulations is partially or totally suppressed or attenuated.... It is an industrial territory in which a series of fiscal and legal privileges are offered to firms of foreign capital (Medawar, 1979:62).

Promotional materials such as these make it abundantly clear that limitations on the rights of workers are part of the bait that EFZs offer to foreign companies in some developing nations.

Lim (1983:14) has argued that locating TNC industrial facilities in developing countries is beneficial to workers in nations where unemployment and poverty are widespread, even if the rights of these workers are minimal. This perspective is manifest in the June 6, 1980 issue of *Fortune* magazine which asks, "Even though the people working on Castle and Cooke's banana plantations in Central America earn far less than the U.S. minimum wage, would they be better off if the company decided to move elsewhere?" However, the economic conditions that TNCs "improve" cannot be analyzed in isolation from the economic domination by foreign business interests that characterizes the history of many developing host nations. Moreover, while the factory work provided by TNCs may improve the incomes of some workers, the dependent development it represents generally results in a distorted economy, a split labor market, and exploitation of women who are the primary laborers in these factories (Amin, 1974; Frank, 1975; Nash, 1979; Wallerstein, 1979).

Direct Influences

In addition to benefiting indirectly from restrictive labor climates, TNCs have at times actively used their economic power in developing nations to limit the rights of workers to organize into unions to protect and promote their interests. In some case, TNCs have used the threat of the runaway shop to discipline workers. For instance, when the Malaysian government indicated in 1983 that it might permit the formation of a union for electronics workers, U.S. electronics firms in Malaysia indicated that, should this happen, they would consider moving their plants elsewhere. Subsequently, the Malaysian government shelved its plans for the union. In a similar case, Control Data Corporation closed a Korean production facility in response to attempts by workers to unionize (O'Connor and Wong, 1983). Such threats or actual incidents of capital flight can have a chilling effect on both labor activism and governmental support for labor rights in nations dependent on foreign investment.

Besides attempts to influence specific policies, some TNCs have used their economic and political power to alter the flow of broader political developments in host nations. In some cases, TNCs have contributed to the elimination of progressive or socialist governments in favor of conservative ones. Activities of this sort are often based on clandestine contacts between TNCs and governments in home or host nations. As a result, relatively little is known about their scope or frequency. However, cases such as ITT's contributions to the overthrow of Allende in Chile, the participation of United Fruit, International Railways of Central America, and Electric Bond and Share in bringing about the downfall of the progressive leader, Jacobs Arbenz, in Guatemala in 1954, and the more recent financial support provided by some U.S. corporations to the Nicaraguan *contras* in their efforts to overthrow the socialist government there, indicate that TNCs are not above using their power to alter the flow of political events in developing nations (Bonner, 1983; Jensen, 1973; Kenworthy, 1973; LaFeber, 1984; Langley, 1985:142–43).

Overall, the combined effects of economic pressures to create a favorable climate for foreign investment, and support by transnational corporate capital for governments or political parties hospitable to their interests, can create a set of structural/legal conditions which allow TNCs in host countries to do what would be illegal in their country of origin. We are not suggesting that all TNCs have taken full advantage of these favorable structural/legal climates, or that all actively engage in efforts to create these climates. We are suggesting that researchers must always be sensitive to the political influences of TNCs on the political climates and legal frameworks of host countries. Accordingly, the laws governing corporate behavior in these nations are a poor starting place for setting the scope of inquiry into corporate offenses in a transnational context. [...]

Notes

1   For example see: Clinard (1946); Clinard and Yeager (1980); Conklin (1977); Denzin (1977); Edelhertz (1970); Farberman (1975); Gels (1967); Hartung (1950); Leonard and Weber (1970); Shapiro (1984); Shover (1980); Sutherland (1940, 1949); Vaughn (1983).

2   See in particular Amin (1974); Chase-Dunn (1978); Frank (1975); Sunkle (1973); and Wallerstein (1979).

3   From the point of view of the TNCs there are limits to the attractiveness of strict controls over labour rights. Regimes that are so repressive as to loose legitimacy can incite significant popular unrest. If the regime is not able to control this opposition, the resulting political instability can negate the benefits of a strong anit-labor government (International Labour Organization, 1985:62–63). The 1986 ouster of Marcos, a strong anti-labor dictator, from the Phillipines is a case in point.

43

Are women human? And other international dialogues
Catherine MacKinnon

[...] Torture is widely recognized as a fundamental violation of human rights.[1] Inequality on the basis of sex is also widely condemned, and sex equality affirmed as a basic human rights value and legal guarantee in many nations and internationally.[2] So why is torture on the basis of sex—for example, in the form of rape, battering, and pornography—not seen as a violation of human rights?[3] When women are abused, human rights are violated; anything less implicitly assumes women are not human. When torture is sex-based, human rights standards should be recognized as violated, just as much as when the torture is based on anything else. [...]

[...] Often the reason given for not considering atrocities to women to be torture is that they do not involve acts by states. They happen between nonstate actors in civil society hence are seen as not only unofficial but unconscious and unorganized and unsystematic and undirected and unplanned. They do not happen, it is thought, by state policy. They just happen. And traditionally, international instruments (as well as national constitutions) govern state action.

First of all, the state is not all there is to power. To act as if it is produces an exceptionally inadequate definition for human rights when so much of the second-class status of women, from sexual objectification to murder, is done by men to women without express or immediate of overt state involvement. If "the political" is to be defined in terms of men's experiences of being subjected to power, it makes some (but only some) sense to center its definition on the state.[4] But if one is including the unjust power involved in the subjection of half the human race by the other half—male dominance—it makes no sense to define power exclusively in terms of what the state does when it is defined as acting. The state is only one instrumentality of sex inequality. To fail to see this is pure gender bias. Often this bias flies under the flag of privacy, so that those areas that are defined as inappropriate for state involvement, where the discourse of human rights is made irrelevant, are those "areas in which the majority of the world's women live out their days."[5] Moreover, the fact that there is no single state or organized group expressly dedicated to this pursuit does not mean that all states are not more or less dedicated to it on an operative level or that it is not a deep structure of social, political, and legal organization. Why human rights, including the international law against torture, should be limited by it is the question.

Second, the state actually is typically deeply and actively complicit in the abuses mentioned, collaborating in and condoning them. Linda "Lovelace" describes her escape from Mr. Traynor: "I called the Beverly Hills police department and told them my husband was looking for me with an M 16. They told me they couldn't be involved with domestic affairs. When I told them his weapons were illegal, they told me to call back when he was in the room."[6] She testified before a grand jury in an obscenity case involving one of the films made of her. The grand jury looked at the films and asked her how she could have ever done that. She said because a gun was at her head. It did nothing.[7] As Linda Marchiano, she later tried to have an ordinance passed that would have made it possible for her to bring a civil action against the pornographers for damages for everything they did to her and to remove the pornography of her from distribution.[8] This ordinance, a sex equality law, was invalidated by the United States courts as a violation of freedom of expression, even though the court of appeals that invalidated it recognized all of the harms pornography did to women and agreed that it actually did those harms. This court held that pornography must be protected as speech in spite of its harm to sex equality—indeed, *because* of these harms, inasmuch as the value of the speech for purposes of protection was measured by the harm it did to women and to their equality.[9] When this result was summarily affirmed by the U.S. Supreme Court, the U.S. government legalized an express and admitted human rights violation on the view that the harm that pornography causes is more important than the people it hurts.[10] This is certainly state ratification of her abuse. It also raises the question, if someone took pictures of what happens in prison cells in Turkey, would they be sold as protected expression and sexual entertainment on the open market, with the state seen as uninvolved? The pornography of Linda continues to proliferate worldwide.

Jayne Stamen wrote her account from the Nassau County Correctional Facility in New York, where she was imprisoned. She was convicted of manslaughter in Jerry's killing by three men she supposedly solicited. Evidence of "battered women's syndrome" was excluded from her trial, to the reported accompaniment of judicial remarks such as "I'm not going to give any woman in Nassau County a license to kill her husband" and "Jerry Stamen is not on trial here but Jayne Stamen is."[11] Prosecution and jailing are state acts. Can you imagine a murder prosecution by a state against a torture victim who killed a torturer while escaping? If you can, can you imagine Amnesty International ignoring it?[12]

In the *Burnham* case, the conviction for marital rape that the wife won at trial was overturned on appeal because of the failure of the judge below *sua sponte* to instruct the jury that the husband might have believed that Ms. Burnham *consented*.[13] There was no standard beyond which it was regarded as obvious that a human being was violated hence true consent was inconceivable. No recognition that people break under torture. No realization that anyone will say anything to a torturer to try to make it stop. When women break under torture, we are said to have consented, or the torturer could have thought we did. Pictures of our "confessions" in the form of pornography follow us around for the rest of our lives. Few say, that isn't who she really is, everybody breaks under torture. Many do say, he could have believed it; besides, some women like it.

This is the *law* of pornography, the *law* of battered women's self-defense, the *law* of rape. Why isn't this state involvement? Formally, its configuration is very close to the recent case Velásquez-Rodríguez v. Honduras,[14] in which a man was violently detained, tortured, and accused of political crimes by a group that was allegedly official but was actually a more or less unofficial but officially-winked-at death squad. He has never been found. What was done to him was legally imputed to Honduras as a state under international law mostly because the abuse was systematically tolerated by the government. The abuse of the women described was not official in the narrow sense at the time it happened, but its cover-up, legitimization, and legalization after the fact were openly so. The lack of effective remedy was entirely official. The abuse was done, at the very least, with official impunity and legalized disregard. The abuse is systematic and known, the disregard is official and organized, and the effective governmental tolerance is a matter of law and policy.

Legally, the pattern is one of national and international guarantees of sex equality coexisting with massive rates of rape and battering and traffic in women through pornography effectively condoned by law. Some progressive international human rights bodies are beginning to inquire into some dimensions of these issues under equality rubrics—none into pornography, some into rape and battering.[15] Rape is now more likely to look like a potential human rights violation when it happens in official custody.[16] A woman's human rights are more likely to be deemed violated when the state can be seen as an instrumentality of the rape. Yet the regular laws and their regular everyday administration are not seen as official state involvement in legalized sex inequality.[17] The fact that rape happens is regarded by some far-thinking groups and agencies as a violation of a *norm* of sex equality. But the fact that the *law* of rape protects rapists and is written from their point of view to guarantee impunity for most rapes is officially regarded as a violation of the *law* of sex equality, national or international, by virtually nobody.

High on my list of state atrocities of this sort is rape law's defense of mistaken belief in consent. This permits the accused to be exonerated if he thinks the woman consented, no matter how much force he used. This is the law in Canada, New Zealand, and the United Kingdom, as well as some parts of the United States, including California, where the *Burnham* case was adjudicated. Another example is abortion's unconstitutionality, as in Ireland. A further example is the affirmative protection of pornography in the United States, including under the case in which Linda "Lovelace" participated.[18] Of course, the United States, an international outlaw of major proportions, is not bound by most of the relevant international agreements, not having ratified them. But other countries where the pornography of her, and others like her, is trafficked are. I would also include in this list of state atrocities the decriminalization of pornography, first in Denmark, then in Sweden. Those were official state acts, however beside the point of the harm to women their prior pornography laws were. No pornography laws at all is open season on women with official blessing. So is the across-the-board legalization of all participants in prostitution.

Why are there no human rights standards for tortures of women as a sex? Why are these atrocities not seen as sex equality violations? The problem can be explained in part in terms of the received notion of equality, which has served as a fairly subtle cross-cultural template for the legal face of misogyny. The traditional concept is the Aristotelian one of treating likes alike and unlikes unalike—mostly likes alike. In practice, this means that to be an equal, you must be the same as whoever sets the dominant standard. The unlikes unalike part has always been an uncomfortable part of equality law, really an internal exception to it, so that affirmative action, for example, is regarded as theoretically disreputable and logically problematic, even contradictory. The Aristotelian approach to equality, which dominates worldwide, never confronts several problems that the condition of women exposes. One is, why don't men, particularly white upper-class men, have to be the same as anyone in order to get equal treatment? Another is, men are as different from women as women are from men: equally different. Why aren't they punished for their differences like women are? Another is, why is equality as well satisfied by equalizing down as up? In other words, if equality is treating likes alike and unlikes unalike, if you get somebody down in the hole that the unlikes are in, in theory that is just as equal as elevating the denigrated to the level of the dominant standard set by the privileged.

The upshot of this approach is what is called in American law the "similarly situated" test, a concept that is used in one form or another around the world wherever law requires equality.[19] As applied to women, it means if men don't need it, women don't get it. Men as such do not need effective laws against rape, battering, prostitution, and pornography (although some of them do), so not having such laws for women is not an inequality; it is just a difference. Thus are these abuses rendered part of the sex difference, the permitted treating of unalikes unalike. Because there are relatively few similarly raped, battered, or prostituted men around to compare with (or they are comparatively invisible and gendered female), such abuses to women are not subjected to equality law at all. Where the lack of similarity of women's condition to men is extreme because of sex inequality, the result is that the law of sex equality does not properly apply.

Sex inequality, in this view, is not simply a distinction to be made properly or improperly, as in the Aristotelian approach. It is fundamentally a hierarchy, here initially a two-tiered hierarchy. Inequality produces systematic subordination, as in the situations of the women discussed.[20] The Canadian Supreme Court in its *Andrews* decision and cases following has come closer than any other court in the world to beginning to recognize this fundamental nature of inequality, leading the world on the subject.[21] To be consistent with equality guarantees in this approach is to move to end sex inequality. Wherever the law reinforces gender hierarchy, it violates legal equality guarantees, in national constitutions and in international covenants as well. [...]

Notes

1 See Convention Against Torture and Other Cruel, Inhuman or Degrading Treatment or Punishment, U.N. Doc. A/RES/39/46 (Dec. 10, 1984).

2 See, e.g., Universal Declaration of Human Rights, General Assembly Resolution 217A(111) (Dec. 10, 1948), arts. 2 and 7; International Covenant on Civil and Political Rights, G.A. Res. 2200A (XXI), 21 U.N. GAOR Supp. (No. 16) at 52, U,N, Doc. A/6316 (1966), 999 U.N.T.S. 171, *entered into force* Mar. 23, 1976, art. 2(1). The Convention for the Elimination of All Forms of Discrimination Against Women, U.N. Doc. A/RES/34/180 (1979). Many nations have explicit sex equality provisions in their constitutions. For examples, see *Constitutions of the Countries of the World* (Gisbert H. Flanz and Albert P. Blaustein, eds., 1971–1994).

3 Since this speech was given and published, some jurisdictions have recognised that rape, at least in official custody or by potentially official forces or when ignored by official instrumentalities, can be torture. See, e.g., Aydin v. Turkey, [1998] 25 E.H.R.R. 251; Mejia v. Peru, Case No. 10.970, Inter-American Committee on Human Rights, Report no. 5/96, OEA/Ser.L./V/II.91 Doc. 7 rev. (1996), available at www.cidh.org/annualrep/95eng/Peru10970.htm. See also M. C. v. Bulgaria, [2003] E.C.H.R. 646 (Dec. 4, 2003).

4 Even among men it is inadequate. Such a definition also excludes racist atrocities often committed against men of color, such as lynching, unless proven done under color of law, and racism generally, and class-based oppression, which harms both men and women.

5 Noreen Burrows, "International Law and Human Rights: The Case of Women's Rights," in *Human Rights: From Rhetoric to Reality* 82 (Tom Campbell et al., eds., 1986). See Eschel M. Rhoodie, *Discrimination Against Women: A Global Survey* 92 (1989) ("This [public/private] dichotomy is deeply engrained in the laws of some countries and thus the law plays a critical role in maintaining gender stratification."). The Convention on the Elimination of All Forms of Discrimination Against Women covers both the conventionally public and private in its guarantees.

6 See Declaration of Defendant-Intervenor Linda Marchiano, above note 7, at ¶ 17, p. 7.

7 Id. at ¶ 21, p. 8.

8 *Public Hearings on Ordinances to Add Pornography as Discrimination Against Women*, Minneapolis, Minn., Dec. 12, 1983, pp. 45–57, published in *In Harm's Way: The Pornography Civil Rights Hearings* 60–68 (Catherine A. MacKinnon and Andrea Dworkin, eds., 1997).

9 American Booksellers Ass'n v. Hudnut, 771 F.2d 323, 329 (7th Cir. 1985) ("Depictions of subordination tend to perpetuate subordination. The subordinate status of women in turn leads to affront and lower pay at work, insult and injury at home, battery and rape on the streets. In the language of the legislature, '[p]ornography is central in creating and maintaining sex as a basis of discrimination. Pornography is a systematic practice of exploitation and subordination based on sex which differentially harms women. The bigotry

and contempt it produces, with the acts of aggression it fosters, harm women's opportunities for equality and rights [of all kinds].' Indianapolis Code § 16–1(a)(2). Yet this simply demonstrates the power of pornography as speech.").

10 Hudnut v. American Booksellers Ass'n, Inc., 475 U.S. 1001 (1986) (summary affirmance).

11 Personal correspondence from Jayne Stamen to the author, March 11, 1988.

12 The New York State Department of Correctional Services Web site lists Jayne Stamen as released on parole on July 17, 2003, after over fifteen years in prison.

13 People v. Burnham, above note 10.

14 Inter-American Court of Human Rights, Velásquez-Rodríguez v. Honduras Series C, No. 4, (judgment of July 29, 1988) (1989), 28 *International Legal Materials* 291.

15 See, e.g., Directorate of Human Rights, Council of Europe, Information Sheet No. 24 (Nov. 1988–July 1989), Appendix XXXII, Declaration on Equality of Women and Men (Nov. 16, 1988). General Recommendation No. 12, Report of the Committee on the Elimination of Discrimination Against Women on Its 8th Session, U.N. Doc. A/44/38 (1989) 81 considering that Articles 2, 5, 11, 12, and 16 of the Convention require states parties to act to protect women against violence of any kind occurring within the family, at the workplace, or in any other area of social life, effectively reading in an obligation to take steps to address violence against women). On efforts to eradicate violence against women within society and the family, see *Report by the Secretary-General*, U.N. Doc. E/CN.6/1988/6 (1987). Regarding pornography, see Directorate of Human Rights, Council of Europe, Information Sheet No. 24 (Nov. 1988–July 1989), Recommendation No. R (89) 7 (principles on distribution of violent, brutal, or pornographic videos). After this speech was given, the CEDAW Committee promulgated its General Recommendation 19, see CEDAW, General Recommendation 19 (11th Sess. 1992), Report of the Committee on the Elimination of Discrimination Against Women on Its 11th Session, U.N. Doc. A/47/38 (1992), interpreting CEDAW's anti-discrimination provision to encompass violence against women and its official condonation. The CEDAW Committee has also recognized pornography's role in violence against women in its General Comment 12: "These attitudes also contribute to the propagation of pornography and the depiction and other commercial exploitation of women as sexual objects, rather than as individuals. This in turn contributes to gender-based violence." Id. at Comment 12. The Human Rights Committee's General Comment 28 on sex equality under the International Covenant on Civil and Political Rights finds that pornography is likely to promote violence or degrading and inhuman treatment. Human Rights Committee, General Comment 28, Equality of Rights Between Men and Women (Article 3), U.N. Doc. CCPR/C/21/Rev.1/Add.10 (2000), para. 22.

16 See, e.g., Prepared Statement of Amnesty International USA, Hearings on Human Rights Abuses Against Women, Hearing Before the Subcommittee on Human Rights and International Organizations, Committee on Foreign Af-

fairs, U.S. House of Representatives, March 21, 1990 ("[S]ome governments do not consider rape, sexual assault and sexual abuse as serious a crime as other types of physical assaults. This is particularly alarming when the perpetrators of the rape are government officals charged with the protection of the public" Id. at 6.). Amnesty International has, since this speech was published, increasingly taken on sexual torture in official custody as part of its mandate.

17 But see U.S. State Dept. Cable, "In recent legislative report language, the Senate Foreign Relations Committee observed that government tolerance of violence and abuse against women appears to be widely practiced and tacitly condoned in many parts of the world. Noting that such abuse is a violation of human rights as defined in existing legislation, the Committee called on the Department to pay special attention to these abuses in the cruelty reports." International League for Human Rights, *Human Rights Abuses Against Women: A Worldwide Survey* (May 1990). See above note 11, at Appendix 2.

18 Hudnut, above note 23.

19 In some places, there are various ingenious methods for cushioning the impact or qualifying the irrationality of the "similarly situated" test, usually by recognizing "differences" in some form, but it remains the main rule.

20 This critique is discussed more fully in Catherine A. MacKinnon, "Reflections on Sex Equality Under Law," 100 *Yale Law Journal* 1281 (1991), reprinted in *Women's ives, Men's Laws* 116 (2005).

21 See Andrews v. Law Society of British Columbia, [1989]1 S. C. R. 143; Regina v. Turpin, [1989] 1 S. C. R. 1296; Regina v. Lavallée, [1990] 1 S. C. R. 852; but compare Regina v. Hess, [1990] 2 S. C. R. 906.

44

The degradation of the international legal order?
Ben Bowring

[...] The late 1980s were a turning point in the fate not only of the (former) USSR, but of international law as a potential source of protection from strong states. In 1986 the United States lost the case brought against it in the International Court of Justice by Nicaragua. And on 15 April 1986 the United States attacked five targets in Libyan territory, having sought and obtained the agreement of Margaret Thatcher for the use of the UK as a staging post for its bombers. Not only for the purpose of this chapter, the events of 15 April 1986 serve as an awful warning for what took place on 11 September 2001. As was recognised at the time, the civilian deaths in Tripoli and Benghazi, if scaled up from the tiny population of Libya to the huge population of the United States of America, would have represented a strike on New York and Washington causing at least tens of thousands of innocent victims. Neither international law nor justice can countenance an eye for an eye, violence for violence. But the action of the United States in April 1986 was at the very least an awful barbinger, and perhaps one of the causes, of the events of 11 September.

However, the purpose of this section is to recall the prophetic words of Professor Paust, writing shortly afterwards. It should be noted at once that Paust was not writing to condemn the United States. Far from it. His conclusion was in essence a premonition of Kosovo and Afghanistan. 'Indeed, if the state dominated system did not recognise that the use of force is permissible when reasonably necessary to defend fundamental human rights, such a denial would inexorably demonstrate its own illegitimacy.' At first sight, of course, this is a non-sequitur, but we will let that pass. More interesting is the path of Paust's reasoning, and the demonstration he offers of the iron consistency of US policy, with regard to international law.

Paust starts with the now forgotten 'Schultz doctrine', enunciated on 15 January 1986, before the bombing of Libya. George Schultz, then US Secretary of State, stated in a speech at the National Defense University: 'It is absurd to argue that international law prohibits us from capturing terrorists in international waters or airspace, from attacking them on the soil of other nations even for the purpose of rescuing hostages, or from using force against states that support, train and harbor terrorists or guerillas.' He added: 'A nation attacked by terrorists is permitted to use force to prevent or pre-empt future attacks, to seize terrorists, or to rescue its citizens, when no other means is available.'

Paust contrasts this assertion with the near-unanimous (the US abstained) condemnation by the UN Security Council of Israel's use of force in 1985 against the PLO in Tunisian territory. The Security Council condemned this action as a 'flagrant violation of the Charter of the United Nations, international law and norms of conduct', and the 'sincere condolences over the loss of life of its citizens' extended to the Government of Tunisia by Ambassador Vernon Walters, when explaining US abstention.

For Paust, 'One is left necessarily then with the following set of questions: is it permissible under international law to attack terrorists on the soil of another nation without the consent of such a nation-state? Indeed, is it permissible to attack states that support, train, or harbor terrorists?'

Having reviewed the UN Charter, the 1970 Declaration on Principles of International Law, and the many authoritative condemnations by a wide range of scholars – two full pages of footnotes – of both pre-emptive and retaliatory reprisal actions, Paust concludes: 'For this reason, implementation of the "Schultz doctrine" by the use of preemptive or retaliatory use of force would place the United States in violation of international law and must be opposed.' [...]

[...] [O]n 2 August 1990 Iraq invaded Kuwait, and – after a remarkably lengthy pause – on 29 November 1990 the UN Security Council adopted Resolution 678.[1] This Resolution appeared to mark the end of the stifling of the Security Council, so much a feature of the Cold War. The system appeared to be about to come into its own.

In part, the delay was caused by the need to win the near-unanimous vote (China was not present) that the United States wanted. In order to win Soviet support for the vote, the United States, according to news reports, agreed to help keep the three Baltic republics out of the November 1990 Paris summit conference,[2] and pledged to persuade Kuwait and Saudi Arabia to provide the USSR with the hard currency it desperately needed – they did so,[3] though only shortly before its demise.

It will be recalled that Resolution 678 '[a]uthorises Member States co-operating with the Government of Kuwait ... to use all necessary means to uphold [the earlier resolutions] and to restore international peace and security in the area'. For the first time since Security Council Resolution 84 of 7 July 1950,[4] recommending unified military action against North Korea, military action was taken with the approval of the Security Council.

Thomas Franck and Faiza Patel were unambiguous in their response to these events.[5] 'The UN System seems politically to be developing the capacity to substitute police enforcement for vigilante violence ... Now, surely, is the time to embrace, to encourage, the new policing system before settling forever for sovereign wars of self-proclaimed self-defence.'[6]

However, there were a number of cogent criticisms at the time.[7] Eugene V. Rostow commented: 'Except for the word "authorises", the resolution is clearly one designed to encourage and support a campaign of collective self-defence, and therefore not a Security Council enforcement action.'[8] Burns H. Weston went further, questioning the legitimacy of the resolution and the action which followed.[9] For him, this had four aspects. First, the indeterminacy of the legal authority of Resolution 678; second, in the great-power pressure diplomacy that marked its adoption; third, in its wholly unrestricted character; and finally 'in the Council's hasty retreat from non-violent sanctioning alternatives permissible under it'.[10]

The Security Council held no meetings on the Gulf crisis between 29 November 1990 when Resolution 678 was adopted, and 14 February 1991, when it met in secret session to discuss the political aspects of the end of the war. On 3 April 1991 the Security Council adopted Resolution 687,[11] Iraq accepted it on 6 April, and the Security Council declared it to be in effect on 11 April.

In one respect, the Security Council did in fact set itself a new precedent; this was indeed to be a new era for the authorised use of force. Christine Gray points out that since Operation Desert Storm the Security Council has authorised member states to take action in Somalia (1992), Yugoslavia (from 1992), Haiti (1994), Rwanda (1994), the Great Lakes (1996), Albania (1997), the Central African Republic (1997), Sierra Leone (1997) – as well as Kosovo in Resolution 1244 and East Timor under Resolution 1264: 'it has not concerned itself with identifying a legal basis for such authorisations beyond a general reference to Chapter VII of the UN Charter.' All were internal conflicts, with the debatable exception of the former Yugoslavia.[12]

But Resolution 687 did not bring about any closure in respect of the war against Iraq. Earlier in 2002 the *European Journal of International Law* devoted a whole issue to 'The Impact on International Law of a Decade of Measures against Iraq'.[13]

Operation Desert Storm was soon followed by Operation Provide Comfort by the USA, UK and France in protection of the Kurds of Northern Iraq in April 1991.[14] Part of the justification for this was that the action was taken 'in support of Resolution 688', ignoring the fact that this resolution was not adopted under Chapter VII, and did not authorise the use of force. In January 1993 the USA and UK carried out attacks on Iraqi missile sites in the no-fly zones. The Secretary General of the UN argued that this action was mandated by the Security Council according to Resolution 678, because of Iraq's violation of the ceasefire resolution.[15] Gray points out that the Secretary General never reverted to this argument, and it has been criticised for arrogating to individual states powers which belong to the Security Council.[16]

Very similar justifications were used to justify Operation Desert Fox in December 1998, in response to Iraq's withdrawal of co-operation with UN weapons inspectors. This operation, which lasted four days and four nights, saw the use of more missiles than used in the whole of the 1991 crisis. The UK and US referred to Security Council Resolutions 1154 and 1205 as providing the legal basis for the use of force. But, as Gray points out, these resolutions had been passed under Chapter VIII, but made no express provision for the use of force. [...]

[...] [On 24 March 1999, after the breakdown of the Rambouillet negotiations over the fate of Kosovo and the Kosovars, Operation Allied Force was launched. This was the start of a 78-day bombing campaign.[17] As Biddle points out, NATO won: not surprising, when it is considered that the combined population of NATO's 19 countries exceeded Serbia's 11 million by a factor of 65; NATO's defence budget was 25 times larger than Serbia's entire economy; and its armed forces outnumbered Serbia's by 35 to 1.[18]

In many ways, the war against Serbia provided the bridge between the wars against Iraq and Afghanistan. 'Even as NATO bombs fell on Belgrade, US and British aircraft were continuing their sustained (if nearly invisible) war on Iraq, one that expended more than 2,000 bombs and missiles in 1999 alone – not nearly the number used in Kosovo but still a sizeable show of force. And the 2000–1 campaign in Afghanistan was both a clear descendant of and a reaction to the military model unveiled in Kosovo.'[19] In his review for *Foreign Affairs*, Biddle makes no mention at all of international law, or of the United Nations.

The argument that the bombing was necessitated by the need to avert humanitarian disaster – a new law of humanitarian intervention – had such moral appeal that critics of the action were few, at least in Northern Europe. There were exceptions. Michael Byers and Simon Chesterman responded polemically on 19 April 1999: 'Nato's unilateral intervention in the Balkans has frightened Russia, isolated China, and done little to help the million or so Kosovars in whose name Serbia is being bombed. Its principal achievements may be to ensure the death of the "new world order" famously heralded by George Bush after the liberation of Kuwait in 1991, and to destroy an institution that has helped to prevent international wars for over half a century.'[20]

Thomas Franck pointed out one of the crucial differences between the Gulf War and the Kosovo War – the distinction between '... mitigation and justification. Neither the US Department of State nor NATO seriously attempted to justify the war in international legal terms.'[21] He was forced to this conclusion by Bruno Simma's unanswerable critique[22] of the war's legality. Franck responded:

... while UN authorisation of collective military action did break new ground, there was little new about armed response to outright aggression. Resolution 1244, on the other hand, endorses the deployment of collective (regional) armed force to counteract, not aggression, but gross violation of humanitarian law and human rights ... There is, however, another notable distinction between Resolutions 687 and 1244. The former established an international regime for Iraq wrought by the triumph of the Security Council-authorised forces. The latter imposed a regime on Yugoslavia after a campaign by NATO that the United Nations had not authorised. Although the Council had previously invoked Chapter VII and 'stresse[d]' the need for a 'negotiated political solution', it had stopped short of authorising NATO to bring about the results it later embraced in Resolution 1244 ... This has made it hard to disagree with the disquieting conclusion of Professor Bruno Simma ... that NATO's military action was in breach of international law.[23]

The main issue, however, was whether the actions of NATO, especially the United States, had the effect of bringing about, in record time, a new creative development in customary international law through state practice and *opinio juris*. That is, did the imperative – as presented by NATO – of averting a humanitarian disaster in Kosovo, namely the genocide or at any rate ethnic cleansing of Kosovars by the Serbs, trump the provisions of the UN Charter prohibiting the use of force? [...]

[...] Legal scholars have not failed to notice the political imperatives which law was made to serve. Christine Gray points out that Kosovo is another instance (following Rwanda, Albania and Haiti) of the desire for legitimacy which influenced the USA, the UK and other NATO states in claiming a Security Council basis for their use of force in Kosovo.[24] She adds: 'It is no longer simply a case of interpreting euphemisms such as "all necessary means" to allow the use of force when it is clear from the preceding debate that force is envisaged: the USA, UK and others have gone far beyond this to distort the words of resolutions and to ignore the preceding debates in order to claim to be acting on behalf of the international community.'[25] Christine Chinkin used an article in the *AJIL* itself to aim the most succinct and deadly criticism of the Kosovo War:

> Finally the Kosovo intervention shows that the West continues to script international law, even while it ignores the constitutional safeguards of the international legal order ... All these incidents serve to undermine the Charter on an ad hoc selective basis without providing clear articulation of the underlying principles, or even assurance of future acceptance by those who currently espouse them. The case of Kosovo may have highlighted the continuing chasm between human rights rhetoric and reality. It does not resolve the way this can be bridged.[26] [...]

Thus, the doyen of American international lawyers, Loius Henkin, was quite firm as to the international law: '... the law is, and ought to be, that unilateral intervention by military force by a state or group of states is unlawful unless authorised by the Security Council.'[27]

Notes

1   See (1990) 29 *International Legal Materials* 1565.
2   Apple 'Summit in Europe: East and West Sign Pact to Shed Arms in Europe' *New York Times* 20 November 1990.
3   T. Friedman 'Mideast Tensions: How US won Support to Use Mideast Forces. The Iraq Resolution: a US–Soviet Collaboration – A Special Report' *New York Times* 2 December 1990.
4   SC Res 84, 5 UN SCOR (Res & Dec) at 5.
5   Franck and Patel (1991).
6   Franck and Patel (1991) p. 74.
7   See also Glennon (1991); Caron (1991); Damrosch (1991); Meron (1991).
8   Rostow (1991) pp. 508–509.

9 Weston (1991).
10 Weston (1991) p. 518.
11 Security Council Resolution 687, 30 ILM 846 (1991).
12 Gray (2002) pp. 3–4.
13 *European Journal of International Law* Vol. 13. No.1, February 2002.
14 Malanczuk (1991); Franck (1995) pp. 235–236.
15 Weller (1993) p. 741.
16 Gray (2002) p. 12.
17 See Murphy (2000).
18 Biddle (2002) p. 138.
19 Biddle (2002) p. 139.
20 Byers and Chesterman (1999).
21 Franck (1999) p. 859.
22 Simma(1999).
23 Franck (1999) p. 858.
24 Gray (2002) p. 8.
25 Gray (2002) p. 9.
26 Chinkin (1999) p. 846.
27 Henkin (1999).

45

Preventive war 'the supreme crime'
Noam Chomsky

[...] The new "imperial grand strategy," as it was termed at once in the leading establishment journal, presents the US as "a revisionist state seeking to parlay its momentary advantages into a world order in which it runs the show," a "unipolar world" in which "no state or coalition could ever challenge" it as "global leader, protector, and enforcer." These policies are fraught with danger even for the US itself, the author warned, joining many others in the foreign policy elite.

What is to be "protected" is US power and the interests it represents, not the world, which vigorously opposed the conception. Within a few months, studies revealed that fear of the United States had reached remarkable heights, along with distrust of the political leadership. An international Gallup poll in December, barely noted in the US, found virtually no support for Washington's announced plans for a war in Iraq carried out "unilaterally by America and its allies": in effect, the US-UK "coalition."

Washington informed the UN that it can be "relevant" by endorsing Washington's plans, or it can be a debating society. The US has the "sovereign right to take military action," the administration moderate Colin Powell informed the World Economic Forum, which also strenuously opposed Washington's war plans: "When we feel strongly about something we will lead," he informed them, even if no one is following us.

Bush and Blair underscored their contempt for international law and institutions at their Azores Summit on the eve of the invasion. They issued an ultimatum – not to Iraq, but to the Security Council: capitulate, or we will invade without your meaningless seal of approval. And we will do so whether or not Saddam Hussein and his family leave the country. The crucial principle is that the US must effectively rule Iraq.

President Bush declared that the US "has the sovereign authority to use force in assuring its own national security," threatened by Iraq with or without Saddam, according to the Bush doctrine. Washington will be happy to establish an "Arab façade," to borrow the term of the British during their day in the sun, while US power is firmly implanted at the heart of the world's major energy-producing region. Formal democracy will be fine, but only if it is of the submissive kind accepted in Washington's "backyard," at least if history and current practice are any guide.

The grand strategy authorizes Washington to carry out "preventive war": *preventive*, not pre-emptive. Whatever the justifications for pre-emptive war might be, they do not hold for preventive war, particularly as that concept is interpreted by its current enthusiasts: the use of military force to eliminate an invented or imagined threat, so that even the term "preventive" is too charitable. Preventive war is very simply, the "supreme crime" condemned at Nuremberg.

That was understood by those with some concern for their country. As the US invaded Iraq, historian Arthur Schlesinger wrote that Bush's grand strategy is "alarmingly similar to the policy that imperial Japan employed at Pearl Harbor, on a date which, as an earlier American president said it would, lives in infamy." FDR was right, he added, "but today it is we Americans who live in infamy." It is no surprise that "the global wave of sympathy that engulfed the United States after 9/11 has given way to a global wave of hatred of American arrogance and militarism," and the belief that Bush is "a greater threat to peace than Saddam Hussein."

For the political leadership, mostly recycled from more reactionary sectors of the Reagan-Bush I administrations, "the global wave of hatred" is not a particular problem. They want to be feared, not loved. It is natural for Donald Rumsfeld to quote the words of Chicago gangster Al Capone: "You will get more with a kind word and a gun than with a kind word alone." They understand as well as their establishment critics that their actions increase the risk of proliferation of weapons of mass destruction [...] and terror. But that too is not a major problem. Far higher in the scale of priorities are the goals of establishing global hegemony and implementing their domestic agenda: dismantling the progressive achievements that have been won by popular struggle over the past century, and institutionalizing these radical changes so that recovering them will be no easy task.

It is not enough for a hegemonic power to declare an official policy. It must establish it as a "new norm of international law" by exemplary action. Distinguished commentators may then explain that law is a flexible living instrument, so that the new norm is now available as a guide to action. It is understood that only those with the guns can establish "norms" and modify international law. [...]

INDEX

GENDER AND CRIME

A Reader

Karen Evans and Janet Jamieson (eds)

Focusing explicitly on questions of gender and crime, Evans and Jamieson guide the reader through a range of classic and groundbreaking studies, highlighting key contributions and debates and providing an indication of the new directions an engendered criminology may take us in coming years.

This engaging reader is divided into five sections, mapping the theoretical, empirical, and practical developments that have endeavoured to identify the ways in which gender informs criminology. Issues addressed by the readings include:

- Female offending
- Gendered patterns of victimisation
- The gendered nature of social control
- Masculinity and crime
- Placing gender in an international context

Evans and Jamieson's powerful concluding chapter clearly sets out the achievements and the challenges that the gender and crime question has posed for criminology. They argue that unless the question of gender remains at the forefront of criminological endeavours, criminology will fail to offer an agenda informed by an understanding of social justice that strives to be attentive to both victims and offenders, whether they be male or female. *Gender and Crime* is key reading for students of criminology, criminal justice and gender studies.

Readings by: *Jon Bannister, Susan Brownmiller, Beatrix Campbell, Pat Carlen, Meda Chesney-Lind, Ruth Chigwada-Bailey, Richard Collier, Jock Collins, Jason Ditton, R. Emerson Dobash, Russell P. Dobash, Stephen Farrall, Lorraine Gelsthorpe, Elizabeth Gilchrist, Annie Hudson, Ruth Jamieson, Nancy Loucks, James W. Messerschmidt, Allison Morris, Greg Noble, Lisa Pasko, Scott Poynting, Lorraine Radford, Marcia Rice, Carol Smart, Laureen Snider, Elizabeth A. Stanko, Paul Tabar, Kaname Tsutsumi, Anne Worrall.*

Contents: *Series editor's foreword – Publisher's acknowledgements – Introduction: Gender and crime – the story – Part 1: Engendering the agenda – Introduction – Criminological theory: Its ideology and implications concerning women – Challenging orthodoxies in feminist theory: A black feminist critique – Girls' troubles and "female delinquency" ' – Twisted sisters, ladettes, and the new penology: The social construction of "violent girls" ' – Part 2: Engendering the victim – Introduction – Women fight back – Typical violence, normal precaution: Men, women and interpersonal violence in England, Wales, Scotland and the USA – Women and the "fear of crime": Challenging the accepted stereotype – Women's violence to men in intimate relationships: Working on the puzzle – Part 3: Gender and social control – Introduction – "Troublesome girls": Towards alternative definitions and policies – Justice in the making: Key influences on decision-making – Black women and the criminal justice system – Women's imprisonment in England and Wales: A penal paradox – Part 4: Engendering masculinity – Introduction – Boys will be boys – Structured action and gendered crime – Masculinities and crime: Rethinking the "man question" – Gender, class, racism, and criminal justice: Against global and gender-centric theories, for poststructuralist perspectives – Part 5: International perspectives – Introduction – Constituting the punishable woman: Atavistic man incarcerates postmodern woman – Globalization and violence against women: Inequalities in risks, responsibilities and blame in the UK and Japan – "You deserve it because you are Australian": The moral panic over "ethnic gang rape" ' – Genocide and the social production of immorality' – Conclusion: gender and crime – the legacy? – References – Index.*

2008 352pp

978-0-335-22523-1 (Paperback) 978-0-335-22522-4 (Hardback)

ETHNICITY AND CRIME

A Reader

Basia Spalek (ed)

> "Basia Spalek has compiled an excellent reader about a much researched and highly sensitive subject. Crucially, she contextualises ethnicity and crime within broadly defined social and intellectual contexts, avoiding the limitation of all too frequently repeated research based solely on statistical measures and policy evaluations."
>
> Simon Holdaway, Professor of Criminology and Sociology, Sheffield University

Issues in relation to race and ethnicity have generated substantial and ever-growing interest from, and within, a multitude of academic, research and policy contexts. This book brings together important material in race and ethnic studies and provides different ways of thinking about race and ethnicity in relation to crime and the criminal justice system.

Ethnicity and Crime: A Reader consists of a collection of works that capture the main themes that arise from within this vast area of work. It is divided into five sections:

- 'Race and crime', racial discrimination and criminal justice
- The racialisation of crime: Social, political and cultural contexts
- Race, ethnicity and victimisation
- Self and discipline reflexivity: Ethnic identities and crime
- Ethnic identities, institutional reflexivity and crime

Each section contains recurring and overlapping themes and includes many different ways of thinking about race and ethnicity in relation to crime. It spans theoretical approaches that might be labelled as positivist, critical race analyses, left realist approaches, feminist, as well as post-modern perspectives.

This is the first title in the new series Readings in Criminology and Criminal Justice and follows the series format of thematic sections, together with an editor's introduction to the complete volume and an introduction to each section.

Contents: Series editor's foreword – Publisher's acknowledgements – Introduction – PART 1 'Race and crime', racial discrimination and criminal justice – Ethnic minorities, crime and criminal justice: A study in a provincial city – Some recent approaches to the study of race in criminological research: Race as social process – Discrimination in the Courts? – The Enlightenment and Euro-American theories of the judicial process – PART 2 The racialisation of crime: Social, political and cultural contexts – The race and crime debate – The myth of black criminality – Tolerance, freedom, justice and peace? Britain, Australia and anti-Muslim racism since 11 September 2001 – Introduction to The Asian Gang – PART 3 Race, ethnicity and victimisation – Racist violence in Europe: Challenges for official data collection – Racial victimization: An experiential analysis – Racism and victimization – Woman abuse in London's black communities – PART 4 Self and discipline reflexivity: Ethnic identities and crime – Political Blackness and British Asians – Racism, ethnicity and criminology: Developing minority perspectives – Constructing whiteness: The intersections of race and gender in US white supremacist discourse – Researching black Muslim women's lives: A critical reflection – Criminology and orientalism – PART 5 Ethnic identities, institutional reflexivity and crime – Can Macpherson succeed where Scarman failed? – (In)visible barriers: The experience of Asian employees in the probation service – Conclusion – Bibliography – Glossary – Useful websites – Index.

2008 488pp

978-0-335-22379-4 (Paperback) 978-0-335-22378-7 (Hardback)